CONFESSIONS OF AN UNDERCOVER AGENT

Confessions of an
UNDERCOVER AGENT

Adventures,
Close Calls,
and the
Toll of a
Double Life

CHARLIE SPILLERS

University Press of Mississippi / Jackson

www.upress.state.ms.us

The University Press of Mississippi is a member
of the Association of American University Presses.

Photographs are courtesy of the author except
where otherwise noted.

First printing 2016

∞

Library of Congress Cataloging-in-Publication Data

Spillers, Charlie, author.
  Confessions of an undercover agent : adventures,
close calls, and the toll of a double life / Charlie Spillers.
    pages cm
  Includes index.
  ISBN 978-1-4968-0520-1 (cloth : alk. paper) —
ISBN 978-1-4968-0521-8 (ebook) 1. Spillers, Charlie.
2. Police—United States—Biography. 3. Undercover
operations—United States. 4. Law enforcement—
United States. I. Title.
  HV7911.S594A3 2016
  363.45092—dc23
  [B]   2015028440

British Library Cataloging-in-Publication Data available

To Evelyn Smith Spillers, my intrepid wife; to our son,
Terry Lee Spillers; and to our beautiful granddaughters,
Michaela Brooke Spillers and Hannah Elizabeth Spillers

CONTENTS

PROLOGUE

Junior, a wiry black man in his late twenties, sat behind the steering wheel of his parked car and held a .25 semiautomatic pistol just below the rim of the open car window, jumpy and ready to shoot at any movement outside the car, be it a passerby or someone getting out of another car. Lips pressed tight with nervous tension and a wild glare flaring in his eyes, he swung his head from side to side searching the area, trying to watch in every direction.

A few moments before I had parked next to Junior's car, a maroon Buick parked facing an apartment complex. I had just slid onto the passenger seat and wore a hidden body wire, ready to buy an ounce of heroin from him. I would give the code word *coke* to trigger the bust. Other narcotics investigators in unmarked cars waited nearby to rush in and arrest both of us. They would pretend to arrest me in order to preserve my cover, and I was unarmed. At the last minute the investigators added a couple of uniform police units to assist with the bust.

I needed to alert the others to the danger.

"*Gun*, man, why you got a *gun*?" I said *gun* loudly and distinctly, hoping the investigators listening over the wire would be able to hear it.

"Man, you don't need no *gun*," I repeated.

He didn't answer and instead jerked his head from side to side, trying to watch everything around us.

I could tell he was strung out. He flinched at any movements nearby and his dilated eyes flashed back and forth from outside the window to me. Junior gripped the gun tightly but his hand trembled and I feared he might shoot at the slightest provocation. My heart pounded in my ears. I tried to keep my voice relaxed and calm to settle him down. I focused. For me the world didn't exist outside the car and I needed to try to control what was going to happen inside.

But I was also in danger from the uniform officers who waited to help make the arrest. In order to protect my cover, they weren't told I was an undercover officer. They thought they would be arresting two drug deal-ers. If any shots were fired from inside the car, then the officers might riddle it and anyone in it, including me.

"You got the money?" Junior asked. His high-pitched voice almost cracked and he spoke quickly as if he wanted to hurry and get away.

"Yeah," I said. "It's eight hundred, right?" But he wasn't paying atten-tion to me any longer. He was staring hard at a man coming out of one of the apartments and walking toward a car. "Eight, right?" I repeated.

He glanced back at me, but his eyes kept darting to our surroundings. "Eight. Yeah, eight," he said loudly, almost shouting, and I felt tension crackling inside the car.

"You got the stuff?" I asked.

Junior suddenly jumped and jerked the gun up as a car rattled past behind us, and he flinched again as a gray cat ran from behind a garbage can.

"What about the stuff, the smack?" I repeated.

He was watching the surroundings so intently that he still didn't hear me, and I asked about the heroin again. He clutched it in his left hand. Reaching across his body, he put the baggie of heroin on the seat between us. He wasn't going to let go of the gun. As I picked up the heroin, he kept scanning the area, jerking around with the gun up when someone happened to walk by the rear of the car. He was becoming more agitated and I needed to set things in motion before he got worse.

"Okay, man, here's the money." I put the heroin down and reached into my front pocket for the money. "It's all here. You can count it if you want." Junior glanced around and then put the gun down between his legs so he could take the money.

"By the way," I said, pulling out a wad of cash, "can you get any coke?"

Suddenly we were in the middle of a deafening racetrack. Power-ful car engines roared and tires squealed. With screaming engines and flashing lights, police cars raced at us from both sides. In an instant, Junior grabbed the gun and was raising it toward his window to shoot the oncoming officers . . .

PREFACE

These stories involve a wide-ranging cast of characters in the criminal world. A wealthy Memphis businessman involved with Mafia and Mexican drug-smuggling operations in Houston, Texas; a cabdriver on the Gulf Coast working with heroin dealers from Mobile to New Orleans; a Jackson, Mississippi, drug dealer meeting suppliers in New Orleans; a safecracker's accomplice; a hospital worker involved in drug trafficking; a PCP dealer arrested with his suppliers in Baton Rouge; and a crime figure sending stolen cars from north Mississippi to Alabama, Louisiana, and Florida. These characters all had one thing in common. They were all the same person, me, a lone undercover agent playing different roles using multiple identities for ten years to make cases on drug traffickers and other career criminals.

As an undercover police officer with the Baton Rouge Police Department (BRPD), and then as an agent with the Mississippi Bureau of Narcotics (MBN), I dealt with memorable criminals and experienced exciting adventures and anxious moments. I often worked alone and sometimes unarmed. Some encounters were heart-stopping moments filled with rushes of visceral emotion—anxiety, fear, relief, and exhilaration. Successfully handling a tight spot felt like barely dodging a horrible accident and winning the lottery all at the same time—surges of relief and elation—and I became addicted to the excitement of working undercover. It was also satisfying to accomplish challenging missions and infiltrate criminal groups, all while attempting to walk the thin line between success and disaster.

At the beginning of my undercover journey I had no idea of the tests I would encounter, and the experiences and challenges that lay ahead.

CONFESSIONS OF AN UNDERCOVER AGENT

MY PATH TO AN UNDERCOVER LIFE

Cajun Roots

I was born in Louisiana into a family with a rich Cajun French heritage. Living deep in the heart of Cajun country, my great-grandparents, Bertrand Borel (pronounced *bow-rail*) and Bernadette Perrilleaux (*pair-uh-loh*), grew sugarcane near New Iberia, and couldn't speak or understand English—they spoke only Cajun French. During our visits, my mother and grandparents, who spoke both languages, acted as interpreters.

My grandmother recalled that she and my grandfather, Amilcar Frederick, met at a "fais-do-do" under moss-covered oaks with wide, low-hanging limbs. The aroma of spicy gumbo in large black iron pots filled the air and foot-stomping Cajun music soared as accordions and violins accompanied plaintive ballads of love and loss sung in Cajun French.

For the first years of their marriage they lived in a cramped, homemade houseboat tied to overhanging trees on a small bayou, a big change for my grandmother, who came from a well-to-do family in Saint Martinville. They lived on game, fish, gardening, and bartering, and their only mode of transportation was a pirogue, a small wooden boat my grandfather paddled on the bayou. After the birth of my mother and her sister, they moved to Krotz Springs, a sleepy fishing village on the banks of the wide and deep Atchafalaya River. My grandfather made his living by fishing in the river with hoop nets in the summer and trapping mink and otter on the bayous in the winter. He never owned or drove an automobile, never had a bank account, and never purchased anything on credit. He was a renowned and widely respected hunter, and villagers talked about his special skill at hunting deep in the swamps.

Growing up, I stayed with my grandparents during summers. Occasionally I accompanied my grandfather and his partner, Adoir (*ad-war*), when they went out on the river in a bateau, a long, wooden flat-bottom boat, powered by a puttering gas engine, to check their nets, an exciting adventure on the wide, deep river. They took the day's catch in Adoir's old pickup truck to Ortiz's fish market in Krotz Springs where they collected ten to twenty cents per pound, depending on the type of fish.

French was dominant at their house. My grandfather listened to the news broadcast in French from radio stations in Opelousas and Lafayette, and he and the men who came by to visit would often talk in French. I couldn't understand them, but was fascinated by the mysterious French sounds and the animated discussions: gesturing hands, expressive eyes, and heads nodding and shaking. Perhaps without realizing it, during those summers I was learning at an early age to pay close attention to body language. When the womenfolk came to visit my grandmother, she served small demitasse cups of strong Cajun coffee even when it was sweltering outside, and they would gossip in French so that I wouldn't know what they were talking about.

In addition to Cajun French and Cajun hospitality, their home was filled with the delicious aromas and tastes of Cajun cooking: game stews made with thick brown roux, steaming chicken and sausage gumbos, spicy jambalaya, crawfish étouffée, and crawfish bisque. My mother cooked Cajun dishes she learned from my grandmother, and now my five sisters carry on the tradition. Instead of turkey, our family Thanksgiving dinners in Louisiana consist of large pots of chicken, sausage and seafood gumbo, potato salad, French bread, and wine.

My grandfather's side of the family came to Louisiana in the early 1700s from Alsace in eastern France near Germany. My great-grandfather Traismond Frederick was a "bayou doctor" who administered homemade potions along with old Celtic-sounding incantations and chants to cure ills up and down the bayous. My great-great-grandparents were Telesphore Frederick and Elizabeth LeBlanc, and after Elizabeth died, the Savoys became part of our family tree when Telesphore married Julie Savoy.

My grandmother's side of the family was pure Acadian French forced from what is now Nova Scotia in Canada to Louisiana. Her grandfather, Pierre Alsace Perrilleaux, fought for the South in the Civil War with the Eighteenth Louisiana Infantry in battles around Corinth and Vicksburg, Mississippi. The richness of our Cajun and French heritage is reflected by the last names in our family line: Borel, LeBlanc, Savoy, Perrilleaux, Berthelot, LeTuiller, Giscair, and Dupuis.

■ ■ ■

My father's side of the family came from England to South Carolina and then westward to Alabama and Mississippi, where Choctaw Indian became part of our family line, and then on to north Louisiana where my father was born and raised. My father was a "tool pusher" in the oil fields, which meant that we moved every two or three years because his work followed newly producing fields. Changing schools became a regular but dreaded routine for me and my two brothers and five sisters. We moved around Louisiana and south Mississippi. In Louisiana we lived briefly in Baton Rouge, Krotz Springs, Cut Off, Vidalia, and Ferriday; in Mississippi we lived in Roxie, Cranfield, Washington, Natchez, Brookhaven, and Magee, where I graduated from high school.

With each move, I was always the new student, the outsider, the stranger, walking hesitantly into a classroom full of kids who had grown up together. We had no shared history and I needed a way to get along with them. Years later those experiences proved to be an asset. While working as an undercover agent I was always the stranger, the outsider trying to find ways to be accepted by closed criminal groups of longtime associates and friends, many of whom had grown up together.

Following graduation from high school, I embarked on another phrase that helped prepare me for the difficult challenges of undercover work.

The Marines

One attribute beneficial for undercover work is an attraction to excitement and challenge. The US Marines supplied ample doses of both and I became seduced by the allure. At seventeen, I joined the Marines on a three-year enlistment. I had an inkling of what was to come when a Marine officer swore in a small group of us in at Jackson, Mississippi, prior to departure for boot camp. After administering the oath, he announced in a commanding voice, "Y'all better give your heart to God because *your ass* now belongs to the Marine Corps."

For thirteen weeks we went through a hard-as-nails boot camp at Parris Island, South Carolina, followed by four weeks of infantry training at Camp Geiger, North Carolina. Following infantry training, I was stationed at Camp Lejeune, North Carolina as a rifleman in a line company. The hand of fortune soon intervened, however, and I was selected for transfer to Battalion Secret and Classified Files, a two-man office at battalion headquarters.

On paydays we frequented bars in Jacksonville, North Carolina, the town just outside base. Those forays often led to memorable escapades.

During one nocturnal sojourn in town, I ran into a little trouble. After closing time for the bars in Jacksonville, I would sometimes amble across the tracks to a black residential area to a house that served as an illicit, after-hours juke joint. The small, white frame house was usually packed with customers, with a jukebox playing in the living room and whiskey sold in paper cups out of the kitchen. I was usually the only white in the place.

One night another customer insisted that I buy him a drink. Having just spent my last dollar, I had to decline, which led to an angry invitation to step outside in the street. We went outside, followed by all the other customers. We squared off in the middle of the street while the crowd gathered around us in a big circle, the scene lit by a yellow glow from streetlights. I put up my fists; my opponent, however, picked up a beer bottle.

"Hey, man," I protested, "where I come from we don't need weapons to duke it out. That ain't right. Drop the bottle, man."

From the crowd came the voices of several guys who were in my battalion, urging the guy to drop the bottle. He hesitated, finally threw down the bottle, and the fight was on. He was taller and had a longer reach, but I was doing well until several others piled in on me from the sides and I went down. As I was getting back up, someone yelled, "He's been stabbed! He's cut!" My assailants and the crowd backed away. Feeling pain in the back of my right shoulder, I twisted my head to that side and saw that the back of my light-blue shirt was soaked red with blood. Someone had stabbed me in the back of my shoulder.

I shook my fist at the crowd, "You sumbitches," I yelled, "you coward sumbitches! Dammit, can't you fight fair?" I was mad—not very smart, but mad. The crowd melted away and I started lumbering toward the tracks holding my right shoulder. A detective driving in the area happened across me and got me to the hospital where they stitched me up. The knife blade that plunged into my shoulder was about one inch wide and left a permanent scar.

Because of the wound I was put on light duty for a couple of weeks and my lieutenant had me give a written statement about the incident. The Marine Corps considered Marines to be government property. If a Marine did something that left him unable to perform his duties, then he could be disciplined, essentially for damaging government property—himself. I wrote the statement and never heard any more about it. I suspect the lieutenant was secretly proud that one of his men had been stabbed in a bar fight, which lived up to our reputation as hard-drinking, fighting Marines. With a painful shoulder for the next couple of weeks, I wasn't up to any more fighting for a while. But more was soon to come.

One payday weekend after I recovered, a couple of Marine buddies, Pete and Gary Wyne, and I drove to South Carolina in Pete's car and picked up two women and brought them back to Jacksonville for a night of partying in the bars. That wasn't a good idea for two reasons. First, I wasn't authorized to be off the base because my liberty card, the pass to be off the base, had been confiscated by MPs the night before due to another minor incident. So I was already in trouble. If I were caught off base without a liberty card, I would be in much deeper trouble. Second, there were hundreds of hard-drinking Marines in the bars in Jacksonville but very few women, resulting in dozens of drunken Marines chasing after each woman. Barhopping with two women was akin to waving a red cape at a restless herd of eager and excited bulls. Nevertheless, we unwisely went barhopping with the women—and we would pay for it.

When we left the last bar at closing time, three Marines followed close behind on the sidewalk, taunting us and calling out to our women. One still had a smirk on his face when I spun around and smashed him in the mouth with my fist. The fight was on. The six of us swirled wildly, fighting on the sidewalk and out into the street. We were frantically swinging away when MPs arrived. The MPs grabbed me first and shoved me face-first against a wall. Then they turned to grab the others. As soon as the MPs turned away, I pushed off the wall and ran. The women huddled in a doorway and I yelled for them to follow me. We ran down the street and disappeared around a corner. Behind us more MPs were arriving, shouting and blowing whistles. We ran until we reached Pete's car two blocks away. Luckily I had his keys; we drove around for a while and then got something to eat at an all-night grill.

The MPs loaded Pete and Gary and the others into a paddy wagon and took them to the MP lockup in town. I knew the routine, so as dawn approached we parked near the lockup and waited. Soon Gary and Pete came out, released after being held in the drunk tank with dozens of other Marines. I had one of the women get them and then we drove the women back to South Carolina, recounting the fight and laughing about the night's events. The other three sat up front during the trip and I lay on the backseat with my head in the lap of one of the women while she caressed knots that had already risen on my head from the fight. It just didn't get any better than that—a night of drinking, a glorious fight, escaping from the MPs, and a woman caressing your wounds as we recalled every detail. A wonderful time was had by all, but those good times would soon come to an end.

Crisis: To the Dominican Republic

As my tour at Camp Lejeune was nearing an end, a crisis erupted in the Caribbean. Our battalion was aboard ships in the Caribbean for a three-month cruise as a quick reaction force when an insurrection broke out in the Dominican Republic. Our ship, the *Boxer*, a helicopter carrier, headed there at flank speed and we flew in at night by helicopter, landing on a soccer field near the Hotel Embajador on the western outskirts of Santo Domingo, the capital city. Except for military flashlights with red lenses, the area was blacked out, not a light to be seen anywhere, not even in the high and imposing resort hotel where refugees from the fighting had gathered. The plan was to assemble the battalion in a defensive perimeter around the field and hotel, start evacuating refugees by helicopter to the ships, and then the battalion would head into the city within the next couple of days.

Meanwhile, an infantry platoon was being rushed that night to reinforce the US embassy, which had been taking sniper fire. The platoon loaded in the dark onto three pickup trucks driven by Dominican policemen. As they were about to leave, I could make out some of my grunt buddies in the back of one of the pickups. "Hey, where're you guys going?" I called out as I went up to the side of a pickup.

"We're going to the embassy. There's been a lot of shooting around it and they're afraid the rebels will try to take it. They need help and we're gonna protect it until the battalion comes."

It sounded exciting—a lone platoon wheeling through a blacked-out city in the dead of night, a dangerous mission through armed groups, rushing to "save" the embassy.

"Man," I said, "I wish I was going with you."

"Hell, Charlie, why don't you come? Come on with us," one urged.

"Yeah, come on, Charlie," another added. "We got room. Come on."

That's all it took. I grabbed my pack and rifle and helping hands pulled me up into the bed of the crowded pickup. The battalion classified files I worked with would remain in safes onboard the ship. Whenever we were ashore in the Caribbean I was assigned to drive the battalion executive officer, a major, but I had no idea where he was that night and my jeep was still on the ship, so I jumped at the opportunity created by the confusion that night. Without using headlights, the pickups moved slowly through our lines and then sped through the dark city, careening through wide, empty streets. Kneeling in the back of the pickup we faced outward, weapons loaded and ready.

In the dark we set up a defensive perimeter around the embassy grounds, digging shallow foxholes along hedgerows and underneath palm trees. I took a turn during the night as one of the lookouts on the roof of the embassy. When dawn broke we started receiving occasional sniper fire. I fired back at a couple of clumps of foliage that could have concealed a sniper. I probably wounded the leaves on several trees.

Late in the morning, a Dominican propeller-driven fighter plane circled high overhead and then suddenly screamed out of the sky in a steep dive toward us. We dove for cover and moments later the plane dropped a bomb in the adjacent block. A big explosion and loud blast shook the earth and showered us with debris. A large plume of black and gray smoke billowed over rooftops from the impact area. Scattered sniper fire resumed.

By midafternoon we realized it had become quiet, eerily quiet, and a rumor quickly made it around the foxholes that this was the lull before the storm. I had joined up with a two-man, 3.5-millimeter rocket team, an antitank team, in their shallow foxhole across a side street running beside the embassy. The side street ran in the direction of the main fighting between rebel and government forces and it dead-ended at a T about four blocks from us. We anxiously scanned the area in the strange silence. Soon we heard the rumble of a tank toward the end of the street in the direction of the T. The roar of a tank engine and clanking tank treads were getting louder, closer. The tank was still out of sight but was approaching. We expected it to turn up the street and come clanking toward us to attack the embassy.

To have a clean shot at the tank, the rocket team would have to fire from the middle of the street, but would be an easy target for the tank's cannon and machine guns. We came up with a hasty backup plan in the event they were shot down. I would dash across the street carrying two rocket rounds, make my way to the top of an apartment building, and, when the tank was moving below, beside the building, I would remove the safety pins, lean over, and drop the rockets on the tank. I had no idea if the rockets would even explode that way. The plan was wildly impractical, but we were ready to try it.

We gripped our weapons tightly and strained to detect movement at the end of the street. Abruptly, the tank engine went silent. We assumed the tank crew was waiting for rebel forces on foot to advance and attack first. This was it—we got ready. Minutes ticked by. After thirty minutes nothing had happened and there was no sign of the enemy—only silence. We sent a patrol toward the T intersection to reconnoiter. They disappeared and returned an hour later, laughing about what they had found. The tank had run out of fuel near the intersection and the rebels had abandoned it and just walked away, canceling the attack.

The next day the forward elements of the battalion finally reached the embassy, suffering five Marines killed and sixteen wounded as they fought through the rebels. The fighting ended quickly and we spent another month in Santo Domingo to maintain the peace. By that time, battles raged on the other side of the world. I had no idea then that I'd be going to war soon.

To Vietnam

At the end of my tour at Camp Lejeune I volunteered for Vietnam and served as a squad leader during 1966 with Lima Company, Third Battalion, Third Marines. We roamed the rice paddies south of Da Nang, facing Vietcong guerrillas instead of regular North Vietnamese Army units, and my war consisted of very light combat compared to the vicious firefights and pitched battles fought later. Vietnam was a small-unit war and it felt natural for me to lead my men on patrols and ambushes and look after them.

For several months, our company was on Hill 22 south of Da Nang and we ran daily squad patrols and nighttime ambushes off the hill. Late one morning a patrol received fire right after leaving the hill and my squad rushed out to assist. A quick-reaction squad from another unit landed by helicopter and joined us in sweeping the area. We spread out on line and began moving through brush and clearings. As the Marine next to me moved through a hedgerow, he tripped a booby-trapped mortar shell, triggering a large explosion. The earth erupted and a shattering blast slammed me to the ground onto my stomach as shrapnel tore a hunk out of the back of my left shoulder. It felt like I had been hit with a sledgehammer. Had I been turned toward the blast or been a few inches to one side, the shrapnel would have hit my neck or head. A large plume of black smoke drifted upward, scattered debris fell, and the odor of exploded powder hung in the air.

The blast momentarily deafened me and then I heard ringing in my ears. I lay on my stomach while a Navy corpsman, "Doc," rushed over and worked on me. He was relatively new in-country and I saw his hands shaking. "It's okay Doc," I said, looking over my shoulder. "I'm okay. I'm all right." Then the irony hit me. "Hey Doc, aren't you supposed to be calming *me* down?" But the light moment quickly passed. As the initial shock wore off, I began feeling sharp pain and clenched my teeth to stifle low groans. Despite the pain I felt a sense of relief, realizing I was lucky to be alive.

The Marine who hit the booby trap was mortally wounded. Two corpsmen worked on him while he lay gurgling and thrashing in a poncho filling with blood. Several others had sustained minor wounds. A medevac chopper lifted me and the dying Marine to the forward combat hospital facility at Da Nang, known as "Charlie Med."

After one night at Charlie Med, I spent a week at NSA, Navy Support Activity, the Navy hospital at Da Nang, enjoying the luxuries of sleeping on a bed and mattress, drinking milk, and eating real food. It was a strange world compared to living in dirt night and day, patrolling in sweltering heat, slogging through ankle-deep muck in rice paddies, eating canned C rations, endlessly scanning dark shadows during night ambushes and constantly watching and sleeping in two-hour intervals night after night.

After the hospital stay, I was sent to battalion rear area to continue my recovery. A corpsman cleaned and dressed the large wound twice daily, but after several days I grew impatient to rejoin my men, so without waiting to be released, I grabbed my gear and jumped aboard a resupply convoy going to my company. My arrival was greeted with surprised smiles; they thought I had been evacuated to one of the base hospitals in Japan and would not be back. I resumed leadership of my squad and was back in the war. The platoon corpsman treated my wound daily until it healed. The shrapnel wound left a permanent round scar the size of a baseball on my shoulder. I now had battle scars on the back of each shoulder, one from shrapnel and the other from a knife wound.

"Grasshoppers"

As the squad leader, I carried an M-79 grenade launcher and the rest of the squad carried M-14 rifles. Unlike the M-16 rifles issued later in the war, the M-14 rifle could fire only semiautomatically unless it had been modified by the armory with a selector switch to allow it to fire fully automatically, like a machine-gun. Unfortunately, only two fully automatic M-14 rifles were issued to each squad. I figured out a way to fashion a homemade selector switch using a spring from an 81-millimeter mortar shell and the cotter pin and pull ring from a grenade. Using those items, I modified all the M-14s in the squad to fire fully automatically.

We planned to go outside the wire the next day to test-fire the rifles to find out if they would really fire fully automatically, but before we could test them, the squad was sent out on long patrol. The patrol route was quite a bit farther than patrols had gone before and much deeper into enemy-controlled territory. We all loaded up with twice the amount of ammunition we normally carried. By that afternoon we were in the open, crossing dry rice paddies, when we got hit with rifle and automatic-weapons fire from tree lines to the front and right side. The squad hit the ground and opened up. A tremendous volley of automatic M-14 fire confirmed that the modifications had worked, and the enemy fire quickly fell off.

When we first hit the ground, my face was pressed to the dirt and I thought I saw grasshoppers kicking up grains of red dirt a few inches in front of my eyes. Then I realized that the dirt was being kicked up by the impact of enemy rounds, not grasshoppers.

I raised my head and began firing my grenade launcher at the tree line forty yards away, repeatedly reloading and firing, the shells exploding with a sharp crash when they hit. We rushed the tree line but the Vietcong had melted away by the time we reached it. A quick-reaction force was lifted in by helicopter and we swept the area without finding anything. We didn't suffer any casualties and the entire squad now had fully automatic weapons, so it was a good day.

"Grasshoppers" brought home to me two lessons. First, humans try to fit new images logically into our usual life experience. Seeing grains of dirt kicked up within inches of my head was initially consistent with dirt kicked up by grasshoppers jumping, but then I realized what it was. Second, although enemy bullets had cracked by my head before, this time I could actually see how close death came to me.

■   ■   ■

After nine months in Vietnam my enlistment was coming to an end and I was pulled from the field to the battalion rear area to wait with a half dozen other short-timers to rotate back to the States. Fortunately I didn't undergo the horrors of heavy combat or suffer grievous wounds. I experienced just enough fighting to appreciate the terrible ordeal that those in heavy combat underwent. As combat veterans know, combat strips life to its bare essentials. The veneers of clothing, wealth, education, property, and the like are meaningless. A grunt lives in the dirt and survives on just enough food and sleep and stamina to keep going, to keep *doing*, day after day. A man's worth is judged by how dependable he is in the field and in combat.

Ironically, while combat strips life to its essentials, it also provides an opportunity to live life to its fullest. The stakes are the highest and life is intense, visceral, and vivid. For many it becomes the defining experience of their lives. For me, life since "grasshoppers" has been all gravy—a gift of extra life, bestowed by inches between life and death. Pure luck. I would need that kind of luck many times in the years to come.

I returned to the States, home from the war. The Marines provided excitement, adventure, and travel. I learned valuable lessons—the importance of accomplishing the mission and of taking care of my men. The Marines also instilled self-discipline and the confidence that nothing is impossible to accomplish, a mind-set I tried to apply to future endeavors.

■ ■ ■

After returning from Vietnam, I married Evelyn Grace Smith in Thomasville, North Carolina. We had met shortly before I left for Vietnam. I proposed soon after returning and we settled down in Thomasville. I went to work for Southern Bell Telephone Company in Greensboro. Using the GI bill, I also started on a new adventure—college. I enrolled in night classes at High Point College in nearby High Point, North Carolina. Learning was exciting and each course was a new adventure. I plunged into it wholeheartedly while working full time. It was the start of a long and rewarding journey. Taking courses as a part-time student, first at High Point, then at Louisiana State University (LSU), and finally at Ole Miss, usually at night, and sometimes having to lay off for years at a time, it took twelve years to get my undergraduate degree at Ole Miss, then another four years to get a law degree.

After a quiet year with the telephone company in Greensboro, I was longing for excitement. Law enforcement had a natural appeal and I left Southern Bell to take a lower-paying job as a police officer with the Thomasville Police Department. Before the year was out we moved to Baton Rouge, Louisiana, and I joined the Baton Rouge Police Department. Forty-two years later, my law-enforcement career ended when I retired after twenty-three years as an assistant US attorney and having served as a Department of Justice attorney-adviser to the Iraqi High Tribunal Court and as the justice attaché for Iraq.

Part I
BATON ROUGE POLICE DEPARTMENT

1
INTELLIGENCE

The Beginning

I joined the Baton Rouge Police Department and had been in uniform patrol for just two months when the chief's assistant, Captain Leroy Watson, called and asked to meet with me at my apartment. We sat and sipped coffee. He wanted to know if I would be interested in working undercover as a member of the new police intelligence unit that he headed. I had just moved to Baton Rouge from North Carolina, so outside of my patrol shift, I wasn't known in the city as a police officer. I thought it over for about two seconds and agreed. It sounded exciting and important, although I had no idea what I would be doing or how risky it would be. He instructed me not to return to my next patrol shift and to stay away from police department headquarters.

Aside from me, only two other investigators, Bud Garrison and Al Saizan, were in the intelligence unit and neither was in a covert role. We had a small, one-room office hidden unmarked and in a discreet location in the old Baton Rouge Junior High School building. I went to the office only occasionally to type intel reports and, as instructed, I signed the reports with the number seven rather than my name, a measure designed to conceal my identity on reports disseminated outside the unit.

Captain Watson's visit to our apartment that day changed our lives forever. I would work undercover for most of the next ten years—rewarding and exciting work that would change me and mark me for life. Our home life changed too. We could no longer tell neighbors where I worked. If neighbors inquired, my wife, Evelyn, told them I was a student at LSU and that we lived on her secretarial salary and that the GI bill paid for college. We changed our home telephone to a nonpublished number and did our best to conceal the fact that I was a police officer. She learned that when the phone rang and the caller asked for "Mike" or "Rick" or whoever, the call was always for me—the undercover me—and she would hand me the phone or tell the caller I was out. Our son, Terry, was almost one year old when I started working undercover and nearly eleven years old when I made my last case. He too learned to be careful when answering the phone. Evelyn had to take care of everything at home because I was gone most of the time, working long hours, usually until early morning and sometimes overnight, with no regular schedule and little time off.

When I was home I spent most of my time writing reports and talking on the phone with criminals and informants. Driving home from working undercover I sometimes had to watch to make sure I wasn't being followed. We had to be careful when we were out together in public because we could run into someone I was working on. So going out to eat or simply going to the grocery store together was no longer routine. Life changed for all of us.

My early undercover work in Baton Rouge Police Intelligence was a learning experience. Daily life teems with people heading to work in offices, stores, shops, and factories, and we are surrounded by a peaceful vision of law-abiding citizens, good neighbors, and caring families. Career criminals prowl beneath this placid surface: an underworld of predators who regard the public as victims and the police as the enemy. I soon plunged into that life in Baton Rouge, working alone to collect intelligence while trying to keep from being discovered. My closest companions became burglars, thugs, prostitutes, and safecrackers.

Randy the Safecracker

As an undercover intelligence agent, I had worked my way into a group of career criminals and our daily hangout was a bar in Baton Rouge. One midafternoon I sat at the bar with a safecracker, Randy, and his crazy sidekick, Candyman, who sat on a bar stool between us.

We were drinking beer and talking when Randy leaned toward us and lowered his voice.

"I got a new piece," he said and reached under his shirt at the waist. He slipped out a black .38-caliber snub-nosed revolver. "Just got it last night. It's hot," he added. Randy handed the gun below the countertop to Candyman, who turned it over in his hand, nodded, and passed it to me.

The gun was loaded and felt heavy in my hand. I wanted to get the serial number but it was too dark in the bar to see it that closely without being noticed. "Hey, Randy, I could use this," I said quietly. "How about I'll get it back to you tomorrow." I slipped it in my pocket, planning to get the serial number before I returned it. Anger flashed across Randy's face, his eyes narrowed to slits, and his nostrils flared, and he demanded the gun back right away, causing me to wonder if there was something special about the gun other than it being stolen. I said something about getting it back to him later on, but he became more agitated. Randy glared at me with fierce eyes. He leaned forward over the bar top and locked eyes with me. "Mike, I want my gun back," he growled.

Suddenly Candyman jammed a gun in my side. "Give me the gun, Mike." I froze inside but tried to look nonchalant by ignoring the gun and taking a swig of my beer. Then Candyman cocked his .38. I tensed at the solid metal click of the hammer cocking. Although barely audible, to me it sounded loud, lethal, and vicious. Glancing down, I saw Candyman's finger on the trigger.

He pressed the barrel farther into my right side and I thought about how easy it would be for the cocked gun to go off, especially accidentally. Just the slightest pressure on the trigger would cause the hammer to slam home and the gun to fire a bullet through my guts. I prayed he wouldn't sneeze or hiccup or twitch or flinch or be bumped by someone walking past.

Candyman leaned close to my ear. "Give me the gun, Mike," he hissed in a low, venomous voice, "or I swear, I'll pull this fucking trigger. Give—me—the—gun, *now*." He jabbed the gun barrel harder against my side.

I looked at him. The veins in his neck stood out. His eyes locked with mine in a hard, furious stare. Then his eyes glazed over into a cold, vacant, wild look, and I felt a chill run through my body. Something inside his head had snapped, I thought, and *his finger is on the trigger*. I picked up my beer, willing my hand not to shake, and deliberately took another drink, and then I handed the gun back slowly and carefully so as not to cause a sudden reaction. I passed the gun beneath the bar top to Randy, reaching past Candyman, who still pressed the gun in my side. Randy took his gun back and tucked it under his shirt.

Candyman started uncocking the gun in my side while I held my breath. Uncocking a revolver is dangerous, especially when it is pointed at someone. With his thumb pulling back on the hammer to keep it from slamming home and firing, Candyman pulled the trigger. Then he started slowly lowering the hammer. If his thumb slipped, the hammer would fall and the gun would fire. A bullet would explode my insides. Uncocking the gun took only seconds but it seemed longer, and I was momentarily suspended between life and death while the "normal" world casually went on around us. Candyman put the gun in his pocket and I sighed with a rush of relief. We finished our beers and left, still buddies, but buddies who could hurt each other.

It was a minor incident, almost trivial, yet it was intense because of how easily and effortlessly the gun could have fired, either intentionally or accidentally. The cocked gun was symbolic. With Randy, Candyman, and the others in the group, the veneer of "normal" life was tenuous and could be shattered in an instant.

Randy, a safecracker by trade, had a reputation as one of the best in the business. His easygoing manner was belied by a hint of violence lurking just beneath the surface, capable of exploding suddenly and savagely. Despite the scent of danger, or perhaps because of it, women were attracted to him. He stood a couple of inches over six feet, had sandy hair and raw good looks, and looked to be in his mid-thirties. A once-broken nose somehow enhanced rather than detracted from his overall appearance.

After I started hanging out with Randy to develop intelligence, I quickly learned that Randy's prominence in the safecracking business brought him both opportunities and problems.

One day a broiling afternoon sun chased me across an oven-hot parking lot and into the bar where we usually hung out. Sweat-soaked, I felt the refreshing chill of air conditioners blowing on full blast. Coming from the blinding white glare outside into the dim, windowless bar, I was plunged into almost total darkness until my eyes adjusted. The only light came from the glow of illuminated beer and liquor signs over the long mirror behind the bar and a riot of lights from a jukebox. Only a handful of customers sat at the bar.

The bartender caught my eye and nodded toward Randy, who sat alone at a table near the back wall. As I neared him, Randy watched me, his eyes narrowed and his lips compressed in a tight line. The pent-up anger was easy to see, and the anxious thought shot through my mind that my cover might be blown.

"Hey, man, what's up, Randy? You look like you're mad about something," I said tensely. "Who you mad at?"

He glared at me a few moments and finally answered. "Frank and Sammy, that's who," he spat out, "the stupid sumbitches."

"Damn, Randy, what'd they do?" I asked with a sigh of relief.

"I'll tell you what they *did*." Randy hunched closer over the table. "They came to my house and woke me up at two this morning. They hit a business last night and worked on the safe for two hours—*two hours*—and couldn't get it open. So you know *what* the sumbitches did then?"

"What?"

"The idiots had the bright idea of bringing it to my house to get me to open it. To my house!" he snarled, spitting out each word. Randy shook his head in disbelief. "My house. Can you believe that shit? Sumbitches woke me up and said they had a safe in the trunk of their car outside and wanted me to open it for them. Damn, I was mad. I grabbed my gun and was ready to shoot the sumbitches. They kept saying how sorry they was and begging me to help them."

"Whatcha do?"

"After I cooled down, I told them to get it away from my house. I finally said I'd open it for half of what was in it. So they took off and I met them. I had that sumbitch open in fifteen minutes," he said with obvious satisfaction, the thought tamping down his anger.

"Damn, that's good."

"It wasn't nothing to get it open, but I got only eight hundred for my half," he grumbled. "I shoulda shot the stupid sumbitches."

I later wrote an intel report on the information. I never knew if anyone tried to follow up, but I doubt it: Frank and Sammy were never charged. Undercover, I collected lots of intelligence about crimes and criminals, but my job as an undercover intelligence agent wasn't to make cases. Unlike today's intelligence operations, we didn't have an intelligence analyst to exploit the information or anyone specifically tasked with using the intelligence to develop criminal cases. And no one then was focused on making conspiracy cases, which would have been a valuable tool for making use of the information I gathered. But it was just as well. Working undercover alone and without surveillance, my security lay in avoiding suspicion. If some of my criminal colleagues suddenly started getting arrested, I would be in greater danger.

■ ■ ■

A couple of weeks after Frank and Sammy's safe job, hanging out with Randy became even more interesting. Because of Randy's reputation, he was sometimes suspected of safe jobs he didn't do. One time that had serious repercussions.

Someone had hit safes in two bars, one owned by Jake and the other owned by Sal, who was believed to be associated with organized crime. Jake suspected Randy and word soon circulated that Jake had put out a contract on Randy. We heard that a hit man from Chicago was in town to take Randy out. Randy was concerned and it soon became apparent there was cause for worry.

I was standing with Randy and Dave in the parking lot of a bar late one night talking when a gunshot cracked. I ducked and reached for my gun. Randy dove to the ground, then jumped up in a crouch with his gun drawn, ready to fire. Dave landed in a heap behind a car and scrambled into a squat, peering over the hood. Randy and I crouched side by side holding our guns while searching the surroundings as cars rushed by on the four-lane street in front of the lounge.

"See anything, Mike?" Randy asked anxiously, his eyes jumping, like mine, from place to place.

"No. You?"

"Nothing," Randy swept his gun from side to side. "Dave!" Randy yelled, without taking his eyes off the street and cars. "Where'd it come from?"

Crouched behind the car, our buddy Dave turned his head only slightly to respond. "I couldn't tell. You guys see anything?"

The cars flowed past in a noisy blur under a necklace of streetlights. The danger seemed to have passed and I became worried Randy might snap off a shot at a passerby.

"Maybe it was an engine backfire," I suggested, straightening up and tucking my gun away.

Uncoiling from his crouch, Randy put his gun in his jacket but kept his hand in the pocket. "I dunno." He thought for a moment. "It didn't sound like no fucking backfire. That was a fucking gunshot." I knew enough from Vietnam firefights to know he was right.

Randy inhaled deeply and blew out audibly. "It's got to be that muth-erfucker from Chicago," he muttered to himself, still watching the street, eyes narrowed and jaw set. "Sal and that goddamn Jake."

I felt Randy's reaction was unpredictable. Who was going to make the next move? Events seemed to be spinning out of control.

Later that night, Randy and I sat at our usual table in the lounge. Customers stood two deep at the bar and the tables were full. The crowd was noisy and the din surged in waves. Two of the dancers sat with us between their sets and the owner stopped by when he could get away from behind the bar. Before long, a half dozen others sat crowded around our table.

Randy was quieter than normal and seemed lost in thought. He didn't say much about the gunshot in the parking lot, but the more he drank, the more he simmered; he was getting worked up. Finally, he leaned close to my ear.

"Mike, that goddamn Jake," he snarled, his nostrils flared. "I'll blow that muth-er-fuck-er away. You hear me," he said, raising his voice. "I'll blow him away!" Randy pulled his gun out and slapped it down heavily on the table, rattling beer bottles. It laid there, a menacing metal hulk with the lead noses of .38-caliber bullets visible in the cylinder.

"Jake's got it coming. I oughta hit him tonight."

"Randy," I objected, "you do that tonight and they gonna know you did it—"

"I don't give a damn. I'll blow the sumbitch away." Randy looked around the table defiantly and was met with approving nods.

"Look, you don't know for sure it was Jake," I protested.

"The fuck I don't! It's Jake and that sumbitch from Chicago. I'll blow their shit away. You hear me? I'll blow his goddamn head off."

Customers at nearby tables glanced uneasily at the gun and whispered to companions who stole quick looks in our direction.

"Randy, you need to put your gun away before somebody calls the heat," I suggested, nodding toward the other tables. He looked around with a defiant stare and then put the gun away. We were interrupted by other dancers joining us and the talk turned to other matters.

Later that night, Randy returned to the subject. "Mike," he said, looking directly at me, "you still got your gun on you?" I looked at him sharply and hesitated a moment.

"Yeah. You got something in mind?"

"I wanna pay a visit to Big Jake's and I need somebody to back me up. Jake and Sal are supposed to have the fucking contract out together," Randy explained, but I already knew about Jake. "Jake thinks I hit his fucking joint too. You back me up?" Randy challenged.

"What you wanna do when we get there?"

"I'm just gonna let that sumbitch know I'm around," Randy said, with a determined look. "But if he starts anything, I might need some backup."

"Okay, Randy. Yeah, sure," I said with a nod. "When you wanna go?"

"Now." I was caught between two bad choices. If I declined to go, I would lose credibility and blow any chance of continuing to gather intelligence with this crowd. But if I went with Randy to Big Jake's, we might wind up in a fight or a shooting with an undercover officer in the middle of it. Of course, if I went, it would enhance my credibility, even if nothing happened. Word would circulate that Randy and Mike went to Big Jake's looking for trouble. Without time to think it through, I chose to go, but felt like I was about to jump off a high cliff into a black void. Randy downed the last of his beer and we left.

As I drove Randy to Big Jake's, a jumble of thoughts whirled in my mind. The gunshot and Randy's reaction propelled us toward a confrontation where anything could happen. Whatever the outcome, it would seem inevitable after the fact, but as we neared Big Jake's, the ending was unpredictable.

When we parked, Randy tucked his gun in the front of his waistband with his shirt hanging out to conceal it. I reached back to confirm that my gun was firmly in place and handy at the middle of my back. I felt anxious, my senses riveted, vibrant and alert.

Big Jake's was half full of customers; a few tables were empty and a smattering of people sat or stood at the bar. The only entertainment in the smoke-filled bar was furnished by two pool tables and the jukebox. When we walked in, heads turned. Jake and three of his guys stood clustered at the far end of the bar. Jake was bent over the counter, smiling and talking, but when he saw us his smile vanished, he stopped in mid-sentence, and he straightened up. He and his men watched warily as we strode to the near end of the bar. While I ordered a couple of beers, Randy and Jake glared at each other. Jake's men looked as alert, focused, and tense as I was.

Jake disappeared into a back room. He emerged a few moments later and rejoined his men. Without taking his eyes off Randy, Jake murmured something and his men squared off, facing us. Twenty feet away, Randy stepped away from the bar and stood facing Jake. Using his left hand, Randy casually raised the bottom of his shirt just above his waist, displaying the gun tucked in front. Randy's other hand lingered within a few inches of the butt. The grim look on Jake's face gradually changed into a wry grin. With a tight smile, Jake held his arms out from his sides, palms upward, and walked to Randy.

"Randy, my man. How are you? How you doing?"

"I heard you looking for me. You looking for me, Jake? 'Cause if you are, here I am."

"No," Jake said, with a shake of his head. "No. Hell, I don't know where you heard that. I ain't been looking for you."

"I heard your safe got hit the other night. You get hit, Jake?" Randy taunted.

Jake's jaw tightened and anger flashed across his face. "Yeah, I got hit. Sal did too," he added pointedly.

"I heard you been saying I was the one that hit you."

"What? Who said that? No, I ain't said it was you, Randy."

Randy smirked triumphantly—he had backed Jake down.

"'Cause I know you wouldn't be that fucking stupid, Randy," Jake said with a sneer.

Randy's smirk disappeared and his eyes blazed.

"Jake, if it *had* been me, you would fucking know it." Randy hissed through clenched teeth.

He and Jake locked eyes. "I heard a sumbitch from Chicago was in town looking for whoever done it," Randy continued. "You know, Jake, if anybody was looking for me they wouldn't have to look far," Randy said, thumbing toward his chest. "I'd hit that sumbitch and whoever sent him. Fuck the mutherfucker."

This is the point, I thought, where violence might erupt and I wasn't sure how I would be able to defuse the situation.

Jake hesitated and seemed to be fighting to suppress his rage. "Hell, Randy, I know it wasn't you," Jake finally said. "Sal's the one that's really jacked up about it. That's him. It ain't me." Jake shrugged. "Anyway, let me know if you hear anything, okay? 'Cause whoever did it is going to pay."

"Yeah, sure," Randy nodded. They had just called a truce. Jake was lying. I could tell he thought it was Randy who had hit his place, but he had handled the confrontation and deftly reminded Randy that Randy still had to worry about Sal.

"Hey," Jake called to the bartender and nodded sideways toward us, "give 'em another beer." Jake turned back to Randy and then threw a look at me. "Yeah, Jake," Randy said, taking the cue, "this here's Mike." Jake and I shook. "We look after each other."

After a couple of minutes of light conversation, Jake walked back to his guys at the far end of the bar. We finished the beers, gave a nod to Jake, and headed for the door. I noticed that one of Jake's men was no longer around. Walking to our car in the dimly lit parking lot, Randy and I glanced at the other parked cars and over our shoulders, just to make sure.

As we drove away, I breathed a sigh of relief.

"You see that sorry ass?" Randy asked with a smirk. "Jake knew I'd blow him away."

"Yeah, Randy, you backed him down. Jake didn't want none of you," I said. "But what about Sal, you know he—"

"*Fuck* Sal! *Mutherfucker*. They know I'll take care of their ass, anything happen."

I kept checking the rearview mirror until we were well away from Big Jake's.

When we got back to the lounge, Randy regaled our friends with his tale of the night's events and how he backed Big Jake down. They listened with approving nods and knowing smiles—*Randy's a bad mutherfucker; we're all bad mutherfuckers* was the unspoken feeling. I, of course, was just a *pretend* bad mutherfucker. I wondered where all this "bad mutherfucker" business in the criminal underworld would lead, especially with me along for the ride.

At closing time, two of the dancers joined us and we loaded into several cars and headed to the notorious "gold coast"—several large, twenty-four-hour nightclubs, the Carousel Club, Candle Light, Nicks, and the Riviera, located across the Mississippi River from Baton Rouge. A favorite after-hours spot for criminals, the gold coast was wide open, with gambling, prostitution, fights, and police corruption.

I took Kathy, Bobby, and Rhonda in my car. We joined up with the others at the Carousel and were immediately swallowed up by a packed and raucous crowd in the dimly lit, cavernous building. The crowd tugged in all directions and Rhonda and Bobby got separated from us and disappeared from view. Several hours after daybreak, Kathy and I walked unsteadily out of the Carousel, squinting and blinking at the bright early-morning light. Rhonda and Bobby decided to stay a while longer and catch another ride back. I dropped Kathy off and drove home for some rest.

Before getting some sleep, I wrote quick notes about the night's events and slept until early afternoon. After a shower, several cups of coffee, and sandwiches, I wrote intel reports at the kitchen table. Just before dusk I went back to the lounge and joined some of our regular group at a table. Kathy and Rhonda arrived for work after dark and sat with us between sets. Randy came in later that night. We talked about Sal and Big Jake and whether anyone had heard any more about the Chicago hit man who was supposed to be in town. Things seemed quiet for the moment.

About a week after our confrontation at Big Jake's, an Italian businessman was killed in a mob-type hit across the river from Baton Rouge. He had locked up his business late one night and the next morning his body was found inside. He had been shot in the head and there was no indication robbery was a motive. Rumors flew around and I suspected Randy might know something about it, but when I brought it up, Randy wouldn't talk about it except to say he heard the guy had it coming.

■ ■ ■

Staying out all night in bars with Randy and the others became a pattern and each night blurred into the next. But one night I made it home from the bars well before daylight, and by midafternoon I was ready to head back to work, feeling refreshed after eight hours of uninterrupted sleep. As I stepped outside and walked to my car, I noticed spring had arrived. Birds chirped, the sky was a cloudless blue, trees budded in vibrant greens, flowers bloomed, and the air smelled of fresh cut grass. It felt good to be out in daylight, soaking up the freshness of springtime. Baton Rouge seemed full of life and bustling with energy. It was a beautiful day.

I headed to a bar that Candyman sometimes helped run during the day for his uncle. I occasionally went by for a drink just to stay tight with him and pick up talk about what others were doing. The bar was a small, windowless brick building in a red-light district located on a street off Plank Road, the road that ran parallel to the Mississippi River and the chemical plants along the river. As I neared the bar, a chemical odor permeated the air and replaced the fresh scents of spring.

When I walked into the bar, it felt like plunging into a dark cave. It would have been difficult to find a bleaker place than the inside of the dim, dank, and dirty bar. It smelled of mold, cigarette smoke, urine, and vomit, and stale spilled beer and liquor sloshed on the bar top, tables, and floor. As my eyes adjusted I noticed several die-hard drinkers, some already in a stupor.

I sat nursing a beer and talking with Candyman at a table when one of the men standing at the bar, a scruffy, middle-aged wino, began leaning sideways and fell to the floor and passed out. Others cast brief glances at him and turned back to their drinks. They had looked at the drunk with disgust and fear, I thought—fear that they were looking at themselves.

On a bar stool near the drunk sat a woman about sixty, with smeared lipstick and caked-on makeup over a road map of deep wrinkles. With a cigarette dangling from the side of her mouth, she looked down at the drunk, frowned, and gave a slight head shake. She looked over her shoulder at Candyman, who was at the table with me.

"Well, ain't y'all gonna do summin about him?" she demanded in a raspy whiskey voice.

Candyman glanced at the drunk on the floor. "Fuck him," he smirked.

The woman turned back to her drink. "At least you could move him outta the way, goddammit," she muttered.

Candyman stared at the woman's back. "Stupid bitch." His eyes burned, and I sensed he wanted to hurt her. A shiver ran down my back. I had seen that same mean and crazy look in Candyman's eyes before, when he jammed a cocked gun in my side. What had this mean bastard done in his nasty life?

No one bothered about the drunk. He lay untouched on the floor. For all they knew, he could have suffered a stroke or a heart attack, but no one bothered to find out. He lay forgotten. It was only midafternoon.

An hour later I left the bar and was getting in my car across the street when another drunk staggered out of the bar and started navigating the sidewalk. A medium-sized man in his fifties wearing khaki work clothes, the drunk swayed and carefully put each foot down in front.

Candyman followed him out and stalked a few paces behind. Suddenly, Candyman sprang forward and hit the drunk in the head from behind. The victim went down like a sack of potatoes, unconscious. Candyman rifled the man's pockets and came up with a few dollars. He stuffed the money in his pocket and then kicked the man hard. Candyman looked around to see if anyone other than me had seen him. He cast me a knowing look and then strolled casually back to the bar and disappeared inside. The victim lay in a crumpled heap in bright sunshine under a clear-blue sky. It was a beautiful spring day.

The robbery happened so fast that I couldn't have done anything to prevent it. And I couldn't do anything about it without burning my cover. Using a pay phone a few blocks away, I called police headquarters and anonymously reported that a drunk was passed out in front of the bar and might have been rolled. Then I headed to another bar. My workday was just beginning. It was still a beautiful spring day, but I now felt dirty and grimy.

A couple of weeks later, that spring day was just a distant memory as I sat talking with Randy and others crowded around our table. It was late Tuesday night, and the bar business was slow. I couldn't keep up with the conversations because Kathy sat next to me, talking nonstop. She must be on speed, I thought, as she rattled on. I got a respite when Randy nudged my shoulder.

"Come on," Randy said with a sideways nod toward the door as he stood up. "We're gonna take a ride." Bobby and Frank joined us and we left the bar and went for a ride in Bobby's car. With Randy providing directions, Bobby drove to the other side of the city to an area cluttered with businesses and small office buildings, all closed for the night.

"There it is, Bobby," Randy said, "there on the right. That's it. Just drive on by right now."

Randy pointed to a single-story, blond brick building. A plate-glass door was in the center and plate-glass windows began chest high on either side of the door and ran the length of the front. The business was dark inside except for one overhead light. A narrow parking area crowded the front and one side and a narrow alley ran along the other side. Other closed businesses and offices clustered the area. This was before surveillance cameras became ubiquitous, so there was no danger of being seen on camera.

We drove by and circled back, and Randy had Bobby pull up and stop in front of the building. Randy strode quickly to the window and we followed. Bobby left the car running. A ceiling spotlight shined down on a large gray safe located several paces behind a desk. Illuminated under the light, the safe stood out from the surrounding darkness. Randy stared intently at the safe, apparently assessing the opportunities and risks involved, and then looked over the front glass door.

"All right," Randy said, "let's go. Let's get outta here."

Randy had Bobby drive down the streets beside and behind the building. He wanted to see the views cops would have on night patrol.

After casing the business, we rode back to the bar. Randy didn't make any comments and no one asked questions. The only reason Randy took us with him, I thought, was because he thought he might need a driver and at least two lookouts. But he never brought up the safe or the business again and I never asked any questions about it.

Two weeks later, Randy told me Bobby and Frank almost got caught trying to hit another business. "I told them to stay away from it," Randy complained. "It was too open, but the stupid sumbitches tried it anyway and almost got caught. The cops came just as they were about to go in. It must have had a silent alarm. They shoulda listened. Stupid sumbitches."

■ ■ ■

A month after I accompanied Randy to case a business, I had an opportunity to become more deeply involved. Randy called and said, "I need to talk to you about something. Meet me at the bar this afternoon."

Late that afternoon I arrived at the bar and joined Randy, who sat alone at a table. We nursed our beers, smoked, and exchanged small talk until Randy got around to the reason he wanted to see me. He paused, looked around, and leaned closer.

"Listen," he said. "This is why I wanted to talk to you. I got a job lined up if you're interested."

"A safe?"

"Yeah. The place is a cash business and the safe'll be full of cash if we hit it at the right time. I need a lookout and a driver."

"A lookout and a driver?" I asked, giving myself time to think. He nodded. "Well," I said, "I can be the lookout if you want. How much you figure we'll get and what's the splits?"

"It'll probably be anywhere from six to ten thousand in the safe. I get half and you and the driver split the rest."

"That sounds good to me. For a driver, how about Joey?" I suggested. "He'll keep his mouth shut and he's reliable."

Randy raised an eyebrow. Before he could raise a question, I added, "Joey and I've done a few things together. We can trust him and I know he'll do a good job."

Randy rubbed his chin with the back of his hand, thinking it over.

"Just letting you know," I continued, "but if you got somebody else in mind then—"

"No. Go ahead and get him lined up. Tell him there'll be three of us. Me and you will be going in the building, and he'll be the driver."

"I'll probably need to let him know when we'll need him for the job."

"Just tell him to be ready. It could be anytime in the next couple weeks."

"All right."

After leaving Randy late that night, I called and alerted Captain Watson, the head of the intelligence unit, about the safe job and then lined up the informant, Joey. Captain Watson instantly recognized the problems: the danger to other officers and the inability to stake out the building with the safe since we didn't know which town and which business Randy planned to hit. This was before vehicle tracking devices were in use, and surveillance using unmarked police cars wouldn't be feasible as they would likely be burned trying to follow us during late-night and early-morning hours from Baton Rouge to and around one of the smaller towns in the area. Unmarked police cars, big four-door sedans without hubcaps, were readily recognizable as police cars. Plus, if Randy discovered surveillance on him, it would likely make him suspicious of me.

During the week I told Randy I had Joey lined up to help out. Randy wouldn't tell me in advance when we would do it and he wouldn't tell me where—only that it would be out of town. He told me to be ready at any time.

This was an opportunity, I thought, but it came with serious problems because Randy and the driver would likely be armed. If a police officer happened upon us they might kill him, and I might be unable to prevent it. A lookout would be the first and biggest danger to a police officer, and that's why I had chosen to be the lookout. If an officer discovered the break-in, I should be able to arrest Randy before he could kill the officer. I would still have to worry about being shot myself by police officers, as they would consider anyone in the building to be a burglar and a danger. An armed driver would be dangerous to officers too, but by using an informant, Joey, as the driver, then Randy would be the only danger to others.

A few days later, Randy called me and told me to get a clean car, one that couldn't be traced to me, and buy three pairs of gloves. I got the gloves and a car and that night, Joey and I picked up Randy at his house. Randy put a zippered bag in the trunk and settled in beside me, with Joey on the rear seat. "Where we going?" I asked, pulling onto the street.

"Just drive across the river," Randy said. "I'll tell you later."

We drove across the Mississippi River to Port Allen and then south on Highway 1 to Plaquemine, about ten miles south of Port Allen. Randy wanted to stop at a bar and kill some time so we stopped at the appropriately named Passer le Temps (to pass the time) lounge on the north edge of Plaquemine. The bar was crowded and noisy. We sat at a corner table nursing our beers.

"All right, here's the deal," Randy said edging his chair closer and hunching over the table. We leaned in, elbows on the table. "We gonna hit the safe in a gas station." Randy said. "It's the gas station on the left side of the highway about a mile outta town. We gonna hit it tonight and I'll take care of the safe," he said, looking at me and then at Joey.

"Okay," I said with a nod. "I'm ready." Randy and I looked at Joey.

"Me too," Joey chimed in.

"When we finish our beers we'll head to the gas station. It could have a silent alarm inside so when we get there, I'll throw a brick through a window and then we'll back off and watch it to see if the cops come. We'll wait about twenty minutes and if they don't come," Randy looked at Joey, who nodded, "Joey, you drop off me and Mike at the station."

"Okay."

"Mike," Randy turned to me.

"Yeah."

"When Joey drops us off, we'll go in and you'll be the lookout while I work on the safe. You don't watch me, you watch the outside. I don't want the cops coming up on me, you hear?"

"Yeah, okay."

"Joey, I'll show you where to wait for us after you drop us off," Randy continued. "When I finish with the safe we'll make our way through a field and along tree line to you. When you see us coming, you crank up the car and be ready, you got me?"

Joey nodded.

Randy had planned the safe job without letting us know beforehand which place he intended to hit. By waiting and telling us at the last minute, he didn't have to take the chance that Joey and I might run our mouths to others and let it slip out. He had played it pretty smart. The only thing he had not guarded against was having an undercover police officer acting as his lookout.

Late that night we left the lounge to do the safe job and headed south through Plaquemine toward the other end of town where the business was located. I drove, Randy sat up front, and Joey was in the back. Rather than taking Highway 1, which went through town, Randy had me take back streets. I drove the speed limit and we watched for police cars. Our talk in the car was in brief, tense clips. "When we get there," Randy reminded us, "Mike, you come in with me and Joey, you take the car."

"Right," I said.

"Okay," said Joey.

"Mike, be damn sure you stay on the lookout—don't watch me, watch the outside, you hear?"

"Yeah, I got it, don't worry."

"All right. When we get there, just drive past so we can look it over first. We'll circle back and I'll throw a brick through the window. Then we back off until we see if it's got an alarm. I'll show you a road across the field from the station. We'll watch from there to see if the heat comes. Mike, you and Joey can switch out driving there. Joey, you'll drop us off. Y'all got it?"

"Yeah, okay," I said as I drove through a dark intersection.

Joey spoke up. "Randy, what if . . ."

Suddenly, *BLAM! CRASH!* A van slammed broadside into Randy's door, with screeching tires, crunching metal, and flying car parts, knocking our car sideways in the street, spinning us in a full circle until the car rocked and lurched to a stop amid smoke, steam, and burned oil. The car sat lopsided, leaning close to the ground on the driver's side. The powerful impact knocked us down inside the car. When the car stopped moving, we slowly pushed upright, stunned. "Goddamn! Goddamn!" Randy muttered, shaking his head slowly and rubbing the back of his neck.

In the back, Joey mumbled something unintelligible. He held his head in both hands, grimacing in pain, his eyes squinted closed. We were all bruised, stiff, and sore, but no one was really hurt except Joey, who had to wear a neck brace for the next couple of weeks. The car was totaled. The van was probably totaled too, but at least the driver wasn't hurt.

Before it happened, I had been looking out for police cars, concentrating on Randy's instructions, thinking about what could happen when we were inside on the job—and never saw the stop sign. The side street had the right-of-way and when I blew through the stop sign, the driver of the van had no time to avoid hitting us. Even if it had been daylight I probably wouldn't have seen the stop sign because it was on a higher-than-usual post and partially obscured by a low-hanging limb.

The wreck put an end to the safe job, but I worried that it would blow my cover with Randy and all the others. The car had swapped-out license plates, guns inside it, and burglary tools in the trunk, and all three of us might wind up in jail. I knew my cover wasn't deep enough to hold up to fingerprinting or the involvement of prosecutors and criminal defense lawyers, so when the police discovered guns and burglary tools in the car and took us to the police station, I whispered to one of the officers that I needed to talk to a police supervisor alone. That was met with a frown and a quizzical look, but finally, a supervisor showed up.

"You wanna talk to me?" he said, too loudly. I cringed. Randy might have heard.

"Alone," I said quietly, and cut my eyes toward Randy, who was in the next room. The supervisor shot a look toward Randy, and then looked me up and down, his eyebrows furrowed in a V. Finally he nodded and led me into a room.

I quietly told him who I was and asked him to call Captain Watson in Baton Rouge to verify my identity and undercover role. I never carried police identification on me or in the car. The supervisor gave me a skeptical look, but he sat down at a desk and dialed the number I gave him, which was Captain Watson's home number. It was well after midnight. After reaching Captain Watson and exchanging introductions, the supervisor briefly explained the situation. Then for next few minutes, the officer listened on the phone, repeatedly saying, "Yes, sir. Yes, sir," to Captain Watson while he occasionally glanced up at me. Two other officers wandered in during the phone call. All this was done outside Randy's presence, but I was filled with dread that I would be compromised now. Not because the officers were untrustworthy, but because too many people now knew I was working undercover. My best safety was secrecy—and when too many people knew something important, it would no longer be a secret. Randy and I were released in the early-morning hours and we left with separate rides. Joey was taken to a hospital and released.

The night had been a whirlwind and a disaster. I finally got home after daylight. I talked with Captain Watson several times by phone during that day and we worked on damage control in an effort to maintain my cover with Randy—but I wasn't optimistic.

Things had gone too awkwardly at the local police department in the aftermath of the crash and Randy was no fool. I felt certain my cover was already blown or about to be. The fact that I was undercover would be buzzing throughout the police department and soon on the streets.

Because there was still a chance that I might be all right, I had to show up at the bar where I hung out with Randy and the crowd. I cringed at the thought of it. The weather that day fit my mood.

Right after dawn the day became overcast and dreary. It was a Sunday, and the empty streets and closed businesses added to the gloom. By early afternoon the smell of rain was in the air, earthy and moist. Wind gusts began picking up; dark clouds hunkered low and scudded over rooftops. Strong wind gusts whipped the tops of trees and bushes, and leaves and debris blew past and swirled in eddies in the streets. Loose boards banged and metal trash cans clanged as the wind hurled them down and rolled them along the street. Heavy droplets of rain began hitting hard and turned into torrents of lashing rain, driving sideways, pounding and drumming furiously. Claps of thunder exploded, rumbled, and reverberated while lightning ripped the air, crackling and crashing.

Because it was Sunday, the bar was closed and I welcomed the delay. It would be best to test the waters by going early, I thought, when only a few people would be around. If things didn't seem right, I would get out before everyone arrived and something bad happened.

Monday I called Captain Watson and told him I felt like everything would be okay and I was going to drop by the bar to check things out. Even though I knew my model 60 Smith and Wesson revolver was loaded, I opened the cylinder and checked it anyway. Five .38-caliber bullets were firmly seated in the cylinder. The sight of the bullets, the sound of the cylinder clicking back into the gun frame, and the feel and solid weight of the weapon felt reassuring. I used my senses of sight, sound, and touch to counter the unease in my mind. Checking a gun to make sure it is loaded makes for good drama in the movies, but I was simply soothing myself. I tucked the gun at the back of my waist, pulled my shirt out to cover it, and drove to the bar.

I had been in a bar when Candyman pressed a cocked gun in my side while Randy looked on. That had happened over a simple dispute about a gun. What would they want to do to an undercover cop who had infiltrated the group?

It was almost dusk when I arrived and parked in a lot across the street from the bar. There was plenty of room to park in front but I didn't want my car to stand out to anyone passing by—at least not until I was certain everything was okay. I felt the handle of the gun at my back—another soothing gesture—and got out and walked toward the bar.

I took a deep breath, pushed open the door, and sauntered in nonchalantly. Kathy and Rhonda sat at a table in the far corner and I planned to join them, but first I stopped at the bar to get a beer and a sense of how the bartender would react to me. He had always been friendly, but now acted sullen and cold. I had my answer as to whether I was burned. I headed over to join Kathy and Rhonda. Rhonda got up and left as I approached. I sipped beer and talked with Kathy but she was tense and gave me clipped responses. Bobby came in, saw me, and veered toward the bar. He and the bartender huddled a few moments and then Bobby hurried out the door.

Kathy watched him leave too.

After a moment she said in a strained voice, "Mike."

"Yeah?"

"Maybe you better go now."

I stood up and looked around the bar. It would be my last time inside, and my mind was already racing ahead—anticipating the possibilities that might be awaiting me outside.

I strode toward the door, feeling hostile stares on my back. I became hyperalert as I pushed the door open and stepped out. It was already dark and now more cars were parked around the bar and across the street. As it turned out, no one waited in ambush, but these are the kinds of things you have to think of when working undercover. Actual dangers are more lethal if you are oblivious to the possible risks.

I walked across the street to the lot where my car was parked, and as I got closer I saw something wasn't right about the back window. It looked like a spiderweb. Someone had shattered the rear window into an intricate web of cracks. The other cars were fine; the only damaged car was mine. Someone had busted the window with a baseball bat, I thought, or maybe a bullet had hit it, causing it to shatter. A shiver ran through my body as I realized I had been targeted. It's an eerie feeling to know that someone is after you—not after those *like you*, as in war, the *anonymous you*, but, rather, after *you* personally.

As I drove away, the rear window collapsed and dozens of pieces of glass fell inside the car and on the top of the trunk. Heading home, I checked for anyone tailing me. After I reached home, I stood inside in the dark and watched out the window for a while just to be sure.

It was over, I thought as I watched the empty street, but at least it didn't end violently. Much later I heard that Randy said he knew I was a cop all along and he had planned to kill me the night we went on the safe job. He was going to shoot me in the head with a .380 pistol. I don't believe it. He *was* capable of killing me, but he didn't know I was a cop.

Working Girls and Shopping

Just before I began running with Randy, I hung out with another group. One Sunday, to get around the Sunday closing law, a nightclub owner had secretly invited select customers to a onetime special event at a house, with his nightclub dancers as the featured entertainment. I was there working as a bartender and had a ringside view of the strip show, which turned out to be an incredible performance.

Joey, the informant who later went on the safe job with me and Randy, knew the nightclub owner, and he arranged for the two of us to be the bartenders at the house. Joey and I loaded up boxes of liquor and beer from the nightclub that afternoon and carried it to the house. The kitchen opened into a large living room where the entertainment would take place. We set up a table in front of the door to the kitchen and began selling drinks as the first customers started arriving. A jukebox in a corner played loudly and the house quickly filled.

It was a rare occasion when I was asked to step out of an intelligence-only mode and provide direct help for enforcement. I wore a wire because we had information that an ex-con was coming to the party that night with thousands of amphetamines. If the drugs arrived, I would utter a code word to trigger a raid by narcotics investigators listening nearby in their cars. As it turned out, he never showed up.

A nude stripper stood in the middle of the crowded house full of men who had each paid forty dollars for a night of entertainment. Accompanied by pounding music, she had just finished a striptease and was now completely naked, her breasts still heaving from her performance. Now, as if doing a magic trick, she made an elaborate show of lighting a cigarette; holding the cigarette up above her head, she flourished it in dramatic waves. As everyone watched in amazement, she then used the lit cigarette in a unique way. Other strippers had performed before her, but this was the highlight of the evening. Her astonishing performance was followed by porno films on a projector and screen. This was to excite the customers for the finale—the girls turning tricks in the three-bedroom house.

As the night wore on and the porno films started, I realized I had drunk too much. I was having a drink for every six or seven drinks I was selling, and suddenly the music and yells turned into a loud buzz, colors ran together in a blur, and the room tilted. I needed to sober up. With the party in full force, I abandoned my bartending duties and staggered to a back bedroom. The lights were out but I could make out two twin beds, both empty. I lay down in the dark but for some reason I chose to lie on the floor in a narrow area between one of the beds and the wall.

During the early-morning hours I was awakened by a noise on the bed. As I struggled to a sitting position in the dark, movement on the bed caught my attention. My sluggish brain dimly registered that one of the girls was turning a trick on the bed beside me. A few inches from me, the john was rhythmically humping while the girl uttered exaggerated sounds of pleasure. I lay down and fell asleep until I was awakened later by another girl turning a trick, and again went back to sleep after briefly observing the sex from a few inches away.

Suddenly I was blinded by a brilliant white light. I blinked my eyes open. The overhead light had been switched on. The party was over and the house was empty except for the club owner, the girls, and me and Joey, the informant. One of the girls had turned on the light. She was nude. When I sat up she asked if I had seen her panties. I got up and helped her look. It was three in the morning by then. After the girls got dressed, we piled into two cars and headed to the notorious "gold coast" across the river from Baton Rouge. We partied until midmorning, and then I headed home.

This was early in my undercover career and I learned a valuable lesson that night. Hanging out at bars and drinking every night was a necessary part of my undercover role, but I would have to learn to pace myself so that drinking wouldn't interfere with my mission.

I got some sleep and went out at dusk to one of the bars where I typically hung out. We usually sat together at a larger table—the owner, his dancers on break, and several others in our group. Other than the girls, none made money by working at a regular job. At night, some dancers occasionally left the table during their breaks to turn a trick, returning to describe something weird, funny, or unusual about the john they had just serviced.

The dancers wore sexy panties and bras for their routines at the club. One night, two dancers decided they needed new outfits and they asked me to pick them up the next day and take them shopping. It turned out that the "shopping" was shoplifting. I drove them to several department stores and waited while they went in and shoplifted. Upon returning to the car, they proudly displayed their haul of new bras and panties. The shopping completed, we had lunch and then I dropped them off and went home for a few hours of sleep before going back out. My routine increasingly blurred into days and nights of bars, prostitutes, thugs, burglars, safecrackers, and the daily dramas among the groups, and I became part of a world thrumming beneath the surface of everyday life.

■ ■ ■

In addition to undercover, my work eventually evolved into collecting intelligence through informants. Through various sources, Bud Garrison, Al Saizan, and I developed information about organized crime, rigged sports betting, corrupt officials (including then governor Edwin Edwards), burglaries, robberies, and, of course, drug trafficking.

2
NARCOTICS

Capital Area Narcotics Unit (CANU)

The change from working undercover intelligence to working as an undercover narcotics officer didn't happen overnight; instead, my role gradually evolved. While undercover in intelligence I kept encountering drug dealers. Over time, I started making undercover drug buys and began developing informants, some of whom I used solely for intelligence gathering and others to introduce me to drug dealers.

Narcotics investigations were jump-started with an infusion of federal funds, which allowed the police department to form and lead a multiparish (multicounty) narcotics unit called the Capital Area Narcotics Unit, or CANU, led by Kline Courtney, with Sam Pruet as second in command. CANU purchased a variety of new cars for undercover work, body transmitters, radios, and office equipment. It paid for telephone lines and office supplies. Courtney led it in the first years and later Sam Pruet, an ex-Marine, took over leadership of CANU and PD Narcotics. We thrived under Sam's steady, calm leadership—just what was needed for undercover officers constantly dealing with unpredictable, stressful, and chaotic situations. Other officers came into narcotics, either undercover or as topside investigators. Bruce Childers, Jack Crittenden, Clyde Evans, and others began working undercover, while Henry "Shot" Breeland, Clyde Porter, and others usually worked topside.

Everything was brand new and plentiful. Most important, we had an abundance of money for buying drugs and paying informants. Instead of buying ounces of marijuana and small quantities of LSD and other drugs, we were able to purchase pound quantities and significant amounts of other drugs, and let the money "walk"—that is, never to be recovered. The ability to make larger buys allowed us to infiltrate higher on drug-distribution chains and focus on midlevel dealers and their suppliers.

If money is the "fuel" of undercover drug investigations, then I became a powerful engine; for years I roared nonstop through drug dealers and distribution networks. In order to meet particular suspects, I sometimes worked cover jobs for brief periods, including working in a laundry plant and as a laborer in the supply department of a hospital. Occasionally I rented an undercover apartment or trailer for brief periods.

Good informants were one of the keys to success and I learned to inspire their best efforts by treating them with respect and bolstering their self-esteem. If they were paid informants, I sometimes paid them more than they expected. I always kept in mind that they risked more than I did. I had a certain level of protection by virtue of my badge and the fact that most criminals would not risk hurting or killing a police officer. But informants had no such protection. Over the years, I did my best to protect informants by concealing their roles and in some cases getting them out of the area, or I would pay a visit to anyone who had threatened them.

Informants could also put me at risk, as some did by forgetting my undercover name and calling me by my real name in front of suspects, by forgetting the details of our joint cover story and telling suspects something different, or by acting visibly nervous when introducing me. Sometimes informants talked too much and word leaked out they were working with the police, which exposed us both to greater danger. They were an asset and an occupational hazard at the same time. When possible, once informants introduced me, I usually cut them out after that and dealt with suspects by myself in future encounters. In some investigations I worked completely "cold"—without ever using an informant, although it was usually more difficult and time-consuming to gain the trust of suspects that way.

I usually worked alone, without an undercover partner and without surveillance, as did Bruce, Jack, Clyde and the others. For all of us, undercover work was exciting; even more so because we had to rely upon ourselves and our own wits. Undercover could also produce anxious moments—as I found out when I met Junior for a drug deal.

Danger from Both Sides

Junior, a wiry black man in his late twenties, sat behind the steering wheel of his parked car and held a .25 semiautomatic pistol just below the rim of the open car window, jumpy and ready to shoot at any movement outside the car, be it a passerby or someone getting out of another car. Lips pressed tight with nervous tension and a wild glare flaring in his eyes, he swung his head from side to side searching the area, trying to watch in every direction.

A few moments before I had parked next to Junior's car, a maroon Buick parked facing an apartment complex. I had just slid onto the passenger seat and wore a hidden body wire, ready to buy an ounce of heroin from him. I would give the code word *coke* to trigger the bust. Other narcotics investigators in unmarked cars waited nearby to rush in and arrest both of us. They would pretend to arrest me in order to preserve my cover, and I was unarmed. At the last minute the investigators added a couple of uniform police units to assist with the bust.

I needed to alert the others to the danger.

"*Gun*, man, why you got a *gun*?" I said *gun* loudly and distinctly, hoping the investigators listening over the wire would be able to hear it.

"Man, you don't need no *gun*," I repeated.

He didn't answer and instead jerked his head from side to side, trying to watch everything around us.

I could tell he was strung out. He flinched at any movements nearby and his dilated eyes flashed back and forth from outside the window to me. Junior gripped the gun tightly but his hand trembled and I feared he might shoot at the slightest provocation. My heart pounded in my ears. I tried to keep my voice relaxed and calm to settle him down. I focused. For me, the world didn't exist outside the car and I needed to try to control what was going to happen inside.

But I was also in danger from the uniform officers who waited to help make the arrest. In order to protect my cover, they weren't told I was an undercover officer. They thought they would be arresting two drug dealers. If any shots were fired from inside the car, then the officers might riddle it and everyone in it, including me.

"You got the money?" Junior asked. His high-pitched voice almost cracked and he spoke quickly as if he wanted to hurry and get away.

"Yeah," I said. "It's eight hundred, right?" But he wasn't paying attention to me any longer. He was staring hard at a man coming out of one of the apartments and walking toward a car. "Eight, right?" I repeated.

He glanced back at me, but his eyes kept darting to our surroundings. "Eight. Yeah, eight," he said loudly, almost shouting, and I felt tension crackling inside the car.

"You got the stuff?" I asked.

Junior suddenly jumped and jerked the gun up as a car rattled past behind us, and he flinched again as a gray cat ran from behind a garbage can.

"What about the stuff, the smack?" I repeated.

He was watching the surroundings so intently that he still didn't hear me, and I asked about the heroin again. He clutched it in his left hand. Reaching across his body, he put the baggie of heroin on the seat between us. He wasn't going to let go of the gun. As I picked up the heroin, he kept scanning the area, jerking around with the gun up when someone happened to walk by the rear of the car. He was becoming more agitated, and I needed to set things in motion before he got worse.

"Okay, man, here's the money." I put the heroin down and reached into my front pocket for the money. "It's all here. You can count it if you want." Junior glanced around and then put the gun down between his legs so he could take the money.

"By the way," I said, pulling out a wad of cash, "can you get any coke?"

Suddenly we were in the middle of a deafening racetrack. Powerful car engines roared and tires squealed. With screaming engines and flashing lights, police cars raced at us from both sides. In an instant, Junior grabbed the gun and was raising it toward his window to shoot the oncoming officers, his finger on the trigger. I grabbed his gun arm with my left hand, struggling to keep him from raising and pointing the gun. "No, man, *don't!*"

Junior jerked his arm away but I grabbed it with both hands and held on. With a flip of his wrist he could have fired into my side and chest, but he was still focused on the officers and trying to raise his arm to shoot.

"*NO!*" I shouted. "It'll be *murder!*"

I was on the verge of throwing off my cover, diving on him and wrestling for the gun. Everything was happening in split seconds amid a blur of motion.

Junior hesitated a moment, then dropped the gun, grabbed the dope, and threw it out the window.

"HANDS *UP!*" We were instantly surrounded. "Don't move! Don't move! HANDS UP!" The investigators and officers crouched at our doors, shouting and pointing guns at us.

Two uniform officers were at my door, pointing guns at my head and yelling. At close range, their gun barrels looked like cannons. Their fingers were on the triggers.

"HANDS UP!" the first officer yelled. "Get your hands up! Don't move! DON'T MOVE!"

I was already obeying his commands, my body frozen with both hands up.

"There's a *gun!*" someone yelled. "A gun's on the seat!" That jolted the officers; wide-eyed, faces flushed red, they jerked their pistols higher, aiming for my head.

"*UP!* Keep your hands up, hands up!" The officer shouted at me with renewed vigor.

The second officer shouted, "Get out of the car! GET *OUT!*"

Careful not to make any sudden moves, I started slowly lowering my right hand to open the door when the first officer yelled, "Keep your hands UP! Get your hands up!"

But as my right hand went back up, the second officer screamed, "Get out of the car! Get OUT! *NOW!*" My right hand slowly started to dip again for the door handle, but the first officer yelled again, "HANDS UP! KEEP YOUR HANDS UP!" With adrenaline pumping hard, neither officer heard the other's contradictory commands. Each thought I was disobeying his commands, and knowing that a gun was in the car, they were hyped up and ready to shoot.

My relief at having just survived a wild, trigger-happy drug dealer vanished and I was becoming desperate. Then someone finally opened my door and jerked me out of the car. I was thrown against the car, my arms twisted and my hands handcuffed behind my back. They locked the cuffs on too tight and the steel vise bit painfully into my flesh. Someone shoved me hard against the car and my head banged against the hood. The investigators handled me roughly to make it look good, but at least I was safe. I hadn't been shot by a drug dealer. And I hadn't been shot by the police.

The officers that day probably never knew how close they came to being shot or shot at. Luckily, a tragic outcome was avoided. The arrest was a close call as well. Too often undercover officers and plainclothes police officers are confronted and mistakenly killed or wounded by other officers who arrive on a scene and are confronted by dangerous and confusing situations.

Preserving my cover not only meant being handcuffed and slammed around as part of fake arrests, but several months after the incident with Junior, it also meant brief jail time.

Angel Dust and Jail: Just Another Workday

I really didn't want to go to jail, but that's where I was headed. I got up that morning and got ready for work, knowing I would be confined in a cell for several hours with drug dealers who would suspect me of causing their arrests. It could be unpleasant, especially since we would be locked away out of sight and hearing of guards.

It all started several weeks earlier when an informant introduced me to Robbie, a PCP dealer. I purchased PCP from Robbie and eventually met his supplier, Gino, a self-taught chemist from New Orleans who manufactured PCP. When I discovered that Gino could supply large quantities of PCP, I started working to set up a buy-and-bust deal, but in a way that might preserve my cover and protect the informant. I needed two other agents as cutouts and more money, and I got them from the Drug Enforcement Administration (DEA). I would introduce one federal agent posing as Joe to make a buy and later a second agent posing as Woody to make the buy-bust. I would tell the drug dealers that Joe introduced Woody to me and vouched for him. Woody would make the arrests and pretend to arrest me too. The arrests would put some heat on me but I could pretend I was duped and point the finger at Joe as the one helping the police. Of course, we would eventually have to reveal my true identity and that of the DEA agents as part of the prosecution but meanwhile the cover I was using should be intact for another few months.

Following this plan, I introduced a DEA agent posing as Joe, and together we bought an ounce of PCP from Gino and Robbie. Several days after the ounce buy, I called Robbie and told him we wanted one pound of PCP, and that a friend of Joe's, a guy called Woody, would be putting up the money. Robbie told me the pound would be ready in a couple of days.

On the morning we were to do the deal, Woody and I arrived at Robbie's white frame house and agents conducting surveillance parked nearby, where they were close enough to listen over the body wire hidden on me. We stepped onto the porch and after repeated taps, a disheveled Gino opened the door. Tall and thin, Gino was barefoot, shirtless, and wearing jeans, yawning and rubbing his eyes, having just awakened. He held a finger to his lips and uttered a "shhusshh." He waved us in and led us to the living room, where he again held his finger to his lips and pointed with his other hand toward two figures sleeping on a quilt on the floor, and then he pointed toward an open door through which I could see two people sleeping in a bed.

"We need to be quiet," he whispered. "Everybody's sleeping." We quietly pulled up three straight-backed chairs together in the middle of the room and sat hunched over in a tight group, knees almost touching.

I leaned close to Gino. "Gino," I whispered, "this is Woody. He's the one I told you about that's putting in money on the pound."

"Hey, man," Gino whispered, shaking hands.

"Gino, you got the stuff?" I asked in a low voice. "Let's do it before we wake up everybody."

"Hold on," Gino said softly. He got up and disappeared into another room. Woody and I exchanged anxious looks. We didn't expect a houseful of people. Gino quietly walked back into the room carrying a baggie of white powder.

"This is it," he whispered, sitting down and handing it to me.

"This isn't a pound," I protested. "It looks like it's only an ounce."

"It *is* a pound," Gino whispered, "a full pound. I came on the bus from New Orleans and I didn't want to carry a whole pound so instead I brought this ounce of pure dust. It's pure PCP. One ounce of pure PCP is the same as a pound. I just finished cooking it yesterday before I came up. I guarantee this. All you have to do is cut it to make a full pound and it'll be as good as any angel dust on the street. See, all you have to do is . . ." Gino explained the type of cut to use and how to mix it.

Now that we had the PCP in our hands, it was time to give the signal over the wire for the bust. "All right, Gino, this looks like some good stuff," I said, handing it to Woody. I nodded at Woody. "Looks good to me," Woody nodded back. Time for the code word for the bust.

While Woody looked at the PCP, I asked Gino, "What about *coke*, man, can you get us *coke*?" At the mention of coke, Woody slowly lowered his right hand behind his back toward the gun at his back waist. I tensed for the loud rush of agents storming onto the porch, shouting and bursting into the house with guns drawn. Moments ticked by. Nothing happened. Silence.

"Well, I might be able to get some," Gino whispered.

Frowning, Woody moved his hand back to his lap.

"Good," I said, "'cause if you can, we'd be interested in some *coke*."

Woody again moved his right hand toward his back. A few moments passed. Nothing happened at the door. If he had to, Woody could single-handedly attempt to arrest everyone but they were scattered and others might be out of sight.

"There's some around," Gino said quietly. "I can check on it, if you want. How much you want?"

"Yeah, check on it," I said, "'cause we'd like to get a couple O-Zs of *coke*." Woody's hand moved slowly toward his back. "Long as it's good *coke*." The wire must not be working.

Woody cast a desperate glance at me and finally reached back and whipped out his gun, sticking the barrel almost under Gino's nose.

"You're under arrest!" Woody announced in a low voice.

"*Huh!*" Gino exclaimed, wide-eyed.

"DEA. You're under arrest," said Woody quietly. "Raise your hands." Stunned, Gino raised his hands.

"What? What's going on?" I asked. With the raid not happening on cue, Woody had forgotten about me.

Woody pointed his gun at me. "You too. You're under arrest," he whispered. "Raise your hands!" I raised my hands.

Woody stood up. "Don't move." He took a few paces backward toward the front door while watching us. He stopped and glanced over his shoulder toward the door then back at us. He was waiting for the raid team, but they weren't coming. Woody couldn't get to the front door without leaving us alone, out of his sight.

"Hey, man, what's happening?" Gino asked. "I don't understand—"

Woody came back to us. "You two get on the floor, on your bellies, and put your hands on the back of your heads."

Gino and I lay face down beside each other, hands clasped on the back of our heads.

Bedsprings squeaked from one of the other rooms, followed by rustling noises. One of the two sleeping on the quilt on the floor raised up on an elbow, squinting. "Hey, what's going on?" Oh no, I thought. Woody's eyes jumped toward the sounds and then back to us. We need help soon, I thought, because this is getting—

SLAM! Agents burst open the front door and rushed in, yelling. *"POLICE! POLICE! YOU'RE UNDER ARREST! POLICE!"*

They rounded up everyone in the house and handcuffed me, Gino, and Robbie with our hands behind our backs.

"We'll take him," said Sergeant Sam Pruet, pointing to me. "Come on, you. Get up." Sam and another investigator took me to their car, put me in the backseat, and drove off, heading to PD headquarters.

"Sam, hurry and get these cuffs off," I pleaded as soon as we were out of sight of the house. "Hurry! They're too tight!"

Sam reached over the front seat while I twisted around so that my hands would be toward him.

After the cuffs were off, I loosened my belt and unbuttoned my shirt and started taking off the wire, squirming and crying out in pain as I pulled off the surgical tape covering the wire that ran from the transmitter at my waist to my shoulder, tearing off chest hair and skin along with the tape. The metal transmitter and battery at my waist had overheated and left a reddish burn. By the time we reached the PD, I was put back together and handcuffed.

To make it look good, I was still being fingerprinted when Gino and Robbie were brought in. We exchanged quick glances as I was led away through a large metal door to the holding cells, where they would soon join me. The investigators put me in a cell, locked the barred door, and left, closing a metal door behind them. I sat alone in the cell, waiting and anxious, knowing Gino and Robbie would suspect me because I had brought an undercover agent to them.

Using logic to plan something was good, but dealers didn't always think or act logically or rationally, so I didn't know if the plan would work. Dealers could suspect you for a good reason, a bad reason, or no reason at all. I tried not to give them a good reason.

The metal door down the hall squeaked open and the investigators herded Robbie and Gino to my cell. My stomach felt queasy as I got ready.

I stood up as they were being ushered through the cell door.

"Hey, what about a phone call?" I called out through the bars. "When do I get to make a call?"

"Don't worry, you'll get your call," an investigator said as he clanged the cell door shut behind Gino and Robbie. The investigators left and the metal door down the hall squeaked and slammed shut behind them. We were alone in a silent vault.

Gino and Robbie turned around and looked at me warily.

Frowning, I looked them in the eye and shook my head slowly. "Man, this is fucked up. All fucked up." They exchanged looks. I sat down on one of the metal bunks. They remained standing a few moments and then sat on the bunk across from me. We faced each other just a couple of feet apart in the small cell. No one said anything. The air felt dense.

Gino squinted at me. "Mike, just how do you know this fucking guy?" he said. "Woody—the narc?" My pulse quickened.

"Man, that fucking Joe," I spat out. "That's Joe's buddy."

"Yeah, but *you* brought Woody to us," Gino said accusingly. "It was you, *not Joe*, who brought him to the house."

"That's what I'm telling you," I snapped. "It was Joe that vouched for the guy. *Not me!*" I nearly shouted. "*Joe!*" They were watching me closely. I stared hard-eyed at both as if I was ready to tear Joe's head off, and theirs too if I got any madder.

"But why did you bring him to us?" Gino persisted.

"That's what we wanna know," Robbie said. "Why'd *you* bring a narc to us?"

"Look," I said through gritted teeth as if seething with anger, looking from one to the other. "I didn't know he was a narc. Joe told me the dude was okay. He told me they were buddies and the dude was cool."

"Why didn't Joe bring him instead of you? Why did—" Gino began.

"Mutherfucker! Wait. That's it!" I exclaimed and bolted upright as if struck by a sudden revelation. "Dammit, that's it!"

"What—"

"I understand now how Joe set this whole thing up."

"What do—"

"That's it! That sumbitch!" I shook my head. "Here's exactly how Joe did it," I declared. Their eyes squinted and their heads cocked slightly to the side as if trying to unravel a mystery.

"See, Joe told me he had a friend named Woody who wanted to buy a pound of angel dust. But Joe told me he owed Woody money on dope Woody had fronted to him and Woody wouldn't sell or front any more to Joe until he paid up. So if Joe brought Woody to you himself, Woody wouldn't front or sell any of it to Joe. But if I took Woody to you, then Woody would front some of it to me for hooking him up. Joe said he would help me move it, as long as I didn't tell Woody. Joe said that's why couldn't bring Woody himself and he wanted me to do it. You see? See how he did it?"

Gino looked at me uncertainly, searching my face and mulling it over. "Yeah," he said after a moment and nodded, "I guess. Maybe." Robbie nodded too. But their faces were still tight, jaws set and hands clenched.

"Now here's the kicker," I added in a low, confidential tone. "Joe told me that if I help Woody get a pound of angel dust from you, then Woody would not only front some ounces to me, he would give me a half-ounce for free!" I looked from one to the other. "So see," I held my palms out and upward, "that's why I brought Woody to you and vouched for him—I thought I would make some easy money." For added effect I slumped over with my elbows on my knees and my head hanging down, and stared at the cell floor. I shook my head slowly from side to side as if finally realizing how fully Joe had scammed us. "Man, oh man," I mumbled, "Joe, that mutherfucker."

When I looked back up moments later, they were visibly relaxed; the tension in their faces was gone. They started cussing Joe too. My explanation was awkward, but plausible. They were finally convinced—Joe must be an informant and I was duped by Joe and Woody. For their benefit I recalled how I had met Joe in the first place and how trustworthy he had seemed. I told them that after I bonded out, I was going to lay low. After several hours in the cell, I "bonded out."

Later on, we would charge Robbie and Gino with the sales to me and to Joe. But for the time being, the real informant was protected and my cover was preserved.

A few months later I arranged to be arrested again during another buy-bust and spent several hours in a cell with three drug dealers. It was easier to overcome their suspicions because I had not introduced a "narc" to them. Instead, after purchasing drugs several times, I arranged to buy a large quantity and the arrests were made during the transaction. We tried to make it look like someone unknown tipped off the police about the deal. After I spent several hours in the cell, investigators got me out by pretending they discovered I was a fugitive from another parish and deputies from that parish had arrived to take me back.

Going to jail was unpleasant even though it was only for a few hours each time, but it was part of my job.

The next day I drove to Prairieville, just outside Baton Rouge, and met Earl Medlock at his store, Medlock's Antiques. He sold fifty hits of acid to me and showed me stolen televisions he had for sale. Two men showed up while I was there and unloaded stolen items out of their car trunk. I found out that Earl and one of his sons was expecting a shipment of powdered acid in the mail from California. I left there and drove to the west side of Baton Rouge and dropped by to see another drug dealer who knew me by another undercover name. I was negotiating to buy twenty pounds of pot, which would be a buy-bust later when it went down. I left there and met with another dealer and bought some heroin. Then I drove across the Mississippi and down to Plaquemine where I was circulating with a different group of drug dealers. Finally, I passed on the information about the acid shipment and a mail watch was put on for incoming packages to the Medlocks. A search warrant for a package resulted in the seizure of twenty-six ounces of powdered LSD, but my cover remained intact because I wasn't named in the search warrant affidavit. It was another typical day.

Who Is He? Is He Me?

Who is he? Tom tried to hide it, but something about him didn't seem right. With piercing blue eyes, Tom looked to be in his late twenties or early thirties, medium height, lean but muscular, with sandy hair. He seemed mature beyond his years. Tom showed up one night, a surprise addition to our regular group of drug dealers and users. One had just met Tom and invited him to join us that night at the Rendezvous lounge in

Plaquemine, Louisiana. Everyone else mingled unguarded and outgoing, while Tom was reserved and his eyes were watchful, guarded, and wary. In response to a joke or a humorous comment he would flash a quick smile or hearty laugh, but it was always fake, never genuine. When Tom didn't think anyone would notice, his eyes would quickly dart around the lounge. He appeared to be afraid of something, but what?

Because operating successfully as an undercover agent depended on it, I had become adept at reading people: at catching a quick look or recognizing a suppressed emotion or a fleeting, microsecond expression flashing across someone's face. Watching Tom, I was convinced he wasn't who he pretended to be—just as I wasn't who I pretended to be. We were both faking it. Did he recognize in me what I saw in him? I hoped not.

"I'm glad Jimmy told you to come," I said. "He's a good dude. And this is a good group. Hey, how about another beer? You ready for another one?"

Later, I leaned in close so I could be heard over the music blaring from the jukebox.

"Say, you been working on oil rigs off shore, man?" I asked.

"Yeah."

"Man, I don't see how you do it." I shook my head. "I know that's some hard work, man. Everybody says that's hard work, the hardest."

"Yeah, damn right," Tom agreed, shouting back, "but it pays good."

"When you go back out, man?" Offshore oil-rig workers usually worked rotations of two or three weeks on and two or three weeks off.

"Maybe in a few weeks," Tom said. "I'm waiting for them to let me know for sure when to come back." It didn't sound right, that he wouldn't know exactly when to go back out.

"You staying here?" I shouted over the noise, trying to make it seem like a friendly question instead of being nosy.

"Staying outside town," Tom said, "until I go back out." He was being vague and hard to pin down—just like me. "What about you, Mike?"

"Me? Got an apartment in Baton Rouge, but I'm getting ready to rent a place outside town."

Tom was being deceptive, but I also felt something else about him. He seemed like he was someone who could hurt you. Someone who could smash your head with a brick or gut you with a knife. It was a vague feeling and I couldn't explain it.

Since Tom wasn't who he pretended to be, the only logical explanation was that he was an undercover agent too. He had to be a Louisiana

State Police (LSP) narcotics undercover agent, I thought. He wouldn't have been federal or local, so he had to be with LSP.

I worked in Plaquemine along with Baton Rouge because we had expanded into a task force to cover six parishes. The next time I called in, I gave Sergeant Sam Pruet Tom's name and description and asked him to check with LSP Narcotics to find out if he was one of their agents.

Meanwhile, Tom became a regular and continued to hang out with us at the Rendezvous. He and I continued to feel each other out and the more we did, the more I was convinced he was an agent. One time when we were drinking beers and watching the dancers, I caught him looking at me a moment too long. He quickly looked away when he saw I had caught the look. Maybe he wondered about me now. After a week, Sam called me and said Tom was not an LSP undercover agent.

"Are you sure?" I asked. "He's gotta be an agent."

"No, he's not theirs, Charlie," Sam said. "They're saying they don't have anyone working Plaquemine. No agents at all."

"But he's gotta be an agent, I'm telling you—something's not right about him."

"Well, I don't know about that. All I know is he ain't theirs."

"Damn, Sam. They don't have any idea who this guy might be?"

"No. They're in the dark. They don't have any intelligence on anyone with that name around Plaquemine."

I was frustrated and puzzled. Something was wrong about Tom and I couldn't figure out what it might be.

My suspicions were answered a couple of weeks later when I walked into the Rendezvous late one afternoon and joined several of the group at a table. One was bursting to tell me something as I was sitting down.

"Mike, hey man, you hear about Tom?" he said eagerly.

"Tom? No, what about Tom?"

"He's an escaped convict."

"What! An escaped convict?"

"Yeah, Mike. They captured him this morning. We just found out. And Tom's not his real name."

"That's right," another added. "Can you believe that? Tom was doing time at Angola prison. He escaped and been on the run since." He shook his head. "Man, he had everybody fooled."

Life can be strange, especially undercover life. I realized Tom and I had some things in common. We were both living fake lives, using fake names and in danger of being discovered at any moment. Both bound by the necessity of living double lives to succeed and survive. Remarkably, our phony lives had briefly intersected. But one of us had been discovered and now he was gone.

It Takes One to Know One

A few weeks after the escaped convict was captured, I was at the Baton Rouge Narcotics office reviewing and signing reports when one of the narcotics detectives, Henry "Shot" Breeland came in.

"Hey Charlie, you hear about Clyde last night? About him stopping the guy with the U-Haul trailer to search it for drugs?' Clyde Porter was a narcotics detective who was known for his brawn.

"No, what happened?" I asked Shot.

"You know that joint on Airline Highway, the one where Clyde has those strippers and bar girls that tip him off? Well, one of them called him last night about a man who was driving a station wagon with Oklahoma tags and pulling a small trailer. The man was in the joint drinking alone and one of the girls thought he might be hauling a load of drugs in the trailer so she called Clyde."

"Okay."

"Well, Clyde goes out and sets up watching the station wagon. When the guy comes out and drives off pulling the trailer, Clyde stopped him and the guy gets out of the station wagon."

"Yeah."

"Well, here's the good part. You won't believe it, but it turns out the guy's a ventriloquist, and he gets out holding his little dummy on one arm, its legs dangling down. Clyde's partner was with him and he told me all about it. I swear it sounds just like something Clyde would do." Breeland then related the conversation on the roadside reported by Clyde's partner, an incident confirmed by two uniform officers who drove by and saw part of it.

"Let me see your driver's license," Clyde said to the driver.

"Yes, sir," the dummy replied to Clyde in a high-pitched voice, head nodding, lips and arms moving. "I've got it right here, Officer." Clyde glanced sharply at the dummy and then back at the driver, who put his dummy down and fished out his driver's license and handed it to Clyde. While Clyde examined the license, the driver picked up the dummy.

"Is something wrong, Officer?" the dummy asked in a high, squeaky voice.

"I'll ask the questions," Clyde said gruffly, looking up at the dummy, then at the driver.

"You from Oklahoma?" Clyde asked, looking at the driver.

"Yes, sir," the dummy replied. Clyde looked at the dummy.

"What're you doing in Baton Rouge?" Clyde asked the dummy.

"Well, sir, we're just passing through," the dummy said to Clyde, "on our way back to Oklahoma."

"We! Who's 'we'?" Clyde asked the dummy.

"Oh," the dummy's eyes shot wide open, "just me and my driver here, Officer," the dummy said, motioning to the driver who held him.

"You have anything to drink back at that bar? How much you have to drink?"

"I just had a couple beers, Officer," the dummy said, shaking its head.

"Okay," Clyde nodded. "Whatcha got in that trailer you hauling?"

The dummy's arm pointed toward the trailer. "Just a few pieces of furniture we picked up in Alabama from a relative," the dummy told Clyde, wiggling its head. "You're welcome to look, Officer," the dummy volunteered in its squeaky voice.

Clyde searched the trailer quickly and confirmed it held only furniture.

He handed driver's license back to the dummy. "Thank you, Officer." The dummy gave the license to the driver.

"All right," Clyde nodded at the dummy. "Drive carefully."

While Clyde was talking to the dummy on the roadside, Breeland said, a uniform patrol officer drove by and saw it and radioed everyone that Clyde was on the roadside talking to a dummy. Another officer who heard it drove to the scene to see for himself and reported back that he was watching it.

"Did you see Clyde talking to that dummy?" the first officer radioed.

"No," the second officer replied, *"the only thing I saw was two dummies talking to each other!"*

Risky Business

"Watch out for you." After working undercover in Baton Rouge for several years and making hundreds of cases, I had become widely known among drug-trafficking groups. My real name and some of my undercover names circulated along with descriptions of me. Those who didn't know me knew of me. Ironically, drug traffickers even warned me about me. I was sometimes told, "Watch out for a narc named Charlie Spillers." More often I was warned to look out for me by one of my undercover names. "Hey, Mike," one advised me, "watch out for a guy named Rick. He's a narc and he drives a . . ." To avoid detection, I kept changing undercover names and cars. Sometimes I used different names and different cars at the same time, especially if I was working on separate groups and planned to round up one group while continuing to work on others. Of course, that tactic had its own risks.

Drug traffickers also circulated descriptions of me. "He's stocky and has black hair and a beard," a description that was accurate but not particularly helpful because so many others had black hair and a beard.

The greatest risk of discovery came from those who could recognize me on sight. To keep this threat from becoming too great, I tried to limit my exposure in several ways. During roundups to arrest drug dealers who had sold to me, we had teams go out and make the arrests while I waited at the police department. The arrest teams would bring their prisoners to an interrogation room and through a two-way mirror I would positively identify the prisoner without being seen. If it had been months since my last purchase, they might not be able to accurately recall my appearance, and in some cases it might take a while for the dealer to figure out who the undercover officer was among their customers even though the indictment showed the dates of the drug sales and my real name.

I limited my exposure even when it was time to testify at trial. I would wait in a room next to the courtroom so that I wouldn't be seen by the defendant and his friends until I took the stand. Even this had its limits. When called to testify in one case, I walked into the courtroom through a side door, was sworn in, and sat down in the witness chair. The prosecutor started off by asking my name and occupation.

"Charlie Spillers. I'm a police officer with the Baton Rouge Police Department."

"Tell the jury what your duties are," he said.

I turned and looked at the jury. "I'm in the Narcotics Division and I work undercover, making purchases of heroin, cocaine, LSD, and other drugs."

As I was answering these standard preliminary questions, the vague mosaic of twelve jurors came into clear focus and I froze as I recognized a juror in the front row and he recognized me. He had sold LSD to me the week before and I was still working undercover on him. Imagine my surprise. Even more, imagine his shock.

When I first turned to face the jury and he saw me full on, his eyes squinted and his head tilted sideways as if he were trying to place me. Suddenly he did a double take, his eyes sprang wide open, his mouth dropped, and he stared directly at me. Recovering, he quickly bowed his head toward his lap to hide his face.

Below the surface, a silent drama played out between the two of us. I didn't give any sign I had recognized him and turned back to face the prosecutor for the next question. Outwardly I pretended everything was normal, but inside I cringed and my mind raced. The LSD-dealing juror obviously hoped I had not recognized him, and for the remainder of my testimony he kept his head bowed and stared at his lap. Occasionally he rubbed his forehead with his fingertips, either to conceal his face or in a sign of distress.

I was tense, but he had to be struggling with a flood of emotions. To him my testimony probably seemed like slow torture as I described making drug buys from the defendant on trial, recording serial numbers of buy money, marking drug evidence and delivering it to the crime lab, and eventually arresting the defendant, all actions he could visualize on his LSD sales to me. The drumbeat of my voice had to slam him like repeated blows, giving him a glimpse into his future. For me this was a temporary crisis: notify the prosecutor and the office, scramble to warn the informant who had introduced me to the LSD-selling juror, and make arrangements for the arrest. But for the juror it was a life-changing event. As the reality settled in, this had to be one of the worst moments of his life.

But if I had had time to think about it, I wouldn't have had sympathy for his distress, then or now. The acid dealer on the jury had boasted about feeding his baby boy small chips of LSD tablets.

The tables would soon be reversed. During an undercover deal weeks later, I would find myself in his position when I came face to face with drug dealers I had previously busted and would experience some of the distress and panic he felt. I faced similar nightmarish ordeals several times, and each time suffered a jolt of abject fear—fear I had to suppress and fight through.

Right after leaving the witness stand, I let the prosecutor know about the juror. At the end of the trial, the jury convicted the defendant. In a noncapital case in Louisiana courts, a conviction requires only that at least nine jurors agree that the defendant is guilty. I think the LSD dealer remained on the jury and all twelve voted guilty.

A criminal defendant is entitled to a jury of his peers, but having a drug dealer as a juror in the trial of a drug dealer may be carrying that principle a bit too far. In any event, three people will never forget that trial—the defendant who was convicted, the LSD-dealing juror, and me.

■　　■　　■

To minimize my exposure I stayed away from the police department unless it was time for a roundup. Even then, I had to have a cover story ready in case someone I was working on saw me going or coming from the PD. For example, I could say I was at the PD to pay a traffic ticket or to find out if some items stolen from me had been recovered. I kept such a low police profile that most police officers knew of me but few had ever met me.

My appearance also changed. After starting out clean-shaven, I grew a mustache and later a beard. My hair grew long and full and I put on an extra twelve or fifteen pounds and went from being lean to stocky.

After several years I had to restrict my exposure when working undercover and stopped hanging out at bars where crowds could see me. Instead, I tried to arrange for undercover meetings and drug buys to take place in cars, homes, and apartments, with only the dealer being present when possible. That still presented problems because I wouldn't know beforehand who else might be present.

Despite these precautions, sooner or later while working undercover I was bound to encounter someone who could recognize me. It happened more than once. My world was getting smaller and undercover work was becoming more risky. All undercover agents who constantly work the same area have a "shelf life." The risks had increased but I was still effective and would continue to work undercover long past my "use by" date. It would be a volatile and stressful journey.

Seconds Count

Wrong place, wrong time to visit Nicole and Cindy (not their real names). These two sisters, both in their early twenties, blonde, and attractive, acted as my informants by introducing me to their former drug connections. They were sunny and pleasant to be around, a joy to work with. Of the two, Nicole was the more level-headed, resourceful, and thoughtful; whereas Cindy was less likely to think things through and more prone to panic. Before becoming informants they had run a successful drug business from their house. Resting on concrete blocks, the white frame house was perched on a corner lot and their motto for their former drug business was "Right on the corner, right on the price."

On a summer day in Baton Rouge I stopped by to see Nicole and Cindy and find out if they had heard from any of the drug dealers we were working on. I was using the undercover name "J. R." We sat talking in the front room; I didn't have surveillance and had left my gun in the car.

Through the screen door to the front porch we saw a car suddenly pull into the yard and park beside my car. The car belonged to one of the drug dealers from whom I had been buying. He had his own close group of dealers he supplied, several of whom often traveled with him. Nicole got up and looked out through the front screen door.

Five men piled out of the car and had almost reached the steps to the porch when Nicole suddenly cried out, "Oh my God, J. R., it's *Tony Franks!*" (not his real name). She was in a panic.

"What? Who?"

"It's Franks! *Tony Franks! He's with them!*"

I jumped up and looked. Franks and the others were already coming up the steps. One my worst nightmares. Months earlier, using another undercover name and a different car, I had busted Franks after making several buys from him. He knew I was an undercover police officer. My heart hammered in my ears.

"My God, J. R., you gotta get out!" Nicole and Cindy were in as much danger as I was if Franks saw me. "*Hurry! Hurry!*"

Within seconds the group ascended the steps, crowded on the porch and one reached to open the screen door. They were just a few paces from me but couldn't see me yet through the screen. I felt trapped. And because of my car, the group would know *someone* was in the house.

"Tell them I walked to the store," I said quickly while backing up. As the screen door was opening, I spun around and dashed through the kitchen to the back door. I heard greetings behind me as I jumped over the back steps to the ground and hurried away, keeping my back to the house so that my face couldn't be seen. I walked rapidly at an angle to get out of their line of sight, crossed the backyard of the next house, then turned at the far side of the house and ran to the sidewalk. Watching over my shoulder, I jogged for several blocks before slowing to a normal pace and catching my breath.

If Nicole hadn't noticed Franks or if they had reached the door seconds sooner, I would have been exposed and confronted.

But my car was parked at the house and surely they had asked about me. I needed to find out what was going on at the house and also give Nicole and Cindy a reason to explain my continuing absence. I found a pay phone and called. Nicole answered.

"Nicole, quick, is everything all right there? You okay?"

"We're fine," she whispered, and then in a normal voice, "We're just sitting around visiting." I heard voices in the background. She whispered again, "I told them you had walked to the store. I think everything is all right, but they're waiting for you to get back."

"Okay. Tell them it's me on the phone. Pretend that I'm tripping on acid, I'm wandering around the streets and I don't know where I am and I'm calling you for help, to come find me. Go ahead, tell them."

As she held the phone, I heard her repeat the story to the others and then heard a mumble of responses. She returned to the phone. "J. R., they said to look around and tell us what you see—what buildings or street signs can you see? What do you see around you?"

"Tell them I'm talking crazy, out of my head. Nicole, I'll call you back later." Then I hung up.

Over the next hour we repeated this a couple of times, until she finally reported that they had left. They had accepted the story that I was freaked out on acid and no one became suspicious. But it might have turned out much differently. Sometimes, timing is everything and seconds count.

Is This Work Dangerous? Kill Who?

From a distance Cindy's boyfriend, David, looked like me—and that wasn't good for him. We both were about the same age, had shoulder-length, black bushy hair, and a full beard, along with a stocky build. What made it worse, and perhaps inevitable, although we gave no thought to it at the time, Cindy, her sister Nicole, and I had used David's old van several times to make undercover drug buys, simply because Cindy happened to have it at the time and it looked really cool.

David didn't know I was an undercover officer. And he didn't know that his girlfriend and her sister were my informants and that for months they had helped me make drug buys.

After a lengthy undercover operation, the roundup finally came and dozens of drug dealers were arrested. In the early-morning hours, teams of officers spread out to make arrests. The arrested drug dealers were hustled to the Baton Rouge Parish jail in handcuffs, but most were released on bond by afternoon. Even those who didn't know each other had opportunities to read the charges and to compare notes before being released. Some quickly figured out that the undercover agent was the guy running with the sisters, the man who had long, black, bushy hair and a beard and sometimes drove a van. That apparently led some to mistake Cindy's boyfriend, David, for me.

On the day of the roundup, Cindy revealed to David that they had helped me make drug cases and the arrests had started that morning. David worked at one of the petrochemical plants lining Plank Road in Baton Rouge and after work he usually stopped at a nearby bar for drinks before heading home. He followed his routine on the afternoon of the roundup.

As David left the bar and walked alongside the brick wall of the bar, a bullet cracked by his head and shattered pieces of brick inches away. David ducked and ran for his van and sped off. Once he cleared the area, he stopped at a pay phone and frantically called Cindy.

Cindy called me crying and nearly hysterical. "*J. R., J. R., David almost got killed! Someone tried to kill him!*" She cried. "Oh my God, he almost got killed. J. R., they shot at him. My God, what're we gonna do, what're we gonna do—"

"What? What happened?" I asked. She kept wailing, jumbling her words. "*Wait,* Cindy, *slow down,* slow down and tell me what happened and where."

She went through it.

"Where is David now?"

"He's on his way over here. J. R., it's got to be the people we busted. It's got to be them. Oh my God, what are we gonna do?"

"Wait there, I'm coming over and I'll have a police car sent over. Just wait there until I get there."

I called headquarters and had a marked police car dispatched to park in front of the house. I went to the house and met with David and the two sisters. I arranged for Cindy and David to stay in a motel for the next few nights. Nicole thought that she would be all right, but I insisted that she leave and stay with one of her relatives for a few days. It was nearly a tragic situation—someone tried to kill me and the bullet missed by inches. Only it wasn't me.

■ ■ ■

Another alarming development connected with the drug arrests occurred a week later. An informant who had no connection to the undercover operation that resulted in the mistaken shooting at David called me. He said two men wanted to hire someone to kill me because I had just busted one of their friends. Neither of the two men had ever met me. To keep them from hiring someone else, I instructed the informant to tell them he knew a hit man they could hire at a reasonable price.

In a unique twist, because they didn't know me, I planned to have the informant introduce me as a hit man they could hire to kill me. The informant told the men he knew someone who was available, but they never followed up. Later I had him check back to find out if they were pursuing it with someone else, but they had dropped the idea, which was good for all concerned, especially me.

Over time I recognized a difficult paradox. Experience lessened some risks but increased others. The longer I worked undercover and the better I became at it, the less dangerous it became. But the longer I worked, the more widely known I became, which increased the risk of being recognized.

Close Encounters with Carl, the Bomb Maker

It was a toss-up as who had the worst luck—me or Carl, a drug dealer in Baton Rouge. We were destined to complicate each other's lives.

Carl Meets Mike

Early in my undercover career, using the undercover name "Mike," I made several drug buys from Carl, a lean redhead about to turn twenty. Carl spent his time selling dope, sniffing chemicals, and making crude homemade bombs by stuffing the contents of shotgun shells in tin cans. Carl was always ready to show me his latest homemade bomb and proudly explain how he had made it.

"Come back here, Mike, and see what I made," Carl said, leading me through a haze of marijuana smoke in the house to a rear bedroom. Shotgun shells, gunpowder, lead shot, and empty tin cans lay scattered around the room. "Look at this one." He held up a tin can packed with gunpowder and lead shot, the ends of the can wrapped closed with black electrical tape. It was crude but lethal looking. Each time I went to buy dope, Carl would display his latest explosive creation.

Finally, during a roundup of drug dealers who had sold to me, the time came to arrest Carl. Because of the dangers posed by his bombs, I accompanied the team assigned to arrest him. He was shocked when I displayed my badge, handcuffed him, and advised him of his Miranda rights. In addition to dope, we seized bomb-making materials at his house. He was a dope dealer with an unusual twist.

Carl Meets Johnny

Two years later, using the undercover name Johnny, I went to an apartment complex to meet Rick, an ex-con, to buy an ounce of cocaine. My informant, Tom, arranged the meeting and would introduce me. When Tom and I arrived at the second-floor apartment, Rick's live-in girlfriend Ginger explained that Rick was out doing some business and would be back soon. She invited us in to wait and the three of us sat at the kitchen table.

"We can't stay long," I said, "because we've got some people waiting on us. How much longer you think Rick'll be?"

"He shoulda already been back, honey," she said. "There's a couple other guys coming to see him about some weed, so he knows he needs to hurry to get back to get up with y'all and with them."

As if on cue, the doorbell rang. "That's probably them now," she said, going to the door. After a mumbled conversation at the door, she let in two men. One was a large, stocky redheaded man who looked to be in his early twenties. "Y'all come on in," Ginger said over her shoulder, leading them to the kitchen table. "Rick'll be back any minute." She motioned to me and Tom. "These guys are waiting on him too."

Tom and I rose from the table, and to find out their names I introduced myself.

"Hey man, I'm Johnny," I said.

"Yeah, I'm Carl, man," the redhead said.

"Roger," his companion said.

As we shook hands, Carl gave me a quizzical look as if he were trying to remember something. He seemed vaguely familiar but I couldn't place him.

The four of us sat at the table and Ginger took a bar stool at the kitchen counter.

"Y'all looking for some stuff?" I asked.

"We got coke to trade Rick for L-Bs," Carl replied, referring to pounds of marijuana.

"Got any O-Zs?" I asked, referring to ounces of coke.

"Yeah," Carl nodded. "Y'all got any weed?"

"Not right now, but I can get some later on. How much you want?"

"Fifty L-Bs." Carl said flatly. "How much coke y'all want?"

"We're looking for a couple O-Zs," I said. "How much coke you got?"

"Right now we want to trade Rick for the weed."

"Well, we're waiting to get coke from Rick," I said. "So that must be the coke he's expecting from you. If your deal with Rick falls through, maybe we can do some business with each other later if everything is cool."

"Yeah, man," Carl said nodding, "that sounds good."

We sat at the table discussing the drug situation on the streets—which drugs were plentiful or in short supply and what kinds of acid were available. After waiting a short while, Carl and Roger decided to leave and come back an hour or so later to catch up with Rick. I told Ginger we were going too and would check back later. I wanted see the car Carl and Roger were using and get the tag number.

Tom and I left and got a bite to eat, but something kept nagging at me about Carl. I had a vague unease that I had seen him before. And I could tell he was trying to remember me. The memory was just out of reach.

Tom and I returned to the apartment complex an hour later. As we walked to the outside stairs leading the second floor, Carl and Roger approached from the opposite direction, just happening to come back at the same time. As the four of us reached the bottom of the stairs, Carl stopped suddenly and stared at me, squinting, his brow furrowed and his head tilted slightly to one side.

"What'd you say your name was?" Carl asked in a rising, high-pitched voice.

"Johnny. I'm Johnny," I said, knowing something was wrong and worried about what might be coming. "What's your name again?"

"Carl," he replied automatically. Suddenly his eyes widened and his mouth dropped open, his questioning look replaced by a flash of recognition and then panic.

"You guys coming back to wait on Rick?" I asked, trying to remain calm.

"No, man. *We gotta go!*" Carl said quickly. He abruptly turned on his heel and hurried away, calling to Roger over his shoulder, "*Come on. Let's go, let's go!*"

At that instant, I remembered him. *Carl! That* Carl! The guy I had busted with dope and bombs a couple of years ago. His appearance had changed since then, but so had mine. Their car squealed out of the apartment parking lot and scurried out of sight.

Tom and I went up to Rick's apartment. I wanted to hurry and make the buy from Rick before Carl called to warn him. Rick wasn't back so we left. Over the next several days, Tom and I tried a few times to make the connection with Rick but the deal never went through. I suspected Carl warned him I was the police.

I was astonished to run into Carl. He probably felt the same way. But Carl and I weren't finished with each other yet.

Carl Meets J. R.

A year later, using the undercover name "J. R.," I arranged to buy two pounds of marijuana from Sam, with the deal to take place at his home. Sam lived in a large single-story brick house in a well-kept subdivision in the Baton Rouge suburbs. His car was under the carport when I arrived and someone's Mustang was parked behind it. I parked behind the Mustang and went to the carport door and knocked.

Sam answered the door. "Hey J. R., come on in, my man just arrived with it. Let's go to the back." He led me through the kitchen, past an opening to the living room, and down a hallway to a back bedroom. As we walked into the room, over Sam's shoulder I saw the other man, Sam's source, whose back was to us. His back was broad, he was stocky, and his hair was red. As the man started turning around Sam introduced me.

"Carl, this is J. R., the guy I told you about."

Turning toward me, Carl raised his hand to shake and when saw me he froze and stared—we both recognized each other this time. It was the same Carl. Carl's eyebrows shot up, his eyes widened, his jaw sagged, and his mouth dropped open. He was stunned. I froze inside and my heart raced. As Carl gaped at me, I grabbed his hand and started shaking it.

"Hey man, glad to meetchya," I said quickly.

"What's your name?" Carl said weakly as a confused look spread across his face. "What's *your name?*" he repeated, dumbfounded, as much to himself as to me.

"It's J. R.," Sam said helpfully.

"Yeah, man, I'm J. R.," I managed to say. "Glad to meet you." I was still shaking his hand.

Carl dropped his hand from mine and rushed out the door, followed by a confused Sam watching him disappear. I wanted to rush away too, but I needed to try to get things under control.

"Hey man," I said quickly, looking at Sam, and thumbing toward the doorway, "is everything okay? Is this guy all right? He okay?"

"Yeah J. R., I don't know what's got into him, but he's all right."

"You sure he's all right? You sure you can trust him?"

"Oh yeah. Don't worry man, he's okay."

"Well, okay, if you say so, Sam. Now, what about the pounds?" I forced myself to slow down and tried to keep my voice relaxed. I didn't know what Carl was doing outside the room. Was he going to return with a weapon? Had he left? Was he calling others to hurry to the house? Was he going to return to the room and warn Sam that I was a police officer? I tried to fight through a jumble of conflicts—trying to focus on Sam while worrying about Carl, trying to appear relaxed while tense and anxious, trying to remain still while wanting to get out, and desperately wanting to be anywhere but there.

"They're right here." Sam got down on his knees, reached under the bed, and pulled out a large paper grocery sack. Getting up, he took two compressed bricks of marijuana out and put them on the bed. "Each one is a full pound, J. R. I've got some scales and you can weigh them up." As he turned to get the scales, I held my hand up and stopped him.

"That's all right, man, I don't need to weigh them. I trust you, Sam. You say they each weigh a full pound, that's good enough for me." I took the money out and gave it to him. "And I'm in a hurry 'cause I got some people waiting on this and I'm already running late."

While Sam counted the money, I put the pounds back in the sack. "I got most of it sold already and I might want to get some more L-Bs before long, if you can handle it," I said, tucking the sack under my arm like a football and moving toward the door.

"Yeah, any time you want, just let me know and I'll get up with Carl for more."

Sam led me down the hallway. As we walked past an opening to the living room, I saw Carl. Wide-eyed, he sat on the edge of a couch chewing on his fingernails while watching me walk by with two pounds of marijuana under my arm. We walked through the kitchen to the carport door. I stopped at the door and shook hands with Sam. "Thanks, Sam, I appreciate it." I made a show of taking my time, trying not to turn and run for my car. "And you're sure that guy's okay?"

"Yeah, man, Carl's all right. I don't know what got into him, but don't worry, he's okay."

"Well, all right then, I guess."

I realized that Carl couldn't leave because my car was parked in the driveway behind his Mustang, blocking it. I forced myself to take my time in leaving. I walked casually to my car, carefully backed out of the driveway, and slowly drove away, remembering Carl's tag number as I did. As soon as I turned a corner out of sight of the house, my fists slammed the steering wheel. "Damn!" I shouted. "Damn! Damn! Damn!" I took a deep breath, exhaled in a rush, and shook my head, *"Damn."*

After that incident, I expected to be burned down with Sam and his crowd, but oddly I remained cool with him. It turned out that Carl didn't warn him I was the police. Later, I figured out why. Carl apparently thought Sam was acting as an informant in arranging the deal. Because Carl thought Sam was working with the police, he didn't say anything; instead, he cut off contact with Sam. Sam must have wondered why his drug source wouldn't deal with him any longer.

Carl Finally Meets Charlie

One afternoon a couple of months later, while filling up my car at a gas station, I recognized Carl filling his car on the other side of the pump. I put the gas hose back and stood and watched. When he glanced up and saw me, his eyes widened—a familiar sight to me by now. I stepped to his side of the pump. He straightened up, not knowing what to expect. Neither did I. There was no training, no model for how to handle our repeated encounters.

"Hey, Carl. You remember me?" He probably thought I had been following him.

"What's your name?" he said plaintively in a high-pitched whine. *"Who are you?"*

"I'm Charlie Spillers and you know I'm a police officer. You're out on one bond facing trial and you're going to be arrested on that two-pound sale at Sam's." I paused to let that sink in. "So you need some help." We talked and Carl became an informant.

We had had an unusual, recurring relationship, but meeting just once would have been enough for me. And I'm certain he felt the same way.

The encounters with Carl produced anxious moments but turned out not to be dangerous. In hindsight, our surprise encounters were even humorous, especially since they ended without violence.

■   ■   ■

Two weeks after Carl and I last ran into each other, I had a reminder of the risks involved in undercover work. After making several drug buys from a dealer named Dent, I negotiated to buy a large quantity of drugs, planning to make that deal a buy-bust. I got a motel room for the deal and asked him to meet me there. Dent agreed but had a warning for me.

"If this turns out to be a bust," he declared, "someone's going to die."

He arrived at the motel with a bodyguard armed with a .45-caliber automatic. Dent came to the room while his bodyguard waited in the car. When Dent produced the drugs, I triggered the bust with a code word over the body wire and pulled out my gun and arrested him. At the same time, investigators conducting surveillance rushed in and surprised the bodyguard before he could use his weapon. Safety dictated that it was best to assume that all drug traffickers were armed.

■ ■ ■

The day after the bust on Dent I went by the office to sign reports, turn in evidence, and get more buy money. Jack Crittenden was there and I told him about the bust on Dent and his bodyguard. Jack had a story of his own.

"Charlie, you know that guy Larry I been buying from?" Jack said. "Larry's the one who's always saying he has something big for me, but when I show up he's always pestering me to give him a ride."

"Yeah, Jack, what about him?"

"I finally cured him of wanting a ride," Jack said with a grin. "I bought a cheap bottle of perfume at the five-and-dime store and emptied the whole bottle all over the inside of my car. Man, it stinks! Awful! Then just before I picked Larry up, I turned off the air conditioner and turned on the car heater full blast as hot as it would go."

"Damn, Jack!" It was July and oven hot. "You could get heat stroke."

"By the time I picked Larry up," Jack continued, "I was already sweating like a pig. When Larry got in the car he almost passed out from the blast of heat and the perfume stinking up the car. Man, hot air was blowing full blast in his face. Larry jerked his head back from the hot air and said, 'Whoa, *Goddamn!* Man, you got the *heat* on! Are you *crazy?*' Before Larry could jump out, I drove off. '*Turn it off, turn it off!*' Larry yelled, but I told him, 'No man, I got to leave it on, I got chills.' We had only gone two blocks and Larry's shirt was soaked through with sweat. He was almost crying and I swear he was about to pass out. As soon as I stopped at a red light, Larry jumped out and took off running." Jack grinned with satisfaction. "Man, you shoulda seen him. I don't think he'll ever want me to give him a ride again."

"Jack, that's pretty good," I said. "That's pretty smart, except for one thing."

"What's that?"

"Now your car is going to be stinking for a month or two from the perfume."

Of course Jack knew that, but he was always looking to devise a clever quirk to his undercover work and took pleasure in the intrigues he created.

Like an actor, Jack assumed the roles and voices of many characters to gain the confidences of drug dealers. To keep one wary drug dealer from being suspicious, Jack pretended to have a serious stuttering problem, an issue that, at the time, might hamper one from becoming a police officer. As Jack and the dealer negotiated price, Jack stuttered and struggled to get the words out. He spoke in a strained voice with his head nodding forward at each sound, "I-I-I-I-*I'll* g-g-g-g-*give* tuh-tuh-tuh-tuh-*two* huh-huh-huh-huh-*hundred!*" With his eyebrows raised and his mouth slightly open, the drug dealer began nodding back at each stutter, waiting for Jack to get the words out, which he finally did and finished off by accidentally stuttering spit on the dealer's face. The dealer wiped his face and backed up a few feet to continue their negotiations. Later on, Jack's informant told him the drug dealer had been making fun of Jack's stutter. When he finally arrested the dealer, Jack announced the arrest and read off the man's Miranda rights without a stutter, which came as an added shock. Jack asked the man if he understood the rights Jack had just explained and the man replied that he did. "One more thing," Jack added, wagging his finger, "let this be a lesson to you not to make fun of people who stutter."

Mike, Meet Charlie

Another drug buy; another crisis.

I had arranged to buy narcotics from Doug, a pharmacy store manager, and he expected me at his apartment that evening. I left my gun in my car in case I was patted down. Doug met me at the door with another man standing behind him peering over his shoulder.

"Hey, Mike, come on in," Doug waved me in. He closed and double-locked the door behind me and then introduced me to his roommate Jim.

The pungent musky odor of burning pot filled the air. A group sat in a circle on the living room floor, smoking pot and listening to heavy rock rolling from large floor speakers. They cast desultory, heavy-lidded glances in our direction and continued smoking.

Except one.

A young blonde woman in the group stared at me, suddenly stood up, and rushed from the room, disappearing down the hallway that led to the bedrooms. Alarm bells sounded in my head. I tensed, but tried to appear relaxed. I didn't recognize her, but I had been working undercover for years and more and more people now knew me by sight.

"Come on, let's go back here," Doug said, leading me past the group and down the hallway. Jim followed behind me. As we walked by one of the bedrooms, I caught a glimpse of the woman inside. Looking anxious, she watched as we went past. Alarm bells rang louder.

Doug led me into a bedroom and leaned over to pull out a dresser drawer. Jim moved around me and joined him. My back was toward the bedroom door, which was not an ideal situation with trouble brewing behind me, but at least Doug and Jim weren't between me and the door if I needed to make a hasty or forced exit.

"I've got it right here, Mike. Like I told you, I got whatever you want," Doug said, reaching into the dresser drawer. "Let me show—"

"Doug! Hey, Doug," the woman called out in a strained voice from the bedroom door behind me. "Can you come here a moment?" I felt rising panic.

"What?" Doug said irritably.

"I need your help with an album."

"I'll be there in a minute."

"No, I need you *right now*," she insisted. "It can't wait."

"All right, I'm coming," Doug called out past my shoulder and glanced at me, some uncertainty now in his eyes. "Be right back, Mike."

"Sure man, but I'm in a hurry. I've got people waiting on this."

Doug shut the drawer and hurried past me.

As Doug left the room, I could hear the woman urging him farther away: "Over here, I need to show you something." Then her voice dropped to unintelligible whispers and I could picture her holding a finger to her lips shushing him and then urgently waving him into a room to warn him about me.

Jim was talking and I was responding to him, but my mind raced, preoccupied with the unknown going on behind my back. I thought of the room full of people between me and the apartment door, and it felt like the world was closing in. Maybe the deal would just fall through. Or would Doug return with the others? Could I talk my way out, bluff my way out, fight my way out? Pressure built in my chest, my skin felt prickly, and I sensed the hair on the back of my neck standing up. It was hot in the room. Something was going to happen soon. I braced myself. Get ready, I told myself. *Get ready.*

A sudden buzz of murmurs erupted from the group in the front room, followed just as suddenly by complete silence; even the music went silent. *Get ready.*

I was saying something to Jim when I caught him cast a furtive glance over my shoulder toward the doorway. Then, right behind me, almost at my back . . .

Doug's voice suddenly called out, *"Charlie!"* A one-second pause. *"Charlie!"*

For an instant my world stopped, and then was spinning out of control. I felt as if I stood alone in the center of an arena filled with an angry roaring crowd, but heard no sounds except the loud thumping of my heartbeat. Just as quickly, sounds and senses returned in a rush and I was back.

"Charlie!"

I didn't react, not even a flicker of having heard anything. I forced myself to continue looking at Jim and to continue talking. A microsecond battle had raged as I struggled to overcome a normal reaction and panic to hearing my name called.

Doug appeared at my right shoulder and moved in front of me, in close.

"Hey, Doug," I said, casually, "we were just talking about—"

"Your name *Charlie*?" he demanded, poking an accusatory finger at my stomach.

"What?"

"Your name Charlie? *Is* your name *Charlie*?"

"Naw, man, I told you, I'm Mike," I replied, indignantly. Then I gave him a puzzled look. "What's this about Charlie? Who's *Charlie*?"

Doug hesitated, searching my face, and then made up his mind.

"Ah, nothing," he eventually pronounced with a shake of his head. "Don't worry about it. Well, Mike, like I was saying," he said, turning toward the dresser. "I have it right here." He opened a drawer and took out a bag of narcotics. We agreed on the price and he sold narcotics to me.

On my way out, we passed through the living room. It was empty. As we reached the front door, Doug stopped. "Hey, Mike, remember when you came in and the girl got up and left the room, the one who came and got me out of the bedroom?"

I thought a moment. "Oh, yeah," I nodded, as if vaguely remembering. "She came to the door."

"She told me you were a narc," he confided.

"Huh! A *what?*" I said, wide-eyed and incredulous.

"Yeah, that's right. She said you were a narcotics agent with Louisiana State Police and that your name was Charlie Spillers."

"*Who? Me?* Ha, that's crazy," I hooted indignantly, shaking my head. "Just crazy. Man, she's all mixed up."

"Yeah, well, she thought you were a narc named Charlie Spillers, but I gave you a test. When I came back in the room I called out 'Charlie,' the name 'Charlie,' and you didn't react at all. You passed my test," he said smugly. "So I knew she was all screwed up."

When I left the apartment, the night air felt crisp and bracing. Walking to the car, I breathed deeply, trying to release the strain and tension. I had made it out without everything blowing up and had made the buy besides. Emotions whirled. Driving away, I stared vacantly at the road ahead and slowly shook my head, muttering, "Damn . . . *damn!*"

I got home about one in the morning. Sitting at the kitchen table, I marked and sealed evidence, then wrote notes about the buy for my report. Nearly an hour later I was finished and stood up and stretched. I was drained but still too hyped up to go to bed. I turned on the television and kept the sound low so as not to wake Evelyn and Terry. I stared numbly at the television, slowly decompressing and not actually comprehending. Just before dawn I began nodding off and staggered to bed. It was close to becoming a routine night.

Guatemalan Intelligence El Commandante Calls BRPD

Constantly working undercover was stressful though we tried to give no sign of it. We sometimes relieved the tension by playing practical jokes. Lighthearted moments relieved the stress and made you feel normal.

Late one night, Jack Crittenden and I were alone at the narcotics office when one of us came up with the crazy idea to call Sergeant Charlie Gouner and pretend to be with Guatemalan Intelligence. Gouner answered.

"Eez thees zee commander of zee narcotic in zee Baton Rouge, zee policia?" I asked.

"Yes, it is," Gouner replied, hesitantly. "I'm sorry, who is this calling?"

"Thees eez El Commandante Riviera, zee head of zee Guatemalan Intelligentsia. Who eez zees person to which I am talking to?"

"*Guatemalan Intelligence! Oh! Yes, sir!* I'm Sergeant Gouner, sir."

"You are zee one in zee charge of zee Baton Rouge narcotic?"

"*Yes, sir!*" Gouner sounded like he was standing at attention. Perhaps even saluting.

"Eez bueno, Serzhant Gonna, we need zee help on somesing verree importante."

"*Yes, sir!* Anything you need, sir. Just let me know what you need, sir, and we will do it."

"Eez bueno. Zee plen with zee beeg load of zee narcotic, she eez coming to your airport late tonight."

"Yes, sir!"

"We need zee help with zee surveillianze when eet land. Eet weel land and re-fooel and zen she take back off."

"Yes, sir! Just give me the information you have and the plane's tail number and when it gets here we will do whatever you need, sir. Sir, could you hold on just a moment please, sir, and let me get a pen and paper. I just need to get, uh, uh . . . I got it! Yes, sir, I'm ready to write it down. What is your name again, please, sir?"

"Commandante Riviera, zee head of zee Guatemalan Intelligentsia."

"Yes, sir, Commandante. How do you spell your name please, sir?"

"Yesss, eet eez R."

"R," Gouner said precisely.

"I."

"I. R-I." Gouner repeated.

I wasn't sure how to spell it, so . . . : "And you *are* zee head of zee narcotic?"

"Oh yes, sir. Yes, sir. I've got R-I- . . ."

"V."

"V. R-I-V."

"And Serzhant Gonna, you have zee plenty of zee men for thees?"

"Oh yes, sir. *Yes, sir*, and if we don't, we can get more, sir. I'll get right on it as soon as we finish talking and I'll get all my men together."

"Goot. Eez verree bueno. Zee plen, eet weel land at zee midnight. You sure to have zee men?"

"Oh yes, sir. You know how big the load is?"

"Zee plen, she eez full of zee cocaina and I weel call you back with zee plen nomber. Eet eez flying to other city and we yoost need surveillianze while eet eez at your airport. What eez your telephono nomber, pleez?"

Gouner recited the number for the narcotics office and assured "El Commandante" that he would be standing by, waiting for his call.

"Bueno. I call you soon, Serzhant Gonna."

"*Yes, sir!* You can count on us, sir!"

Hanging up, we howled at how well the joke had played out. We had recorded the call; replaying the recording, we laughed again. But the recording reminded us that Gouner had promised to call out *everyone*. Sure enough, within minutes we got a call that Gouner needed everyone to rush to the narcotics office for a meeting. Something *very big* had come up.

The joke was getting out of hand; the whole police department was getting alerted. Gouner had even called the chief of police. It was time to call off the joke—if we could.

The Commandante called Gouner one more time. When Gouner answered the phone he sounded rushed, busy calling out all the troops.

"Ah, Serzhant Gonna, thees eez Commandante Riviera here—"

"*Yes, sir,* Commandante, I've called out the whole force and they are arriving now," Gouner said breathlessly, "and I talked to the chief of police and—"

"Serzhant Gonna, Serzhant Gonna, zee plans, they have chenge."

"Oh yes, sir, whatever you need, sir."

"Zee smuggler eez no going to zee Baton Rouge after all, zhey change zee plan and go to other place, so we no need zee help with zee plen."

"Oh—Yes, sir."

"I zhank you verree mouch for zee cooperaseeon."

"Yes, sir, Commandante. We are happy to help, sir. If you need anything else, *anything at all,* just let me know, sir."

"Eez bueno. Zhank you, el Serzhant. I go now. Eez verree beezy wit thees."

"Yes, sir. Yes, sir. Thank you, sir."

Although the Baton Rouge Police Department did not have to assist Guatemalan Intelligence after all, Sergeant Gouner proudly told his colleagues all about the call he received from El Commandante, and as the story spread, Gouner's stature rose. It was not until much later that he was told of the prank, long after we had left the department and we were at a safe distance.

"Don't I Know You?"

I was sat with Ken, my informant, and two lounge dancers at a table in Big John's, a crowded red-light district bar in downtown Baton Rouge. The dancers were taking a break between their sets on the stage. A gray fog of cigarette smoke dulled the dim glow of bar lights and a roar filled the room. During breaks the jukebox was turned down but the crowd noise rose to a fevered pitch in a buzz saw of boozy conversations.

Ken leaned close. "I see a guy I know. Want me to check with him and see if anything's happening?"

"Yeah. You know what to do."

"Be back in a minute."

Ken weaved through the crowd toward the back of the bar and sat down at a table with two men, disappearing from view as the crowd closed in behind him.

He returned a few minutes later just as the two women were leaving to begin another set on stage. Before Ken even sat down, I could tell that he was anxious to report on his conversation with the men.

"What you find out?"

"The guy I know, well, the guy with him's got some Ds for sale," Ken smiled, looking like an angler who may have just hooked a big one.

"Dilaudid?"

"Yeah."

"What kind of Ds?"

"He didn't say. I told them I had a friend who wanted to score. We're supposed to meet them in the alley." Ken glanced toward the entrance. "That's them leaving right now. We better hurry." He started to get up but I grabbed his arm.

"Hold on, Ken, tell me what you told them about me so our stories'll be straight."

"I just told them that you're Mike."

"What else? Quick, anything else? Where I live, where I work, how long we known each other?" Earlier, Ken and I had gotten our cover stories straight but I had to make sure he hadn't strayed from the cover or filled in areas we had not discussed.

"No, I don't think so." Ken bit his bottom lip trying to remember, then shook his head. "No, that was all—just that you're Mike and you're cool."

"Okay. Good. Let's go. Just follow my lead." We made our way to the door.

"What about the guy with the Ds, what's his name? You know him?"

"His name's David. I don't know his last name but I can find out."

"You ever dealt with David, Ken? Ever bought from him?"

"No, but I heard of him before, he deals a lot of shit."

"How many Ds does he have? How much does he want for them?"

"He didn't say, but he can probably do whatever you want."

"What about the guy with him, the one you know?"

"Oh, that's just Robert. I've known him a good while. He deals a little pot. I forget his last name, but I can get it and I know where he lives." Ken was beginning to catch on to the routine.

We stepped out of the bar to find the two men waiting at the curb. As soon as they saw us, they turned and walked hurriedly down the street and Ken and I followed a short distance behind. They turned into a narrow, dark alley and stopped when they were out of the light from the street.

"Ken said you got some Ds," I said to David.

"Yeah," David said, "how many you want?"

"How much you want for them?"

"Twenty-five."

"Tell you what, I'll give you fifteen a piece for three."

As David and I haggled over price, I got a closer look at him in the pale light cast by a distant streetlight. Suddenly I recognized him—he knew I was a police officer. My heart was pounding. Maybe they could hear it.

David was a onetime informant for Bud Garrison, a police intelligence agent. Six months before, I was introduced to David while he was being debriefed by Bud and Al Saizan at the intelligence office. At the time I asked David a few questions about drugs, and then left while they continued the debriefing. David helped Bud only a short time after that and then reverted to drug dealing.

Standing in the alley, David had not recognized me yet. I needed to get the deal over as quickly as possible and get away before he remembered me. I quickly agreed to twenty dollars per tablet and fished the money out of my pocket. As David was handling the tablets to me, I caught him peering closely at my face.

"Hey, don't I know you, man?" David asked, a quizzical frown on his face.

I squinted at David as if trying to place him and then shook my head. "No. No, you don't look familiar to me," I replied, deliberately. I handed the money to David.

"You sure we never met, man?" he demanded. "Where you live, man?"

"I got a house trailer on the east side of town. Where you live?"

"I live off Park," David said, keeping his eyes fastened on mine. "What about your job, where you work, man?" he persisted, his tone surly. He somehow knew it was important for him to remember me, to try to place where he had met me. His memory was giving him a vague warning.

"Hey, look, man, why you asking so many questions?"

"Man, you just look familiar, man. I seen you somewhere before." David's eyes abruptly narrowed and his eyes locked on mine. "You ain't got a brother that's a cop do you?" he said, accusingly, his voice rising. Cop! I fought to push the panic down.

"No, man," I said, trying to keep my voice casual. Did it come out that way, I wondered. I couldn't tell. "I ain't got no brothers."

"You sure you don't have a brother that's a cop? Working at Winbourne police station?"

"Hey, man," I said sharply. "I said I ain't got no brother that's a cop," I insisted. "But I have been to that station before to see about paying a ticket, and while I was there someone said they had a cop who looked like me." It flowed out, spilled out, forming a smokescreen, and I said it without any thought. I had begun speaking without knowing what I was going to say until I heard the words at the same time as David. Does the brain react instinctively to danger using thoughts, words, and body language necessary to fend off a threat, just as the body reacts instinctively to danger by ducking or throwing up an arm to ward off an unexpected blow?

David was watching me closely but his face relaxed slightly and his brows unknitted.

"Maybe that's it. 'Cause I was there once and saw someone who looks like you." He paused. "Yeah," he said, nodding and rubbing his chin. "That must have been it," he said, as much to himself as to anyone else.

"Well, that's probably what it was," I offered. "Maybe you were there when I was seeing about a ticket or you saw the cop who looks like me, but I'm telling you, man, I ain't got no brother that's a cop." I wanted to remind David that the issue was whether I had a brother who was a cop, not whether I was a cop.

"Okay, man, okay." David held up his hand signaling a truce. "Okay."

"All right, what if I wanna score some Ds later, maybe in a couple days? Can you fix me up?" I needed to play it out.

"Yeah, man, I'll be around here."

David and Robert turned and walked out of the alley through the pool of light under the curbside streetlight and disappeared into darkness. I took a deep breath and sighed as Ken and I walked back to the bar. My heartbeat was returning to normal. Even though it was a cool spring night, sweat had formed on my forehead and I wiped it away. As we entered the lounge, the music from the jukebox and the din inside were faint, but as my adrenaline finally ebbed, the music blared loudly again and the raucous noise resumed.

■   ■   ■

I got a break from the streets when the department sent me and Sergeant Sam Pruet to Washington, DC, to attend a ten-week DEA narcotics investigators course. Without realizing it, I probably needed the rest. I had been living on constant stress and adrenaline. I told drug dealers I was working on that I was going out of state to lay low from the law for a while. The course was conducted at DEA headquarters in downtown DC and Sam and I stayed at the nearby Burlington Hotel. About thirty investigators were in the course, including several from other countries. It was a great experience and a welcome rest. When we returned to Baton Rouge, I resumed my undercover roles and was soon immersed again in the drug-trafficking world.

Tight Spot

Crisis, stress, and looming disaster continued to be unfortunate parts of my undercover life. The only question about each was how I would handle it and how it would end.

I had gone several months without being caught in a tight spot, and since then my undercover drug buys had been uneventful. That was about to change.

My informant had arranged a drug buy from a dealer named Bob and we would meet him at an all-night diner. Late that night, the informant and I sat in a booth, waiting for the meet. It was a routine buy and I didn't have surveillance. Since we expected only one man and would meet in a public place, I had left my gun in my car, as I often did.

My back was to the door and the informant sat across from me so he could watch the door and spot Bob when he arrived.

"There he is," the informant said excitedly, looking over my shoulder, "coming in the door now. That's Bob. That's him." I looked over my shoulder and saw a big man with a beard.

"Standing at the door? With the beard?"

"Yeah, that's him."

Bob stood just inside the door, his eyes searching the tables and row of booths. The informant rose slightly and Bob saw him. Just then another man came in the door and Bob nodded for him to follow. They headed toward us. Over Bob's shoulder I got a look the other man and recognized him—John! The pit of my stomach felt as if a roller coaster had just plunged underneath me. He knew I was a cop—I had arrested him the year before. I was heavier than I was then, but he was certain to recognize me. Now John and Bob were closing in and would be at our table in a few seconds.

I quickly turned my head away so he couldn't see my face. My mouth went dry and panic surged. I dreaded what would happen when he got a good look at me.

"I don't know the other one," the informant said.

"He knows me! He knows I'm a cop!" I whispered urgently. "Let's get them outside in the dark *fast*."

Suddenly they were at our booth. I covered my face with both hands while faking a big yawn. John slid in the booth beside me, his body pressed against mine. Bob sat down beside the informant.

"Man, my head's hurting," I complained through my fingers. "This light's hurting my eyes. Let's go outside. Damn, my head."

John glanced at me. Head bowed, I held my head in both hands, rubbing my forehead with my fingers, hiding my face in the process.

"Yeah, Rick's head's bothering him bad, let's get outside," the informant added.

"Let's go to my car." Bob said.

John and Bob slid out of the booth and led the way out of the grill. I lingered, letting the informant get in front of me. We followed Bob to his car. Fortunately it was parked in a dark area of the lot and faced away from the brightly lit grill. I trailed at the back of the group and used the informant's body to shield me from John. Bob and John got in the front of the car and the informant and I took the rear seat. While the doors were open the inside dome light lit up the interior and I cringed until the light went off and we were in the dark. I sat directly behind John so that he couldn't see me without twisting completely around.

I had to get this over quickly and get out of the car, away from John, before they discovered my identity. John couldn't see me without twisting around but he still might recognize my voice, although I was trying to alter it with a deeper, gruff tone.

Following introductions, I glanced at Bob. "Ya'll got it, man? I need to go, my head's killing me. Damn." Head bowed, I rubbed my forehead

"Yeah." Bob replied and nodded to John. John reached under his seat and handed a package to Bob. Bob looked around the parking lot and then handed a bag of dope over the seat to me. We agreed on a price and I passed the money to him.

"Thanks, man," I said. "Gotta go take care of my head."

The informant and I got out. I carefully kept my back to the car as we walked away. When I heard Bob's car finally driving off, I breathed a deep sigh of relief. Then I shook my head at how close that had been—too close. Much too close.

But I had another tight spot to deal with that night, although very minor by comparison. I left the parking lot, dropped off the informant at his apartment, and got home well after midnight. I had a midterm exam in my economics class the next night and wasn't the least bit ready for it. I had missed most of my classes and needed to stay up and study. I had been trying to take college courses part time, but it was proving difficult because I kept missing classes.

Evelyn and Terry were sleeping soundly when I got home. After quietly making coffee, I sat at the kitchen table writing notes for my report of the drug purchase, and then marked and sealed drug evidence. It was two o'clock in the morning and I was on my second cup of coffee by the time I opened my economics textbook and began studying for the exam. The close call earlier that night kept interrupting my thoughts and I cringed recalling the tension and utter anxiety I felt just a few hours before. The memory seared me and I kept trying to push it away. By dawn, I was on the second pot of coffee. I could force myself to physically keep going but my mind had become sluggish. Words in the text began running together and I read and reread paragraphs about economic theory without being able to absorb anything. I finally closed the textbook and slept for several hours. I had another drug deal set for shortly before the exam and needed some rest.

As it turned out, I missed the exam because of the drug deal, a pattern that would be often repeated. It wasn't the first time my studies suffered because of my work, nor would it be the last.

Roadside Ballet

There was no one tip-off.

On a pitch-black night, well after midnight, we drove miles from Baton Rouge and sat idling on the side of a deserted narrow road with no sign of life or houses. My fellow undercover agent, Bruce Childers, and I were in a car with the go-between, David, waiting to buy fifty pounds of marijuana from David's source, who arranged to meet us on the road.

We planned to do a buy-bust, to arrest David and his colleagues during the delivery. We knew danger escalates on deals for large quantities because either side might try to rob the other of money or drugs.

Late that night we had picked up David and followed his driving directions. We traveled away from Baton Rouge for more than thirty minutes to a narrow road, a secluded area on Jefferson Highway.

"Here, stop here," David said. Dense woods crowded the road edges, and large tree limbs looming overhead enclosed us in a black tunnel. It was isolated—no traffic was on the road and no houses were nearby.

"What? Here?" I asked, slowing down.

"Yeah, stop here. Right here," he insisted.

"I can't pull over, there's no shoulder on the side of the road," I protested. "You want to just stop in the middle of the road?"

"Yeah, this is good, right here. Here. *Right here.*" He knew exactly where he wanted our car. I stopped and put the transmission in park. Our headlights illuminated a leafy tunnel underneath the trees and a light fog lingered a couple of feet off the ground. From outside, the car probably seemed to be floating on fog.

"What'll we do now?" I asked, wondering if he had anyone hidden in the forest next to us.

"Just wait here," David said. "He'll be here."

"When?"

"Any moment, just wait, he'll be right here." David's voice was rising. "Turn off your lights and the engine." I turned off the engine and headlights. Complete blackness enveloped us. Pitch black and silent. I doubted I would be able to see my hand in front of my face. I couldn't see what David was doing but at least Bruce sat right behind him. This was getting a little hairy.

"What'll we do now?" I repeated, trying to control the rising tension in my voice.

"Just wait, just wait, he'll be here in a minute."

Fuzzy headlights suddenly flashed on and off in the far distance, perhaps a mile in front of us, dimmed by the fog and curling mists.

"Flash your headlights on and off," David said.

I turned them on and off.

"What now? What's going on?" I asked. "Is that him?"

"Yeah, that's him. That's him." David's voice was high-pitched, tense. "Just wait."

The distant headlights came back on and slowly moved toward us.

"I need to take a leak," David said abruptly, and started opening his door. Something's wrong, I thought. Why does he want out of the car? This is no coincidence.

"Me too," I said quickly, and opened my door.

"Yeah, I do too," Bruce added from the backseat. It was a two-door car and Bruce squeezed out from the back. The interior car light was disabled and we moved in darkness except for the distant headlights that were still too far to reach us.

We lined up alongside the right side of the car, with David in the middle, facing the trees. David was to my left and silhouetted against the distant headlights. I watched him out of the corner of my eye in case he went for a gun. After we unzipped, David's right hand rose slowly toward the front of his waist. I slowly raised my right hand toward my back waist where my gun was tucked. David's hand went back down and I lowered mine. Then his hand went back up and mine followed to my back again. He lowered his hand and I lowered mine again. We were engaged in a tense, synchronized ballet.

After we finished, David lingered, obviously not wanting to get back in the car. Something wasn't right and I knew we weren't getting back in the car without him. The three of us stood, each side trying to wait the other out. The headlights were getting closer. We couldn't wait any longer.

"Come on," I said, turning to the car. "Let's get back in."

"I'll just wait out here," David said.

"No, let's all get in the car," I commanded. I stood facing him. "We'll wait in there. Come on."

Bruce climbed in. David hesitated, and then got in. I went around and got in behind the steering wheel. The oncoming car's headlights illuminated the interior of our car and I could make out an anxious look on David's face.

"What now? What's he gonna do?" I demanded.

"Nothing, just wait."

"Does he have the fifty pounds with him?"

"Yeah. He's got it. He's got it."

The car slowed to a crawl as it drew beside us. It stopped for a moment and then continued uncertainly past and sped up. The driver apparently expected David to be outside the car. I watched the car's red taillights in the rearview mirror and tried to watch David at the same time. The car stopped in the road a half mile behind us, backed up, maneuvering to turn around, and then headed back in our direction, its headlights looming closer in the rearview mirror and lighting up the back window of my car.

"What's up? What's he doing?" I demanded anxiously. "What's going on?"

"Nothing. Just wait. Wait." David's voice trembled, almost cracked, close to panic.

The headlights stopped about forty yards behind us and then were switched off, casting us in total darkness. We needed to seize control of the situation.

"What about coke," I said, "can you get us some coke?" *Coke* was the code word to make the arrest, and Bruce responded immediately.

"POLICE!" Bruce pressed a gun barrel against the back of David's head and grabbed him around the neck with his other arm. "Police! You're under arrest. Keep your hands up. Put them on the dash. NOW!"

I reached over and patted David down for weapons, not finding any.

"You tell us, *now!* Quick, what's going on?" I commanded. "What's going to happen? How many are in that car?"

"Nothing. Nothing's gonna happen."

"What's about to happen? Goddamn it, tell us now, right now."

"Nothing. I don't know nothing."

"Bruce, hold on to him, I'm getting out."

I got out and closed my door quietly. It was so dark I couldn't see the other car or even the edges of the road. I reached back and felt the handle of my gun for reassurance and carefully stepped in the direction of the other car. I couldn't see the pavement under my feet or get any orientation so it felt like I was walking blindfolded, one step at a time, feeling my way with my foot. When I had gone about twenty yards I heard a whisper in the black void ahead of me, maybe ten yards away.

"David?" a voice called out in a low whisper, almost inaudible. "David?" The voice closer now, searching. "David?"

A black shadow suddenly loomed in front of me.

"David," he whispered, surprised, "is that *you?*"

I didn't answer and he moved closer until we were almost touching. *"David?"*

"No, man, David's at the car."

"Where's David?" he said, alarmed, still whispering.

"David's in the car, he's waiting on you. He told me to come get you."

"Where is he?"

"At the car. He's waiting for you."

The shadow moved beside me and we walked side by side toward my car, unable to see it until we were within a few feet.

"Where's David?"

"He's inside," I said, and dropped a half pace back and grabbed my gun. As he reached the back of the car I shoved him over the trunk and pressed the gun at his back.

"POLICE! Hands on the trunk! Get your hands on the trunk. You're under arrest." Holding the gun against his back, I patted him down with one hand and took a knife out of his pocket.

"Who's with you?" I demanded. "Anyone in your car?"

"What? What's going on?" He started to straighten up and turn around; I pushed him back down.

"Don't move! Hands on the car! Keep your hands on the trunk. You're under arrest. Anyone else with you? Who's in your car?"

"Nobody, no one's with me," he said in a strained voice. "I'm by myself."

I recited his Miranda rights as Bruce got David out of the car and turned on the headlights so that we could see. We got a two-way radio out from under the seat and called for the investigators on surveillance.

No drugs were in the other car. The license plate had been removed and lay on the back floorboard. A loaded .22-caliber rifle rested at an angle on the front seat, the butt next to the driver's position, within his easy reach. A bullet was in the chamber, ready to be fired.

They had planned to rob us but we had disrupted the plot before they had the chance. One of the men confessed to the planned robbery and became a witness against the other. Later, I heard that while on bond, one of the men robbed a drugstore.

Jack Crittenden had arranged the fifty-pound deal but came down with the flu and Bruce and I stepped in at the last minute. The deal didn't seem right from the beginning and we shouldn't have allowed the bad guys to choose the location. Nothing bad had happened, but if they had gotten the drop on us, the outcome would have been different. Bruce and I might have gone for our guns and come up firing. Someone would have been hurt or killed.

Sometimes timing is everything. It was for us that night.

The attempted robbery was just one more close call. Despite the growing number of tight spots, it never crossed my mind to stop working undercover. The Marines had instilled the attitude that accomplishing the mission was all important—no matter how tough or difficult. So the fact that working undercover was becoming more hazardous was irrelevant. It was my job. And I was oblivious to the toll of constant stress. That would come later.

Too Close to Home

Over the years I had made hundreds of undercover buys and with each roundup, more and more of my defendants were out on bond. The arrests generated two types of threats: Some might want to eliminate me because I was the key witness and others might want to retaliate. Not surprisingly, reports occasionally surfaced of threats or plots against me, although none was serious.

I was careful not to expose my wife Evelyn and our son Terry to danger. I never let suspects know where we lived, which was much easier to conceal in those days, before the Internet and Google searches. Although I gave out my home phone number to suspects and informants, it was a unpublished number and couldn't be traced without a subpoena. We were discreet at home and very few of our neighbors ever knew I was a police officer.

One summer we bought a mobile home and placed it in a spacious new mobile home park off Airline Highway on the east side of Baton Rouge. The park had landscaped lawns, a well-equipped playground, swimming pool, and separate sections for people with children and without children. If a mobile home park could be upscale, ours was it. It was not only nice, it was safe. There was little likelihood that drug dealers would ever live in the neighborhood or even visit it. A couple who were close friends lived in the same park. The husband was a contract police agent who occasionally worked with me undercover. Aside from one other family, no one else there knew I was a police officer. At first Evelyn and I felt comfortable and secure. That feeling came to an abrupt halt one hot summer Sunday.

I had just returned from running an errand and was sitting at the kitchen table writing reports on recent undercover buys. Evelyn and Terry were at the playground located in a large common area behind our mobile home. The door suddenly swung open and Evelyn rushed inside carrying Terry, her face flushed red.

"Charlie! Charlie!" she cried out breathlessly. Her eyes were wide with fear, an almost desperate look on her face. Holding Terry on her hip, she quickly shut the door.

"Evelyn, what is—"

"Charlie! There's a man out there. He wanted to know if 'Mike' lived in this trailer," she said rapidly, rushing the words, still breathless. "He saw your car in the driveway. I told him I didn't know any Mike, I didn't know who lived in this trailer."

I sprang up, hurrying to a window, holding my gun. "Where is he? What else did he say?"

"I don't know where he went. I got Terry and started walking away like I was going to another trailer." She put down Terry, locked the door, and hurried from window to window closing the curtains. Gripping the gun firmly, I went from window to window, peering out from the edges.

"You see what kind of car he was in?"

"No, he was walking when I saw him."

"What'd he look like?"

"It scared me so bad I didn't pay attention. He was a black man, tall and big, maybe in his thirties."

I scanned the areas on both sides of the trailer, front and back, but didn't see the man or any strange cars. I doubled back to each window and checked again.

"How long ago did it happen?"

"Just a few minutes ago. I walked away toward Dorothy's trailer and when I looked back he was gone, so I ran back here." It was a brave thing for her to do, to come back to the trailer. She and Terry were in danger, but she knew the man was coming after me and she had to warn me.

I tucked my gun in my waistband in the small of my back and pulled my shirt out to conceal it. "Lock the door behind me and don't unlock it for anyone but me."

"Don't go out there!"

"It's all right," I assured her. "Don't worry. I'll take care of it. I'll be right back."

Outwardly, I tried to appear calm for her benefit, but I was worried. Now they knew where we lived, our protective shield was gone. Was there only one? The thin metal walls of the trailer would not stop bullets. Instead of calling headquarters to send police units, I rushed out to deal with any immediate danger. I went out the door and down the steps and heard the door lock behind me.

Our trailer park was not on a main street and was only accessible through a winding drive. Whoever confronted Evelyn had not just happened by, but had obviously come searching for me. He had recognized my undercover car and he knew I was Mike. I was frightened by the close call Evelyn and Terry just had. I had been confident, perhaps recklessly confident, that I could take care of myself and that my family was protected as long as defendants didn't know where we lived. Now that protection had just been stripped away and Evelyn and Terry were vulnerable because of my work.

I walked around the trailer, looking in every direction for any sign of the man or any strange car. I got in my undercover car and drove slowly around the trailer park, making two passes on every street. Satisfied that the park was clear, I drove to the road outside, pulled to the side, and scrutinized every car that went past. After ten minutes I drove to a nearby strip of retail stores. It was Sunday, so the stores were closed and the parking areas were empty. Satisfied that the man was no longer in the area, I returned to our trailer. Evelyn unlocked the door with a look of relief.

"Did you see anything?"

"Nothing. I checked the whole park. He's not here. I checked out the road and the shopping center and didn't see anything there either. He must have left right after he talked to you. You remember if he had a mustache or a beard?"

"I don't know, I just saw that he was big and tall. It scared me so much, especially because Terry was there, that I just didn't notice what he looked like. Who do you think it was? What do you think he wanted?"

"I don't know. Probably someone I busted while using the name Mike, and he recognized my undercover Camaro. It could be anyone. But don't worry. He probably thought he was mistaken about it being the same car. There's plenty of red Camaros just like that one."

I called several informants and instructed them to scout for any street talk about someone gunning for "Mike." I called other narcotics investigators to let them know what happened and asked them to have their informants check for street talk. I wanted the officers to know about it in case something bad happened before I was able to write it up in a report. An hour later I drove around and checked the area again. Everything appeared normal.

Evelyn put Terry in his bed to take a nap and she left to pick up a few items at a convenience store. I resumed writing reports, but still worried. Evelyn had been gone only a few minutes when someone knocked hard on the door. Looking out, I saw a large black man standing at the foot of the steps. Tucking my gun at my waist under my shirt, I opened the door.

As the door swung open I recognized him—it was Eurl, an acid dealer. I had bought LSD from him and had busted him a month before. Eurl glared up at me. In an instant, I decided that if we didn't wind up in a shootout, by the time Eurl left he would be an informant. That would be the only way to neutralize him as a danger to my family. Now that he knew where I lived, they would be vulnerable. The first moments would be crucial, and I needed to seize control from the start.

"Hey, *Mike*," he snarled, his face sullen. He had spit out the name *Mike*.

"Eurl!" I smiled broadly. "Hey, man, I'm glad you're here. Come on in." I stepped back. "I've been wanting to get in touch with you, to talk to you about the case on you."

Eurl hesitated, staring. He didn't expect this reception. "Come on in," I repeated, waving a hand toward the inside. He watched me closely as he climbed the steps and stepped inside, drawing himself up into a confrontational stance in front of me. I smiled and closed the door.

"Here, sit down, Eurl," I said earnestly, motioning to the kitchen table. "I need to talk to you, man."

He hesitated, wary; his eyes darted quickly around the room. He looked back at me and then sat down at the table, angrily staring at me. I wondered if he had a gun. I sat down across from him and rested both forearms on the table. He was watching me carefully, but I could sense that whatever he had planned to do was momentarily thrown off by his surprise at the welcome. We were both wary, although I suppressed my true reaction. I watched his every move, facial expression, and body language. I had to assume he was armed and had come to retaliate. But even if Eurl came only to verbally confront me, it could erupt into a vicious fight or later threats to my family. I plunged ahead to maintain the initiative.

"Look, man, you know that I'm a police officer and that I was the one who made the case on you." He was surprised—he had apparently expected denials and evasions. But this also built my credibility because I confirmed what he already knew. "I wanted to get in touch with you because you are facing some heavy charges. The DA and the judge don't like acid, Eurl, and just think how you would look to a jury. On an acid case they usually want to put the guy in the joint and throw away the key. You know what I'm talking about."

"Yeah, but—"

"Look, Eurl, the cases on you are airtight and there's no way out. That's why I wanted to talk with you. You're a decent guy. You're not a rip-off artist like a lot of people dealing drugs. You don't need to go to the joint, Eurl. I don't want you to go to the joint. You don't want to go to the joint, do you?"

"No. But tell me one thing, Mike."

"If I can."

"Why did you bust me, man?"

"Eurl, that's my job. I'm a cop. If you're dealing dope, you're eventually going to get busted—if not by me, then by someone else. Anyone dealing for any length of time is going to get busted, either because the cops are after him or because of just plain bad luck. You know that. You know what I'm saying is true, right, man?" He nodded, a tip-off that what I said was having some effect.

I continued, "But you know you were doing wrong, Eurl." I looked him in the eye. "Especially selling acid. That's not like selling pot, man. You were breaking the law and you got busted. Even though I like you, Eurl, and I want to see you help yourself out, if you were out here selling again I would bust you again. You see where I'm coming from?"

"Yeah, I guess so, Mike. But what can I do? I don't want to do no time."

"That's why I wanted to talk to you. You made a mistake, but you don't belong in the joint. But I can't help you unless you help yourself. I can tell the DA what a good guy you are, but that won't mean anything to him. You've got to give me something to bring to the DA so I can show him you're a good guy, that you've turned around and helped us. You see what I mean, Eurl?"

He arched an eyebrow. "What I gotta do?"

"You've got to give me something so I can help you out. You've got to help me make some cases."

"Then I won't have to do no time?" he asked.

"Look, Eurl, I can't promise you that you won't get any time. The only thing I will promise is if you help me and you're straight with me, I'll make the DA and the court aware of how much you helped. Most of the time they follow my recommendation, but I can't guarantee that they will. If you're willing to help make some cases, you'll be doing the best thing you can do for yourself. If you go to trial, you'll be convicted and get the book thrown at you. You understand?"

He nodded, rubbing his chin with his hand, pensive.

It was time to bring Eurl over the threshold, to pull him over to my side. "But I've got to know today, right now, if you're going to help yourself out. Not everyone gets the opportunity to help and there's some I won't let help because they need to be off the streets."

"Well, Mike, I—"

The trailer door swung open. Carrying a grocery bag, Evelyn was on the top step outside the door, looking over her shoulder back toward the street.

"Charlie," she called out. "There's a car parked—"

She froze as she turned her head toward the kitchen table where we sat, her mouth dropped open, and her sharp intake of breath was audible.

"It's all right," I said quickly. "It's okay. You can come in."

Evelyn stepped into the trailer, her back against the door, hesitant to come further.

"It's okay," I repeated, rising from the table and taking the bag. Eurl rose too, a good sign.

"This is Eurl, the guy I told you I need to talk to. Eurl, this is my wife Evelyn."

He nodded at her. Evelyn's terrified expression melted away as she realized everything was okay, even though Eurl knew she lied to him at the playground.

I placed the bag on the kitchen counter and Evelyn busied herself putting the groceries away while Eurl and I sat back down.

"Mike, can I think this over and let you know something later?"

"No, Eurl, I've got to know right now, before you leave here, whether you're going to do the right thing. I've got more than enough to do, and plenty of people are helping me already, so if you do this, it's mainly to help you, not me."

"What about the guy who introduced you to me? Was he helping you?"

"Eurl, I'm not going to tell you whether he was or not, just like I'm not going to tell anyone if you help me, except the DA and the judge. And I don't want you to tell anyone, not your girlfriend, not your best friend, no one. If everything goes okay, no one will ever know you helped me."

He was silent. I waited. After a few moments, he asked, "How long I gotta help you?" I had him now; it was just a matter of working out the details.

Before he left, I locked in his cooperation by having him identify his supplier and other dealers. Then I had him make a recorded call to his supplier from our trailer. After another thirty minutes of conversation and a couple of cups of coffee, Eurl left with my office number and instructions to arrange a meeting between me and his supplier.

I was relieved and elated after Eurl left, the same sensations I experienced during close calls on drug deals. Eurl had not only been neutralized as an immediate threat, but he was now also an informant.

It had been a terrifying experience for Evelyn. She had enough to worry about with my work, wondering whether she would ever see me alive again each time I went out. The work wasn't that dangerous, but she worried that even routine undercover meetings could end in unexpected violence. Now my work and its potential dangers suddenly slammed into our home life and thrust itself on her and our son. This wasn't the sedate and comfortable life she expected when we married, when I was fresh out of the Marines and working for Southern Bell Telephone. Nor was it the normal life our neighbors enjoyed.

Life eventually returned to normal in our household, but our sense of security had been shattered. Not long after this incident, we sold our mobile home and bought a home in Indian Mound subdivision, outside Baton Rouge. Indian Mound was remote and two other police officers lived in the subdivision. It was quiet and safe, and a sense of security returned.

Eurl helped on his acid supplier and on a couple of other deals. Through one of his introductions, I arranged to buy twenty pounds of pot and planned to make the bust when the delivery was made. The deal was set for late one night on an isolated street. Wearing a wire while several investigators were nearby on surveillance, I drove to the meeting place and parked on the street. A car drove up and parked behind me. Five guys got out, and we went to the trunk of their car. They opened it and showed me the twenty pounds, tightly compressed in one-pound bricks. I uttered the code word for the bust and then pulled out my pistol, a .22-caliber two-shot derringer. Facing five guys with a small two-shot pistol wasn't ideal, but I announced the arrest in a loud, commanding voice and confidently ordered them to raise their hands as if I were holding a cannon. They hesitated, and then, finally, to my relief they complied and the other investigators quickly arrived.

Not a Normal Life

The drug dealer's surprise visit to our home was a reminder that our home life was a little different from that of most families. I stole a rare afternoon off to take Evelyn to a movie in downtown Baton Rouge. We had parked and were walking across the four-lane street in front of the theater when I saw two drug dealers I was working on undercover. Evelyn looked really straight, not at all like someone who would be with a drug dealer, and we couldn't be seen together without it damaging my cover and exposing her. The two guys were approaching to our right front, walking on the sidewalk that ran in front of the theater. Our paths would quickly carry us smack into each other and they would see us together if they happened to look our way.

Softly but urgently, I said out of the side of my mouth, "Evelyn, keep on straight. Keep walking, keep walking!" I veered away from her and headed toward the dealers. She immediately realized we had run into some kind of undercover problem and kept walking without a glance in my direction, pretending to be alone. As she went on to the ticket booth, I met the men on the sidewalk.

"Hey, man, where you dudes going?" I said, walking up to them and shaking hands.

"Hey, Rick, what you doing here?" one asked me.

"I gotta see a dude who wants to get something," I confided, "doing a little business and I'm running late. What about y'all? What y'all up to?"

We talked a few minutes and parted, walking away in opposite directions. I walked around for fifteen minutes to give them enough time to clear out of the area, then doubled back to the movie theater and found Evelyn inside and sat beside her. The movie had already started.

"Everything okay?" she whispered close to my ear.

"Yeah, it's okay. I saw two guys I'm working on. They were near the front of the theater. Did you see them?"

"I was afraid to look," she said softly, "but I could tell you met someone."

"I talked to them and they left. Everything's cool. They didn't see us together. Don't worry. What have I missed so far?" When we left the theater, I had Evelyn walk out first and followed a few steps behind, just in case. I have no idea what the movie was about.

On another occasion, Evelyn and I were standing in line at a snowball (snow cone) stand when a finger pushed me in my back. Turning, I was surprised to see a drug dealer I was working on.

"Mike!" he exclaimed, "I thought that was you. Whatta you doing?"

I turned completely around to face him, with my back to Evelyn, in an effort to obstruct his view beyond me.

"Hey, man. Just getting something to cool off," I said. He glanced over my shoulder but I kept talking to keep him focused on me. "What about you? What're you doing here? You just passing by or you getting something?"

While he and I talked, Evelyn moved to the window, got her order and quickly walked out of sight. After I got mine, I told him good-bye and walked away in the opposite direction. She and I met at our car later. On our drive home, I explained who the guy was. My undercover life kept crashing into our private life, but Evelyn was cool and she had come to expect the unexpected.

The Battle for the Baton Rouge Police Department and a Price to Pay

Headline: "Charlie Spillers: The Narc Who Turned."

Louisiana was notorious for corruption. It was ubiquitous at every level of state and local governments and deeply entrenched. Based in New Orleans, the Carlos Marcello Mafia family had spread its influence throughout the state; Teamsters Local Number 5 was a powerful and intimidating presence in Baton Rouge labor markets; good ole boy networks flourished with contract awards, favors, and kickbacks; and gambling and slot machines were common even in small mom-and-pop grocery stores. Widespread corruption may not have been welcome, but people were accustomed to it, expected it, and endured it; they were resigned to governmental corruption as a fact of life, just as they expected and endured the brutally humid Louisiana summers. It is only a slight exaggeration to say corruption was tolerated more than rudeness, a cardinal sin in the Deep South.

It was all the more surprising when we challenged corruption from within. It happened spontaneously. A minor incident sparked a months-long public battle, constant turmoil, and an upheaval in the police department. It drew in the newspapers, the chief of police, the district attorney, and the mayor. It affected careers, changed lives, and transformed the police department.

It started when a patrolman stopped a civilian car that was flashing police lights around the LSU campus. The suspect turned out to be a wealthy developer connected with a high-ranking officer in the Baton Rouge police department. Police Colonel Howard Kidder went to the scene at 3:00 a.m. to intervene and the media picked up on the story. Soon afterward, my close friend Bruce Childers, who was in the Intelligence Division, was contacted by a source who reported that he had witnessed the same businessman and his bodyguards beat a man at a nightclub. Bruce learned that a high-ranking police officer met with the businessman and concluded that the alleged beating was not a police matter. Following these incidents, Bruce started investigating possible corruption in the department, focusing on Kidder. That was the beginning of the end of Bruce's police career.

Soon after Bruce started making inquiries, he was quickly ordered to stop. Then he called me. That phone call began the end of my Baton Rouge career as well.

"Man, Charlie, you're not going to believe what just happened," said Bruce. "Are you ready for this?"

"What? What happened?"

"You know what happened on the LSU campus with the businessman with the police lights?"

"Yeah."

"Well, I started looking into it, I talked with the officer who stopped him and I called Records to get the reports on it. And man, holy cow, guess what just happened." Bruce lowered his voice and spoke in hushed tones: "I just got a call from the major who wanted to know what the hell I thought I was doing. I mean, just like that! And he said I better leave it alone. Damn, man, I mean, what do you think I should do?"

I hesitated.

"What do you think, Charlie?"

"Okay, Bruce, let's do this, you lay low on it. I'm in a better position to fade heat than you and I'll start looking into it high profile and we'll see what kind of heat we draw. Is that all right with you?" Like Bruce, I had heard rumors about possible high-level corruption.

"Man, that's fine with me," Bruce said. "But you sure you want to do it?"

"Yeah, no problem."

"Okay, then, whatever you think. I hope you get further than I did."

By pure chance I was thrust into a corruption investigation. With Bruce trying to work discreetly, he and I began making calls, developing leads, and meeting with individual officers to gather information about possible corruption. The investigation didn't take long to draw heat.

A threat to the status quo was certain to prompt resistance and I expected pressure, but was surprised where it came from first. The district attorney, Ossie Brown, approached police chief Rudy Ratcliff about me. Following the DA's visit, Chief Ratcliff called me to meet him that night at his home. When I arrived, Chief Ratcliff wanted me to explain the investigation. I trusted the chief and I told him everything Bruce and I had found out so far, including information about Kidder. When I finished, Chief Ratcliff told me to continue the investigation and to report directly to him and no one else. The chief refused to stop the investigation. That was the beginning of the end of *his* career.

The DA's attempt to stop the investigation had failed. The mayor, Woody Dumas, tried going directly to me. He summoned me to his home one weekend to discuss the investigation. I was driven to his home by one of his plainclothes police bodyguards. The mayor was too smart and politically savvy to be explicit when we met, but I left with the impression that it would be in my interest to stop investigating.

After Chief Ratcliff refused to stop the investigation, Mayor Dumas replaced him with Howard Kidder, the very police colonel we were investigating. Chief Ratcliff went on leave to recover from knee surgery and the mayor appointed Kidder acting chief, an appointment the mayor intended to make permanent three weeks later. On Kidder's first full day as acting chief, he ordered me transferred from narcotics to uniform patrol. He told the press he transferred me because my cover was blown and I was no longer effective as a narcotics agent. Kidder then ordered me to report personally to him at his office the following week.

Showdown Looms

The news media had been following the saga since the incident at LSU. "A showdown between Kidder and Spillers looms during the new week" reported the Baton Rouge newspaper, the *Morning Advocate*, May 12, 1974, in an article entitled, "Gag Rule Reported Back for Policemen." I expected Kidder to order me to reveal everything about our investigation, including the names of those who had been cooperating and providing information, which included allegations of wrongdoing by Chief Kidder himself. As chief, he had that authority and if I refused he would be able to fire me on the spot.

Given what was at stake, as well as the media attention and the public interest, Kidder would have prepared for the meeting and planned how he would handle it. He had been forewarned by a newspaper article the week before. The news article reported, "Sources say that Spillers will refuse to hand over the information gained in his investigation to Kidder."

The uncertainty of what awaited and the anxiety that my police career was in jeopardy weighed on me as I was ushered into Chief Kidder's office for the meeting. Kidder sat behind a big desk and several high-ranking commanders sat arrayed to each side. It felt like an inquisition.

With his lips pressed tight, Kidder sat with his upper body hunched forward over the desk, arms crossed on the desktop. He nodded to a chair directly in front of his desk and I sat down. The tension was palpable. He cast a quick glance at the others and then started to speak, but before he could I went on the offensive.

"Why did you transfer me from narcotics to patrol?" I asked.

He frowned, momentarily taken back. "Because your cover is blown and you're no longer effective," he replied, repeating the line he had given the newspaper. This was something I could contradict.

"You're a liar," I said. His face flushed red. "My cover's not blown."

"It is—everybody knows your name. Your name's been in the newspapers. You can't work undercover any—"

"It doesn't matter if my name is known. My name's been in the newspapers for years while I've been working undercover. Every time I testify my name is in the papers, but it doesn't affect me because I use different undercover names. I make undercover drug buys all the time and I just made some."

Kidder shifted in his chair. No one likes to be called a liar or directly contradicted, particularly when they know they are in the wrong. I had the momentum but knew I would soon be on the defense.

"So my cover is not blown and I'm still effective in narcotics," I continued. "You only transferred me to stop the investigation."

"Well, I say your cover is blown so you're going to patrol," he announced angrily. "And you cut your hair and shave your beard before you report," he said, jabbing a finger at me. "That's a direct order. Do you understand me?"

"Yes." We stared at each other until finally he glanced at the others in the room.

Kidder cleared his throat. "Now let's talk about this investigation you've been doing. Who are you investigating and what are you investigating?"

"You." I took a deep breath. "We're investigating you and others for possible corruption."

Kidder's eyes flared and his lips tightened. "All right." He leaned forward and hunched over the desk. Our eyes locked. "Now, you tell me what you have found out. Everything."

"No. I'm not telling you any—"

"I'm ordering you to tell me," Kidder declared.

I took a breath and exhaled and shook my head slowly. "I can't."

Kidder stiffened. "What do you mean, 'you can't!' I'm giving you a direct order."

"I can't tell you because Chief Ratcliff ordered me to report only to him and no one else about the investigation."

"Well, I'm the chief now and—"

"No. No, you're not," I said, shaking my head. "You're *acting* chief. Chief Ratcliff is still officially the chief and I'm bound by his orders. So I can't tell you even if I wanted to." Audible grunts and low murmurs came from some in the room.

Kidder's brow furrowed into a V. He cocked an eye and exchanged looks with the others in the room. His look was met with raised eyebrows. They hadn't expected this. I was anxious because I didn't know whether this maneuver would work. Maybe the media attention would make Kidder hesitant to reject it out of hand. Kidder turned his attention back to me.

"I will get back to you about this. For right now," he jabbed a finger at me, "you report to patrol, understand?"

"Yes, I understand."

I left Kidder's office feeling like I had won the first battle, but aware it would only delay the outcome. When Kidder officially became chief, he could then order me to reveal everything. Plus, he already had the power to affect my career, which he demonstrated by transferring me to patrol.

The battle drew in not only the chief, the mayor, and the DA, but also the fledging new police union, which was organized several months before by a small group of young officers. I wasn't a member but they came out and publicly criticized Kidder for transferring me. Although Chief Ratcliff would be on leave for a couple of weeks after being replaced by Kidder, he was still officially the chief of police until the end of his leave, and he issued a statement supporting Bruce Childers and me.

A drumbeat of fast-moving events played out daily in the newspapers and on local television news programs. *State-Times* headline: "FOP Ask Breather in Union's Battle with Police Chief":

[Acting Chief] Kidder has come under fire from the union for transferring a narcotics officer to the patrol division and for going to the scene of a 3 a.m. investigation last Thursday involving a complaint about sirens and red lights on a car owned by [a] local developer. . . .

The transferred narcotics agent is Charles Spillers. Kidder had Spillers in his office today and said he asked the young officer about the reported investigation being conducted in connection with the alleged smoking of marijuana by two local judges.

Spillers was doing special investigations for [Chief] Ratcliff, Kidder said. The acting chief said he transferred Spillers to the patrol division because he had no special investigations for the young officer to conduct. Spillers has been off on compensatory time but is due back for duty Wednesday. Kidder said today that he informed the officer to shave his beard and cut his hair before reporting back to duty.

Spillers refused to give him any information on the investigation, Kidder said. The officer said that he had been instructed to conduct the investigation by Police Chief Rudolph Ratcliff and to report only to Ratcliff, Kidder reported.

Spillers noted that Kidder is still only the acting chief, although Mayor Dumas has indicated that he will become the permanent chief. Kidder said that he could not argue with the point that he is still only the acting chief and that he plans to ask Ratcliff about the investigation.

State-Times/Morning Advocate headline: "Only Few Want Kidder as Chief in Local Survey":

When the 350 parish residents were interviewed last Friday, just 7.7 per cent said they thought Kidder should be named police chief. . . . While Kidder might have come off poor in the poll conducted by Economic and Industrial Research Inc. (EIRI), Mayor-President Dumas, a staunch defender of Kidder, was rated fairly good by those interviewed.

Morning Advocate headline: "Chief Ratcliff Backs Officers in Probe":

Police Chief Rudolph Ratcliff said Tuesday that he fully supports officers Charles Spillers and Bruce Childers, whose investigation of public officials was allegedly halted by acting police chief Howard Kidder in one of his first official moves.

Morning Advocate headline: "Kidder Appointment Reportedly Opposed":

Chief of Police Rudolph Ratcliff and other close advisors to the mayor tried to stop the hiring of Howard Kidder as acting police chief, according to sources close to Ratcliff and other sources close to the mayor. . . . As Ratcliff was about to leave office, Dumas said that he would appoint Kidder, despite the opposition, because there were many rumors about things Kidder had done, but no proof. . . .

Dumas reportedly called Ratcliff into his office and asked him whether he was going to run for the Livingston Parish Sheriff's post in November 1975. . . . [Dumas] at that point requested Ratcliff's resignation, sources say. The sources say they do not know why Dumas felt Ratcliff should leave the chief's position 18 months before the election. "If we knew that, I think we'd know something," one of the sources commented.

Ratcliff was to stay on for three more weeks, according to statements in the initial meeting, and was not going to leave the chief's post until May 15, the day before he was to have knee surgery.

The second mystery occurred about three days after the meeting. Ratcliff was reported pressured to quicken his move from the office and Kidder stepped in more than two weeks early. Again, sources say, they have no explanation for this move. The sources also say that Ratcliff advised strongly against Kidder for the acting chief's position in that first meeting and that Ratcliff was told that Kidder would just be an acting chief and would make no personnel or departmental changes.

Instead of reporting for patrol duty, I took two weeks of vacation time. It would temporarily keep Kidder's power at bay, but time was running out. Once he officially became chief, Kidder would be able to make me disclose details of the investigation, including the names of sources. Not only that, he could order me not to pursue any investigations. Before my vacation was over, I put in to take several months of compensatory time built up over the years and turned in my resignation effective at the end of that time. Kidder first denied my comp time request, but the city determined I was entitled to it. With my comp time and resignation, I was released from his power and oversight, and continued on my own with the investigation.

Kidder retaliated against Bruce. He transferred Bruce from Intelligence and put him walking a uniform beat downtown. One of the veteran sergeants told the newspaper that Bruce suffered from "diarrhea of the mouth." At one point, Bruce was summoned to meet with the DA, Ossie Brown, and one of Brown's men. As Bruce suspected, they simply wanted to find out who had provided information to us. But prior to the meeting, Bruce had conferred with the US attorney, who gave him suggestions on how to handle a demand for the names of our witnesses. Acting on the US attorney's advice, Bruce told Brown he would reveal the names of corruption witnesses only to a grand jury and he would tell the grand jury that they had the right to summon the witnesses to testify.

Bruce eventually left the department. Meanwhile, he and I continued with the corruption investigation. The Baton Rouge newspapers, the *State-Times* and the *Morning Advocate*, became interested in the struggle. During the ensuing months, Bruce and I shared much of what we found with Bob Anderson, a bright, hard-working investigative reporter with the newspapers.

Weekly and sometimes daily newspaper and television reports detailed some of the findings. I deferred from giving interviews to the paper but later gave a lengthy interview with the weekly *Gris Gris*, which the cover titled: "Charlie Spillers: The Narc Who Turned." I hoped the article would encourage others to come forward with information.

As new sources came forward, the investigation expanded. Police officers, including uniform and detectives, patrolmen and sergeants, began seeking us out to reveal incidents of corruption that they had witnessed or heard about. Over the course of several months, either singly or together, we met with dozens of individual officers. Most of those meetings were covert because just being seen talking to us could subject the officers to retaliation. We met at night with officers in their homes, at the homes of mutual friends, or in parked cars in driveways, parking lots, and even alleys. Sometimes we picked up an officer and drove around talking. We also refrained from talking freely over our home phones.

Officers reported that some police supervisors kept them from enforcing the law or taking action on particular bars. When shootings or other crimes occurred at particular bars during times or days when they were illegally open, some shift supervisors intervened and had patrolmen suppress the facts or falsely report that the crimes had occurred elsewhere. The incidents officers reported to us fell into several categories of possible corruption, most centered on protecting bar owners, prostitution, and bookmaking. In some cases, officers had just made arrests at bars when supervisors showed up and ordered the officers to release the prisoners. Officers identified certain supervisors who intervened and prevented them from making arrests. Fortunately, there were only a few, but because of their rank or position they could influence the work of an entire patrol shift. We took written and signed statements from the officers.

The struggle took unexpected turns. Following numerous media reports, Kidder temporarily took a leave of absence and sued the newspapers for libel. I was stunned when he won the lawsuit in the trial court. After the win, he resumed his position as police chief. The appeals court upheld the trial court's verdict. I couldn't understand how the court could have found in Kidder's favor. Later, when I read the court's decision, it seemed to me that the court never grasped the true facts or situation. Bruce and I were painted as "disgruntled" officers, instead of officers who fought corruption. Even more disturbing, the appeals court inexplicably pointed out that Bruce and I shared information with the newspaper but refused to share it with Chief Kidder. The court went on to cite the testimony of various witnesses about corruption, but observed there was no proof, apparently discounting the value of witness testimony. Eventually, the Louisiana Supreme Court reversed the verdict for Kidder. The Supreme Court pointed out that bar owners and other witnesses were in a position to know and should not be disbelieved because of their backgrounds and that officers who came forward were credible witnesses.

The Louisiana Supreme Court's decision came too late to change anything. Kidder had long been back as police chief and he wasn't leaving. Despite the risks to their jobs, many officers had come forward about corruption and testified at trial. Kidder retaliated. Officers suffered setbacks in their careers such as involuntary transfers or undesirable assignments, or they were passed over for promotions, and there were other forms of retribution as well. Bruce and Jack Crittenden both left the department, as did some other officers who had stepped forward with information.

There were attempts at more ominous payback. Two investigators who were close to Kidder approached an acquaintance of Bruce's who had been arrested on a routine traffic stop with a small amount of marijuana and a handgun. The investigators told the man that Bruce had tipped off the police and caused the man's arrest, which was not true. The investigators returned the man's gun and told him the charges would be dropped if he gave them "useful help" in making a case on Bruce. The man later told Bruce about the plot and admitted that he was so mad after being told that Bruce caused his arrest that if he had found a way to get into Bruce's house that night, he would have planted drugs and called the investigators. I was the focus of another effort. An investigator with the district attorney's office tipped me off that someone in the DA's office was trying to get one of my former informants, a call girl, to go before the grand jury and testify that I wanted her to frame two judges, which wasn't true. In fact, she had reported to me that a notorious crime figure who controlled organized gambling had paid her to service two judges and she had used drugs with one of the judges during their tryst, although I was never able to substantiate her allegations. In still another plot, a high-ranking officer instructed an investigator to try to make a criminal case on Greg Phares, a narcotics detective who had assisted the corruption investigation. Greg learned of the scheme when the investigator told one of Greg's sources about it and the source secretly recorded their conversation.

After Kidder retired years later, the officers and investigators who stood up to corruption became supervisors and leaders in the department and role models for others. Kidder had transferred Greg Phares from narcotics to patrol. Greg later became chief of police and served in that position for ten years. Kidder had transferred Sam Pruet from leading the Narcotics Division to working on the booking desk, a change for Sam that was akin to being banished from real police work. After Kidder left, Sam became head of narcotics again. After enduring years of setbacks and delayed careers, many of those officers and investigators rose again in the ranks.

The more important part of the story was not as dramatic, but it was more profound and long lasting. The Baton Rouge Police Department changed forever. By courageously stepping forward, young officers and veterans served notice they would not tolerate corruption in the department. The few supervisors who had protected bars, prostitution, and bookmaking could no longer order officers away with impunity. The department could never go back to the old ways. A new generation came into its own because police officers risked their careers. "The ultimate measure of a man is not where he stands in moments of comfort and convenience, but where he stands at times of challenge and controversy," said Martin Luther King Jr. Those officers embodied that truth.

Grady Partin, the Head of the Teamsters, and "Marshal Matt Dillon"

Powerful Teamsters Local Number 5 and its head, Grady Partin, were notorious and always big news, not only in Louisiana, but nationally, with Teamsters' strikes marked by threats and violence. During the time I was in Intelligence, the Teamsters were striking against a local milk creamery plant in Baton Rouge and were trying to disrupt the creamery's operations.

One of my intelligence informants attended a Teamsters meeting about the creamery strike. During the meeting the group discussed ways to interfere with the tanker trucks used to transport milk to the creamery. Someone suggested placing dynamite under parked trucks and others urged the men to use ice picks to puncture the thin milk tanks on the trucks. After the meeting I warned Captain Watson, the head of Intelligence, about the potential violence and wrote an intelligence report about it.

After I had left the PD and was working closely with investigative reporters, Local Number 5 and Grady Partin were in the news and I happened to mention the Teamsters meeting about the creamery strike to the editor. He thought the meeting was newsworthy and published a story about it in the newspaper, naming me as the source of the information.

Partin responded to the article by writing a letter to the newspaper denying the allegations. Partin wrote, "Charlie Spillers must think that he's Marshal Matt Dillon," a reference to the popular television western series *Gunsmoke* starring actor James Arness as Marshal Matt Dillon.

Shortly after that, I learned that Partin was in the hospital for observation for possible heart problems. I suspected the hospital stay was merely a ploy to postpone one of his court hearings. The next day I went to the hospital and showed up at Partin's hospital room. Several Teamsters types were sitting together and smoking in the lobby downstairs— beefy men with scowls and craggy faces.

I tapped lightly on the door to his room. "Come in," someone grunted. Surprisingly, Partin was alone. He was sitting up in bed, looking healthy and normal when I walked in and introduced myself.

"Grady?"

"Yeah," he growled.

"I heard you might be looking for me. I'm Charlie Spillers."

His eyes widened. "Well, if it ain't 'Matt Dillon.'"

"You looking for me?"

Grady and I had a friendly chat. I told him I was no longer interested in him and the Teamsters, and Grady said he bore no ill will. I left relieved not to have to worry about the Teamsters.

■ ■ ■

It was time to leave the Police Department and Baton Rouge. The police chief, the district attorney, the mayor, and the Teamsters weren't too happy with me. Neither were the drug dealers. Six years of undercover had been a life-changing experience, one filled with drama, excitement, and tight spots. There was more to come.

Part II
MISSISSIPPI BUREAU OF NARCOTICS (MBN)

It is not the critic who counts; not the man who points out how the strong man stumbles, or where the doer of deeds could have done them better. The credit belongs to the man who is actually in the arena, whose face is marred by dust and sweat and blood; who strives valiantly . . . who spends himself in a worthy cause; who, at the best, knows in the end the triumph of high achievement, and who, at the worst, if he fails, at least fails while daring greatly, so that his place shall never be with those cold and timid souls who know neither victory nor defeat.
—Theodore Roosevelt, "Citizenship in a Republic," speech at the Sorbonne, Paris, April 23, 1910. This quotation was included in the Mississippi Bureau of Narcotics agent manual.

3
JACKSON

Introduction to the MBN

I became familiar with the Mississippi Bureau of Narcotics (MBN) when the Baton Rouge Police Department sent me and Sergeant Sam Pruet to Washington, DC, to attend the DEA ten-week narcotics investigators course. The class was composed of about thirty investigators including several from the national police forces of foreign countries. With only a limited number of student slots available nationwide, I was astonished to learn that the class included six agents from a single agency— MBN. Although it had only been recently established, MBN was already regarded as an elite state drug agency, professional and on the cutting edge of law enforcement. The MBN agents in the course included Kent McDaniel, Jim Walker, Danny Lowery, Steve Ford, James Brantley, and Richard Allison. I was impressed by their professionalism and pride in the bureau.

When I left the Baton Rouge Police Department during the battle over corruption, I applied for the Louisiana State Police and MBN. During the application process with LSP, a group of high-ranking state troopers interviewed me. For months my name had frequently been in the newspapers and occasionally on television news in connection with the struggle against corruption. During the LSP interview, a grizzled captain asked me with a sneer, "If you're hired, is it going to be in the newspaper every damn time I go take a crap?" I don't have a chance of joining LSP, I thought, but it was a fair question.

MBN's selection process was advanced and rigorous for the times, with psychological testing, polygraphs, physical-agility tests, interviews, assessment-center testing with role-playing scenarios, and in-depth background investigations. Months after completing the selection processes, I received acceptance letters the same week from LSP and MBN. I chose MBN and went through an eight-week MBN Basic Agent School.

Of the more than 350 who had applied for MBN, twenty-nine were selected and attended the Basic Agent School, which was held at the Mississippi Law Enforcement Officers Training Academy outside Pearl and run by MBN agent Joe Madison, a former Army Special Forces soldier. The class was composed of men and women, black and white, a diversity that was rare among some law-enforcement agencies in the deep South at the time.

The training was physically and academically challenging—the attrition rate was just over 50 percent; fourteen of twenty-nine finished the school. We were on probationary employment for a year; before the year was out, MBN dropped four more, leaving ten out of the fourteen who had finished the academy. After graduation from the MBN Basic Agent Course, I began working in Jackson, sometimes alone, but often working at first with agent Earl Pierce and later with agent Sara Niell.

Evelyn and I sold our home in Baton Rouge and moved to Jackson. Terry had started school in Baton Rouge but now he was uprooted in the middle of the school year and enrolled in school in Jackson. It was reminiscent of the moves my family had made when I was young and had to keep changing schools. In Baton Rouge, Evelyn took care of everything at home, which allowed me to focus entirely on undercover work. She paid the bills, balanced the bank account, enrolled Terry in school, took care of the housekeeping, and worked as a secretary. When I took college courses part time, she helped me study for tests. We moved several times in Baton Rouge and she did all of the apartment and house hunting and took care of arranging utility services, packing, and organizing the moves. Now she did all of that in Jackson, and enrolled Terry in school and went job hunting.

We didn't have any family in Jackson and didn't know anyone there. But joining MBN was like joining a family for both of us and that helped with the transition to our new surroundings.

Caught in a Lie

Are two lies better than one? I found out when a drug dealer pointed a gun at my undercover partner.

Agent Earl Pierce and I had been working undercover together in Jackson, Mississippi. Our informants, a young man and his wife, helped us make buys from several dealers, including Robert, a drug dealer who led his own crew of dealers.

The couple had called earlier that night to let us know that Robert had become suspicious of them and they were scared. The danger wasn't just from Robert; it was also from his men.

We went to the couple's apartment that evening to get more information and reassure them. While we were there, Robert made a surprise visit. He showed up at the door with three other men, all with sullen faces and hard stares. I could sense that he was in a confrontational mood, but whatever plans he had for the couple changed when he saw us. He and his buddies came in and pretended they just dropped by for a friendly visit. There was a strong undercurrent of tension in the room, but on the surface it was all friendly chatter with a contentious edge, accompanied by drinking and LSD use by Robert and his pals.

They had been in the apartment for about an hour when Robert suddenly pulled out a gun and confronted Earl, who sat about ten feet away on a bar stool at the kitchen counter. Robert sat on the floor, his back against the apartment wall, his feet flat on the floor and his knees bent. His forearms rested on his knees, and both hands gripped a loaded .357-magnum revolver. Robert pointed the gun at the center of Earl's chest and accused him of lying.

As I sat on a bar stool next to Earl, my heart raced but I tried to stay calm. Not only did I have to worry about Robert, but also the other three men. My .38 pistol was tucked in my waistband at the center of my back and my right hand rested on my thigh. I wondered if I could slowly move my hand toward my back without Robert noticing. If so, I could grab my gun, whip it around, and shoot. Would I be able to get to my gun before Robert noticed? Would I be able to shoot before he pulled the trigger? Were the other men armed too?

"Huh! Hey! Hey, man, whatta you doing!" Earl protested, ducking his head down and holding his palm up as if it would shield him from a bullet. "Goddamn, don't point that gun at me!" Earl instinctively tried to shrink himself smaller, like a turtle pulling its head into its shell, wanting to disappear completely, as would anyone.

"You lied to me." Robert stared over the gun barrel at Earl.

"What are you talking about, man? Lie about what? I ain't lied to you, man."

"You told me you're working at Red Ball Trucking in Meridian. And you don't work there. You lied."

"Hey, man, I *am* working at Red Ball." Earl insisted, but it was weak because it *was* a lie and now, maybe, just maybe, he had been found out.

Ever so slowly, I began inching my hand up my thigh toward my waist.

"No. A friend of mine has been working there a long time and I asked him about you, and you know what he said?" Robert demanded. "Huh? You know what he said?"

"What?"

"He's never heard of you. He's been working there for years and he's *never* heard of *you!*" Robert said angrily. His face contorted with rage.

"Well, see, I just started," Earl explained, "so maybe we just haven't met yet."

"No. He knows everyone. *Everyone.* And you don't work there. You lied to me. Why did you lie to me?" Robert demanded. Earl was trapped.

Robert pulled back the hammer on the gun.

CLICK. It was cocked.

His finger was on the trigger. The gun was ready to fire.

Even joking around, pointing a cocked gun at someone is dangerous. A slight pressure on the trigger is all it takes, intentionally or accidentally. And Robert wasn't joking around. He was deadly serious.

He was a drug dealer and he had caught an undercover agent in a lie. Perhaps Robert was bluffing; maybe he just wanted to scare Earl and didn't intend to pull the trigger. But a cocked gun makes a bluff effective. Logically, he wouldn't be able kill someone in front of witnesses and get away with it, but angry drug dealers aren't always rational.

I slowly moved my hand higher up my thigh, closer to my waist.

Robert's eyes narrowed over the gun barrel, his nostrils flared, and his jaw muscles tightened. "Now," he said. "Why—did—you—*lie?*"

Silence. Complete silence. Loud and seemingly endless.

Earl's face flushed red. What was he going to say? What could he say?

"Well, man, . . . uh . . . well, see . . . ," Earl stammered.

I was close to grabbing for my gun.

"Uh, see, . . . I can't let it get out that I'm out running around seeing women and doing drugs, 'cause, see, uh, I'm married and I can't let my old lady find out. And if my probation officer hears I'm running around doing drugs, then he'll revoke me and send me to the joint . . ."

I couldn't tell exactly where this was going, but at least Earl was talking and Robert had lifted his head slightly from sighting down the barrel at Earl's chest.

". . . and I tell people I work in Meridian because that way if word gets back to either one about me, they'll think it's just someone from Meridian with the same name as me. That it ain't me. So that's why I tell people I work at Red Ball in Meridian."

Whether that was going to be good enough for Robert, it was definitely good enough for me. I could have hugged Earl. How in the world did he come up with that so fast? Being on the point of death makes one focus. Under pressure, he did some quick thinking.

"See, that way, they'll figure that it must be somebody else—somebody from Meridian—and not me since I live here."

"Why didn't you just tell me the truth to begin with instead of telling me you worked at Meridian?" Robert wondered.

"Well, see, that's just it, man. I trust you, but you know how people can talk and if word starts getting back to my wife or my probation officer, I'm cooked, I'm done for, so I can't take a chance."

"Well . . ."

"I'm sorry, man," Earl pleaded. "I didn't mean to lie to you. I was just trying to stay outta trouble." Earl acted properly chastised and submissive.

Robert pointed the gun barrel upward and put both thumbs on the cocked hammer. Holding the hammer back, he pulled the trigger, and using his thumbs, he let the hammer down slowly and carefully so as not to fire the gun. Earl blew out an audible sigh of relief. So did I.

Relief flooded my body and I suddenly felt drained as the adrenaline rush wore off. I could only imagine what Earl felt. If we had been ready to end the entire undercover operation, we would have taken Robert down right then and hustled him out in handcuffs, but we needed to keep going while it was still productive and protect the informants.

"You can't lie to me and get away with it." Robert said with a triumphant smirk. "Why did you think you could get away with lying to *me?*" he gloated. Robert had a big ego and it went on like this for a while until the room calmed down. Robert and his men finally left. As soon as the door closed behind them, we all blew loud sighs of relief. It had been a trying ordeal and we were all emotionally drained.

Years of undercover experience kept me from reacting prematurely. Had I grabbed for my gun when Robert first pointed a gun at Earl, people likely would have been injured or killed. Robert could have shot Earl before I could have gotten off a shot. Having survived tight spots before, I knew there was a possibility of a good outcome, which fortunately turned out to be the case. But the outcome was not preordained.

For an undercover agent, a lie can cut both ways. It can trap you or it can save you. Here, within just a few minutes, it did both.

New Orleans Strip Clubs and Careful Dealers

After working briefly with Earl Pierce, I began working regularly with a new partner. MBN agent Sara Niell and I began working together in the Jackson area, frequenting bars and presenting ourselves as "a couple."

With beautiful, lively eyes, a bright smile, and long, light-brown hair, Sara's looks and engaging personality attracted people to her. She was enthusiastic about working undercover, had a sharp mind that never stopped spinning, and could work nonstop for days with little rest.

We made a perfect team. We enjoyed working together and were both attracted to the excitement, adventure, and satisfaction of undercover work. Our minds worked alike in assessing undercover situations, calculating opportunities, and overcoming obstacles. Like me, she appreciated the skills and nuances of undercover work. Most important, she had the passion, energy, and intelligence for it.

We lived in the same condo complex, which made it convenient to get together and go out working at a moment's notice. Pretending that we lived together, we gave Sara's phone number to drug dealers, and when they called for me she would tell them I had just left and would be back in a few minutes. I would walk over to Sara's apartment and return the call and sometimes wait at her apartment for return calls.

One night at one of the bars, we happened to meet David Abramowitz, who used the name "David Steele," and he sold us an ounce of hashish. In his late twenties, David was medium height with light-brown hair and a bushy handlebar mustache. The three of us went outside to his car and Sara and I bought the hashish. He was vague about his background, except to say that he was from New Orleans and had only recently come to Jackson.

David confided that his drug connections were in New Orleans and that they could supply larger quantities. A week later I bought one pound of hashish from David. For that deal, we met in McComb, Mississippi, at an entrance ramp to Interstate 55. He parked his car and had me drive him all the way into Louisiana and then back to McComb before he sold me the pound. I suspected he was testing me to find out if I would travel out of state. During the deal I told him we were interested in getting fifty pounds of pot and David said he would check with his connections in New Orleans.

Sara and I had an undercover apartment, a duplex, in Brandon during that time. To enhance our credibility for doing the larger deal, we took David to the apartment for a visit, and I left briefly, supposedly to collect money owed to us by dealers to whom we had fronted drugs. I returned with a brown paper sack holding $18,000 in loose bills, MBN funds to be used for a "flash roll." In front of David, I dumped the money on the coffee table and asked him to help us count it and bundle it into one-thousand-dollar stacks. By doing this, Sara and I had not only shown a flash roll but also bolstered our standing as drug dealers.

Several days later, David told us the deal for the fifty pounds was on, but we would have to travel to New Orleans first to meet the connections. The next weekend, Sara and I drove to New Orleans and met David. Instead of taking us to his drug sources, David led us on a tour of strip joints in New Orleans. During the night, one joint blurred into another and we lost track of how many we had visited. David drank heavily.

We kept prodding him about meeting his connections, but he would say, "Wait. We have to wait."

"Wait for what?" I asked.

"Just have to wait until they're ready."

Using pay phones, David made a couple of calls during the night, and after each pronounced that we had to wait a little longer. Finally, he said it was time to go meet the connections. He staggered out of the strip joint and we went to the car.

Following his directions, we drove out of New Orleans, north across Lake Pontchartrain, on the twenty-eight-mile causeway. He kept passing out during the ride. When we shook him awake, he mumbled and said, "Keep on going." When we reached the other side, we shook him awake, but he kept leading us down wrong roads and passing out. He was stone drunk and had no idea where he was. A couple of hours before daylight, we stopped at a motel and put him in one room and Sara and I took the adjoining room, and slept for a couple of hours on separate beds.

After we got him up at midmorning, David had sobered up and he led us back to New Orleans to an apartment in the French Quarter and introduced us to his connections, two men in their late twenties. It was clear that this visit was so that they could get to know us and check us out. As we sat and talked, a couple of other men visited the apartment. It seemed to be preplanned that they would come by and look us over. I suspect they knew some area narcotics agents by sight and had come to see if they recognized us.

While we were there, one of the men wanted to use our car for just a few minutes to pick someone up. It was another way they could check us: secretly going through our car for hidden radios, badges, guns, or anything else that would indicate we were actually agents. We kept our undercover car "clean" of those items and I readily let them borrow it. In fact, I was proud to let them see it. To keep the car looking legitimate, Sara and I never threw away hamburger wrappers, empty milk cartons, potato chip bags, or anything else. The floorboards were inches deep in smelly debris.

After a long visit, we left and drove back to Jackson, both exhausted from lack of sleep.

But we passed their check and the fifty-pound deal was set. The following weekend, Sara and I drove back to New Orleans and did the fifty-pound deal in a parking garage. As the deal went down, New Orleans PD, DEA, and MBN agents rushed in and made the arrests. Searches of the apartment produced ounces of cocaine. One of the men cooperated and helped the DEA make a clandestine lab case.

It's difficult to make significant cases "working cold," without an informant, but that turned out to be a good example of how working cold can occasionally pay off.

Sara and I continued working together in the Jackson area. Drug dealers were naturally wary of anyone new, but by pretending to be "a couple," we lessened some suspicions. Sometimes that wasn't enough, however. When one dealer became suspicious of me, I showed up at his house late one night and pretended that Sara and I had an argument and she kicked me out. I spent the night in a spare bedroom at the dealer's house and left the next morning to try to "make up" with Sara. When some other drug traffickers became suspicious of Sara, MBN issued a press release announcing Sara's arrest in her undercover name, Sara Houston. The arrest articles ran for two days in the Jackson newspaper, the *Clarion-Ledger*, and helped take some of the heat off of her.

Clarion-Ledger
Brandon, Miss.
Sara Houston, 22, of Hernando, was held in the Rankin County jail Thursday following her arrest on drug charges, the State Bureau of Narcotics said. A Bureau spokesman said Ms. Houston was arrested in the county Wednesday night by state drug agents and local officers. She is charged with possession and sale of dilaudid and possession with intent to deliver LSD. Bond was set at $3,000 on each charge.

A 22-year-old Hernando woman was arrested in Rankin County about 10:30 pm Wednesday by agents of the Mississippi Bureau of Narcotics and charged with several hard drug offenses, a spokesman for the bureau said today. Sara Houston is charged with possession and sale of dilaudid and possession with intent to deliver LSD. Members of the Rankin County Sheriff's Office assisted in the arrest. Bond was set at $3,000 per count and she is being held in the Rankin County jail, the spokesman said.

Fortunately the extra measures Sara and I took helped preserve our covers. Undercover work presented challenges that required not only quick thinking but also imaginative responses—although we could never be certain of the outcomes.

4
NATCHEZ, MCCOMB, AND VICKSBURG

After working together in the Jackson area for a few months, Sara and I split up and I began working undercover around Natchez, McComb, and Vicksburg. I soon began working up another buy-bust, but one that had some unusual twists.

It's Always Best to Keep Your Gun Loaded—Except When It's Not

The Hard Times was legendary and so was "Papa Cool." The Hard Times nightclub is a honky-tonk joint located on a lonely corner of Highway 61 where 61 is joined by a long, narrow road that winds to Alcorn University, an all-black college at the time. It was well named. Squatting on a bare patch of dirt and gravel, it was a ramshackle structure of old, weathered boards, warped and long since turned gray, scoured bare by decades of wind, sun, and rain, topped by a rusty tin roof. The Hard Times, like its customers, tilted slightly to one side. It stood forlorn during the daytime, but come nighttime, it was the place to be, its dusty parking lot filled with cars crowded in a widening circle and customers packing the joint. Papa Cool owned and ran the Hard Times club. "Cool" was a tall, lanky black man maybe in his forties, and he was as widely known as his joint.

Early one evening just before dusk, I drove up to the Hard Times and went in alone, "cold," without an informant. I wanted to get there early so that I could try to meet Papa Cool. It would be easier to seek him out and talk to him before he got busy. A few customers were already there. As the only white, I drew questioning looks and some long stares, but ambled in and ordered a beer at the counter like I was where I belonged, relaxed and comfortable.

At the time I was working undercover in Natchez, where I had an undercover apartment. An informant I had worked with in Jackson, a black male, would come down and stay with me at times. I had him trying to find out what was going on in the black clubs and to work me in for undercover drug buys when he could. Meanwhile, I was working cold, making buys from white dealers. The informant heard about Cool up at the Hard Times, and although he never went there, others told him that Cool could deal in quantities. I thought it best to make the approach cold, directly to Cool—to take a gamble.

"A friend in Natchez told me you're all right, that I could trust you and we might be able to do some business together."

"Who's your friend?" I gave him a name and he thought he recognized it.

"What kind of business you talking about?"

"He said you could do some quantities, and if you can, that's what I'm interested in, quantities, not a onetime thing, a regular thing."

"Yeah, I might be able to do that, depending on what you want."

It turned out that he could move large quantities of pharmaceutical drugs, narcotics and depressants, quantities that could be obtained only by having a good inside source or through drugstore burglaries. We arranged a deal.

Several days later, we met at an abandoned gravel pit, an isolated, desolate landscape, barren and moon-like, with dark forest and deep shadows looming over the rims of the pit. It was a hot summer afternoon. No breeze, no movement, no sound. I didn't know if this was going to be a setup and rip-off, but felt better about it when he drove up alone. He opened his trunk and I bought $2,000 worth of pharmaceuticals from him.

Later I bought from him again, and then started negotiating to buy fifty pounds of marijuana, planning to make it a buy-bust because I wouldn't be able to let that much buy money walk. But the negotiations dragged on and I needed to do something to jump-start it and get it moving. I got a $15,000 flash roll of hundreds and twenties, filled a paper sack with the money, and drove to the Hard Times. It was late night and the joint was full and hopping, the music blaring in the lot. I went in and got Cool and brought him to my car, telling him I wanted to show him something.

"Take a look at this, Cool." I handed him the paper sack and he opened it and looked inside. After taking a quick look around to make sure no one was close, he reached inside and brought some of the bills up toward the light and thumbed them. I could tell it was having the desired effect. "I've got $17,400 together for the fifty pounds already and wanted to show you that. I'm on my way to Jackson tonight to get the rest from some friends who are putting in money on the deal. I'll have it all together late tonight. You think we can do it tomorrow?"

"Yeah. Tell you what, call me in the morning and I'll tell you where to meet me, maybe meet up around ten. It'd probably be on the side of the highway below Vicksburg."

We talked the deal over a little, and then Cool said, "Let me show *you* something." He stretched and reached into his pocket, pulling out a bottle of cough syrup. It still had a seal on the cap. "Man, we been getting this stuff from Baton Rouge. It's over the counter, but, man, talk about getting you off."

"Cough syrup!"

"Yeah, I'm telling you. Man, you take this and next thing you know, lightning bolts be shooting through your body, all the way to your balls!" He was excited just talking about it. "Man, this some good mutherfucking stuff." He unscrewed the cap and held it out, "Here man, try it, I'm telling you, you gonna like it."

"Cool, I don't want no cough syrup," I protested.

He kept on and on, and then took a long swallow himself, titling the bottle and chugging it down.

"Come on, try it," he held it out to me, "I guarantee you gonna like this mutherfucker."

I took it, raised it to my lips, and pretended to take a taste.

"Naw, man, you gotta get a good swig to do any good." He was motioning upward with his palm.

I tilted it upward, stuck my tongue in the opening to block it, and pretended to drink, but then his face was next to mine. "Come on man, you got to get some down."

Since it was over-the-counter cough syrup and had a seal on it, I figured it wasn't spiked, and went ahead and took a big swallow, and with Cool in my face, a couple more big swallows.

"That's right, that's right." He was pleased.

After the meeting with Cool, I drove to McComb and checked into the Holiday Inn after midnight, getting a room on the second floor. It was going to be a busy day in the morning, starting first thing, and I needed a few hours' rest, but first I made a series of calls to arrange for surveillance in the morning and to plan the buy-bust. I put in an early wake-up call and turned out the light and went to sleep.

I jerked awake with my heart beating rapidly and my face flushed hot, nervous, my body trembling. What was happening? I jumped up and rushed to the sink and threw cold water on my face, but it didn't help. My hands were shaking. Suddenly, I felt lightning bolts shooting through my body down to my balls, just like Cool said would happen.

Left to right: MBN agent Fred Macdonald, the author, and Jefferson Parish detective Kenneth F. Smith aboard the shrimp boat *Gulf Stream* at a remote inlet on the Gulf Coast minutes after smugglers had unloaded 20,000 pounds of marijuana from the boat onto a tractor-trailer truck. The three of us made our way in darkness though woods and a swamp toward the boat while the cargo was being unloaded. Macdonald reached it first and single-handedly captured the boat, firing his .44-magnum pistol as he charged. The hole in the pilot cabin window was made by one of his bullets. Not long after this night, Detective Smith was killed during a drug raid in Jefferson Parish. He was twenty-five and left a wife and two small children.

The weekly Baton Rouge paper *Gris Gris* carried an interview with the author about our ongoing struggle against corruption. Intelligence investigator Bruce Childers started an investigation into corruption and was quickly ordered to stop. When I took up the investigation, the district attorney and the mayor got involved. The police chief, Rudy Ratcliff, backed us and ordered us to report directly to him. The mayor then replaced Chief Ratcliff with a police colonel who was the subject of the investigation. On his first day in office, the new chief transferred me and Bruce to uniform patrol and soon ordered me to disclose all our findings to him. I refused and resigned and Bruce and I continued the investigation on our own. Despite the risks to their careers, many police officers courageously came forward with information about corruption.

MBN agent Faron Gardner, an ex-Marine and Native American, poses with an award at the FBI Sniper Course. Sent to work undercover in Greenville for just one night, Faron had two close calls within six hours. As a result of negotiations for a large drug deal, drug dealers thought Faron had a large sum of money in his motel room. When Faron answered a knock at the door, armed men kicked open the door and tried to rush in and rob him. Just a few hours earlier, another dealer had whipped out a gun and he and Faron struggled over it until Faron was able to subdue the man. (Courtesy of Faron Gardner)

MBN agents Sara Niell (center), Bill Taylor (left), and Larry James (right) with a large quantity of cocaine and a gun seized during a drug operation. Sara and the author worked undercover together in Jackson and New Orleans posing as a couple. Sara later worked undercover in north Mississippi in rural areas that were so lawless and dangerous we called the region the "Arizona Territory" and "Tombstone." During a heroin deal outside Columbus, she and her partner Jerry Dettman were ambushed by a hidden sniper and Jerry was wounded. Sara wounded one of the attackers and rescued Jerry. (Courtesy of Sara Niell)

MBN agent Jim Kelly, an ex-Marine who led an especially exciting life, was first involved in a gunfight outside a nightclub in Jackson when he and agent Jim Wallace confronted a gunman standing over a victim he had just shot. Later, during an operation in south Mississippi, Jim shot and wounded a heavily armed man who was waiting in a wooded area to ambush MBN agents moving toward him on a trail. (Courtesy of Randy Wallace)

The author's Baton Rouge police ID. I looked like that for only my first two months in uniform patrol. For the next ten years I worked undercover and my main companions were drug dealers, safecrackers, prostitutes, thugs, car thieves, smugglers, and similar characters.

Rogue's gallery of my undercover looks in Baton Rouge.

"Narcs Die Young" warning in south Mississippi meant for MBN agents. Unfortunately, the warning was prophetic. Several MBN agents died on duty and agent Lane Caldwell was shot and killed as he struggled with a kidnapper. He was twenty-five and left a wife and two young sons.

Mississippi State Penitentiary at Parchman. Inmates at the state pen compiled and circulated a "K.O.S." (kill on sight) list of MBN undercover agents, with descriptions and undercover names. MBN was tipped off and seized the list and launched an investigation. Agents on the list included the author, Steve Mallory, and Doug Cutrer, along with others.

MBN agent Jerry Dettman (*right*) undercover with a suspect in front of the Pizza Haze, a bar MBN operated as a front in Southaven. When MBN learned that a drug organization in Texas had put out a contract on an informant working with us in the Pizza Haze, Jerry directed MBN agent Mike Tyson to sit in a corner inside the bar watching the door and to kill anyone who came in and tried to kill the informant. Fortunately, no one showed up.

The author's taxi ID card in Gulfport in the undercover name Michael Warren. When I first began working undercover on the Gulf Coast to infiltrate heroin trafficking, I drove a taxi as a cover.

The author in a dugout on Hill 19A near Da Nang, Vietnam, while serving as a Marine squad leader. Alfred Price, one of the Marines in his squad, later wrote: "[Sergeant Spillers] was my squad leader when I got to Nam, a great leader, teacher, smart and dead serious, a Marine to be respected and admired." Price was wounded and decorated several times for bravery.

The author on Monkey Mountain in Vietnam, where he served as a Marine squad leader in the area south of Da Nang.

MBN agents and state narcotics agents from Louisiana, Texas, Alabama, Tennessee, and Georgia pose for a photo while attending the MBN Air-Marine Smuggling Investigator's Course in Jackson. In the 1980s, numerous multistate drug organizations were involved in smuggling by aircraft and vessel throughout the southeast United States. MBN recruited sources along the coast and at airfields, identified airstrips used by smugglers, and conducted surveillance of smuggling groups, sometimes across several states. *First row:* Jim Wallace, later MBN director, is on the bottom row at the far right. Jerry Dettman is standing beside Wallace, Don Richards to the left of Dettman, and Barry Newsome second from left. *Second row:* Kent McDaniel, now Rankin County Judge McDaniel, is on the second row, on the far left. James Newman, now sheriff of Franklin County, stands beside McDaniel, Randy Day is third from left, and Dempsey Newman is on the far right. *Third row:* Veteran agent Doug Cutrer is on the far left. Rick Humphreys, who became a district supervisor and later joined the DEA, stands beside Cutrer. Sara Niell, the author's undercover partner in Jackson, is the lone female and is on the third row. *Fourth row:* On the far left, Bill Turcotte, James Newman, second from left, James Brantley, third from left, and Danny Blackledge, fourth from left. (Courtesy of Sara Niell)

MBN agent James C. "J. C." Denham standing behind the author, in a photo taken during the MBN Basic Agent Academy. Drug dealers shot up Denham's home in Meridian, nearly killing his wife. J. C. later served as the chief of police in Waynesboro, Mississippi. He passed away in June 2015.

The MBN Pistol Team posing with trophies they won in competitive shooting matches. Agent Lou Guirola, now a US district judge for the southern district of Mississippi, is seated on the left and agent Steve Ford is seated on the right. *Standing left to right:* Agents Jim Wallace, Charlie Lindsey, Ron Johnson, and Fred Lovett. (Courtesy of Randy Wallace)

MBN agents Randy Corban (*left*) and Earl Pierce (*right*) in MBN Basic Agent Academy. Randy worked undercover in the violent, lawless areas and nightclubs of north Mississippi; areas so rough that his female informant carried a hammer in her purse for fights. While posing as a hit man, Randy was hired by thugs to kill one of their adversaries. After catching Earl Pierce in a lie, a Jackson drug dealer pointed a cocked .357-magnum at Earl and demanded to know why he had lied.

MBN agent Steve Mallory holding a derringer and posing as a biker. One night while undercover in Grenada, Steve and another agent were robbed by several men during a drug deal. One of the robbers put a pistol to Steve's head and pulled the trigger but the gun misfired. Minutes later, as Steve and the other agent struggled with two men inside a car, the windshield was shot out; Steve knocked out one man by hitting him in the head with a gun and then was almost shot by sheriff's deputies who came upon the struggle and saw Steve pointing a gun at the other assailant. (Courtesy of Steve Mallory)

University of Mississippi professor Steve Mallory in his former life as an MBN undercover agent. Mallory's undercover appearance bears a striking resemblance to the killer in the movie *No Country for Old Men.* Steve later changed his looks when he assumed an undercover role as an outlaw motorcycle gang member. He retired as the deputy director of MBN, earned a PhD, became head of the Criminal Justice Department at the University of Southern Mississippi and the interim head of the Legal Studies School at Ole Miss. Steve still teaches at Ole Miss and is chairman of the Mississippi State Board for Police Officers Standards and Training. (Courtesy of Steve Mallory)

MBN agents at the Pizza Haze bar in Southaven, getting ready to remove equipment the night the bar closed for good. MBN operated two bars as undercover fronts, The Hut in Columbus and the Pizza Haze in Southaven. Undercover agents made numerous drug purchases at the bars, many of which were videotaped. *Left to right:* Agents Monty Montgomery, Mike Turner, Randy Corban, Dennis "Mac" McAnally, and John "Doc" Riddell. In an earlier undercover operation, Dennis worked deep cover as a radio station disc jockey in Tupelo, becoming a well-known radio personality. Dennis left MBN, earned a master's degree in religious education, and became a pastor. John "Doc" Riddell perfectly played his part as one of author's business associates in the undercover operation that infiltrated Mafia and Mexican smuggling operations. (Courtesy of Mike Turner)

One of the author's many undercover driver's licenses, this one in the name Michael J. Burns. Including a middle initial allows the same driver's license to support several first names with the explanation that the undercover agent goes by his middle name. For example, with the "J." on this license, I could go by names such as John, Jerry, Joe, Josh, Jake, James, and Jim.

MBN Agent Richard Allison. In a solitary and dangerous assignment, Richard worked deep cover for two years as a bartender in a strip club on the Mississippi Gulf Coast to gather intelligence on organized crime, the Dixie Mafia, and corruption. Leroy Hobbs, Harrison County sheriff, was a silent partner in the strip club and was later convicted on federal charges in another case. (Courtesy of Richard Allison)

A Beech 18 twin-engine airplane, the type of plane William Wayne Mahaffey flew to smuggle drugs from Jamaica to the United States. On a return flight from Jamaica, Mahaffey ran low on fuel and landed in Belize, Central America, to refuel. Authorities there found 1,500 pounds of marijuana on board and arrested Mahaffey and his copilot Julian Sirmons. Mahaffey and Sirmons were sentenced to three months in jail. A short time later, during an undercover meeting with the author in Clarksdale, Mahaffey explained that his organization had paid bribes to get him secretly released after three days in jail. Mahaffey said his arrest had a silver lining because he had developed high-level contacts in the Belize government for future smuggling trips to Belize. Following the seizure of the Beech 18, the smuggling organization provided Mahaffey with an Aero Commander twin-engine plane.

MBN agents Jim Wallace (*left*) and Fred Macdonald (*right*), weary from a long night of surveillance during a smuggling investigation on the Gulf Coast. (Courtesy of Randy Wallace)

MBN agent Terry Spillers with a truckload of marijuana plants. Terry Spillers, my son, followed in my footsteps in law enforcement. He served as a police officer with the Madison, Mississippi, police department and then joined MBN, worked briefly undercover, and is now an MBN district supervisor.

The author and his wife Evelyn in Baton Rouge. My undercover work unfortunately intruded on our home life. When I was away, Evelyn took daily phone calls at home from numerous drug dealers and informants calling for "Mike," "Rick," "John," or "Frank." When we went out together, we sometimes encountered suspects who knew me in my undercover role. When a drug dealer I had arrested showed up outside our home and approached Evelyn looking for "Mike" who had busted him, she was terrified but handled it well.

Sergeant Sam Pruet was the author's immediate supervisor in Baton Rouge PD Narcotics. Sam, an ex-Marine, provided steady leadership. Sam was one of the police officers who came forward to fight corruption, and as a result, his career suffered. Sam later wrote: "[Charlie Spillers] was a hardworking, dependable agent who was a tireless worker. He often worked undercover for the full twenty-four hours in day. He always exhibited high integrity and ethics in everything he did. . . . I retired with the rank of Captain after thirty years, and without a doubt, Charlie is the best undercover agent I ever had under my command." (Courtesy of Sam Pruett)

Seized tractor-trailer truck with 20,000 pounds of marijuana that smugglers had loaded a few hours earlier from the shrimp boat *Gulf Stream. Left to right:* MBN agents Ron Johnson and Dean Shepard. (Courtesy of Randy Wallace)

Drug load from the *Gulf Stream.* Smugglers off-loaded 20,000 pounds of marijuana from the shrimp boat *Gulf Stream* onto this tractor-trailer truck, which is seen parked at a cabin used by some of the smugglers. MBN and DEA agents followed the truck from the coast to the cabin and a nearby warehouse hidden deep in a wooded area. (Courtesy of Randy Wallace)

The author undercover on the Gulf Coast.

Life after undercover. A federal prosecutor at the helm of his sailboat in Florida before the boat was destroyed in Hurricane Opal.

The author at Landing Zone (LZ) Washington in the Green Zone, Baghdad, Iraq, in 2010, awaiting a helicopter flight while serving as the DOJ justice attaché for Iraq. As an assistant US attorney, the author volunteered and served three tours in Iraq for the US Department of Justice, the first two as an attorney-adviser to the Iraqi High Tribunal (IHT), the court that tried Saddam Hussein, Chemical Ali, and other high-level regime members, and the last as the DOJ justice attaché for Iraq. His work related to Iraq was commended by the president of the IHT, the FBI director, the deputy attorney general, the first secretary of the Italian embassy, the British ambassador, and Britain's minister of state for the Armed Forces.

The author at Camp Victory near Baghdad International Airport in 2009. In a letter commending the author's work as the justice attaché for Iraq, the FBI director wrote, "The outstanding rapport you have developed with Iraqi Government officials has strengthened our ability to fulfill our investigative mission. . . . Your strong advocacy has been essential to advancing numerous counterterrorism investigations involving complex international legal issues. The impact of future FBI operations in Iraq will be significantly enhanced as a direct result of your exemplary contributions."

Cough syrup couldn't do that, I thought; it had to have been spiked with a drug, maybe LSD or PCP. My body was out of control, heart beating even more rapidly, nervousness increasing, skin flushing hotter. I had to get to a hospital fast before I freaked out. If I was on acid or PCP, I might freak out driving, so I called the nearest agent to come pick me up.

My .38 was on the nightstand. I might be a danger to myself or others with a loaded gun if I freaked out, so I opened the cylinder and emptied the bullets into my hand. I opened the door, went to the balcony, and flung the bullets as far as I could. I didn't carry extra ammunition because if I had to use my gun undercover it would be over in seconds and I wouldn't have time to reload.

The agent picked me up and rushed me to the hospital. I identified myself to the doctor as an agent and explained about the cough syrup and the symptoms, suggesting that the cough syrup may have been spiked. He diagnosed it as simply an overdose of regular cough syrup, and gave me a shot, which caused the symptoms to immediately subside. A little later, while I was still in the examination room, a kindly looking grandmother of a nurse stuck her head in, looked at me, and shook her head, with an accusatory yet sorrowful look. "And you're supposed to be catching them," she said. "Shame on you. Shame on you." She left. I already felt bad enough, and now felt even worse.

I got back to my room at daylight and called Cool to confirm the deal was on and the time and location for our meet. We were to meet on the side of Highway 61 south of Vicksburg at 10:00 a.m. I would be rushed. He was pleased when I told him about the lightning bolts.

Following the conversation with Cool, I made quick calls to agents with the meeting location and time, along with a description of Cool's vehicle, a Ford Mustang. It would take me at least an hour and a half to drive from McComb to the meeting place south of Vicksburg, so I had to hurry.

I stopped briefly to meet an agent on the roadside to pick up a two-way radio so that I would be able to communicate with the agents on surveillance. He didn't have any .38 ammo; he only had his .357. I couldn't take his gun or wait any longer, so I sped up the highway with an empty gun to meet Cool. Cool might not wait if I was running late and I had no way of contacting him. I arrived late but Cool's blue Mustang was still there, parked on the side of the highway. I notified surveillance on the two-way radio, then switched it off and shoved it under the seat. I pulled in behind him and hurried to his window. He had a woman with him.

"Hey, Cool, sorry I'm running late—I got tied up. We ready?"

"Yeah, I'm gonna get it. You wait here and I'll be back in a few minutes. It ain't far. When I get back, you just follow me."

He drove off, heading north on highway 61, and I notified surveillance to try to follow him to the source. I listened to the radio traffic as they followed him to a mobile home. A Lincoln and another car were parked at the mobile home. Some agents stayed and watched the mobile home while others followed Cool as he drove back to me.

As he was passing next to my car, Cool slowed down and motioned for me to follow him. I pulled out behind him. With the radio in my lap hidden from Cool's view, I shouted out directions to the agents trying to follow us. I didn't know if he had picked up the dope or if it was stashed and he was leading me to it, so we couldn't take him down yet. Cool turned right off the highway onto a narrow, hilly, winding blacktop road, crowded on both sides by the forest, a road where surveillance can't keep you in sight without driving on your bumper. They had to hang back, far back, out of sight.

After traveling several miles down the road, Cool topped a hill, jammed on his brakes, and made a sharp left turn off the road and disappeared into the forest. He had taken an overgrown rutted track, indistinguishable from the dense forest unless you knew it was there and were looking for it. I followed and my car was swallowed up by the woods, becoming invisible from the road. My car crawled through the woods, rising and falling in the ruts, as brush raked the sides of the car and low branches scraped the top; inside the car, the racket sounded like being inside a car wash. I shouted at the radio that we had turned off but I was unable to describe where. I switched off the radio and shoved it under the seat. I knew the agents would not be able to locate the track where we turned off. I was out of contact and on my own. With an unloaded gun.

After a hundred yards the track ended in a small circle, just enough room to turn around to head back out. Cool stopped when he reached it. The dense woods crowded close on all sides, blocking out the sky overhead, the shadows deep and dark. My mind was racing with possibilities. Was I walking into a trap?

A buy-bust has more risk than a normal drug deal because of the large quantity of drugs and the amount of money involved, enough for each party to be wary of a rip-off and, therefore, to be armed and on the lookout for anything suspicious. Was Cool armed to protect himself from a rip-off? Was he planning to rip me off for the money? Did he have partners hidden in the woods, their guns trained on me? If so, I would be an easy target when I made a move to arrest Cool. I could imagine a sudden burst of gunshots, and cringed at the thought.

Cool's door opened and his leg swung out as he stepped out of the car. I got out and we met at the back of his car.

"You got it?" I asked.

"Yeah." He turned to his trunk and opened it. "It's right here."

A large cardboard box held fifty pounds of marijuana, each pound tightly compressed into a brick.

"It's fifty? All here?" I asked.

"Yeah, I made sure it was weighed out, and it's right."

"Good. We can put it in the trunk of my car."

Cool and I carried the box and put it in the trunk of my car. I had a paper bag in the trunk filled with stacks of paper cut to the size and shape of currency.

"Here's the money, Cool." I handed him the bag and closed the trunk. "It's all there."

He started walking toward his car and began opening the bag. The forest felt like it was closing in on me but, whether he was armed or had partners watching, I needed to make my move before he discovered it was only paper. I reached toward my back for my gun and braced for what might happen as I pulled it out. I tensed, expecting the woods to explode with gun blasts or Cool to go for a gun, when he saw me.

"Hey, Cool!" I was swinging my gun up.

"Yeah?" He was turning toward me, holding the partially open bag.

"*POLICE!*" I shouted, pointing the gun at him. "POLICE! You're under arrest! Hands UP! Get your hands UP!" He hesitated a moment, then . . . dropped the bag and raised his hands.

He was staring at my gun. Realizing that he might be able to see the empty cylinders and would know that the gun was empty, I suddenly pointed it downward toward his feet so that he couldn't see the cylinders. As I pointed the gun downward, Cool hopped up, apparently thinking I was going to shoot his foot.

I made him get down on his stomach with his hands over his head and his feet toward me. I yelled for the woman to get out of the car with her hands up, but she didn't move. I moved closer to the car, pointed my gun toward her, and yelled again. Finally she got out and I had her lie down on her stomach beside Cool.

I had everything under control for the time being, but I needed to get someone there quickly with a loaded gun. While watching Cool and the woman, I backed to my car, got the radio, and tried to make contact on our MBN surveillance channel.

"839 to surveillance, over." Nothing. "839 to any unit, over." Nothing.

They were out of range and the radio was picking up mostly static and a few broken words. After a few minutes I was able to make contact and I started talking them in to my location. Soon, I heard sounds of car engines approaching and then cars lurched into sight and agents bounded out with loaded guns. I took a deep breath and sighed with relief.

As agents handcuffed Cool and the woman, I walked up to Cool's car. Both doors were still open, and then I saw it. A large revolver lay on the passenger floorboard. It looked like a cannon. Mother*fucker*, I thought.

The woman was probably holding the gun while Cool was with me. I shook my head thinking about what could have happened deep in the woods—what almost happened.

A couple of hours later I was at the county jail fingerprinting Cool. While talking with another agent I mentioned that my gun had been empty. Startled, Cool froze and shot a questioning look sidelong at me, one eyebrow cocked.

"Hey, man, yo' gun wasn't loaded?"

"No, it wasn't."

"Huh?" He was incredulous. "Yo' gun was *empty*?"

"Yeah, it was empty."

Cool was puzzled.

"Why didn't you have no bullets in it?" asked Cool, squinting.

"'Cause, Cool," I paused, and looked directly at him, "I like you, man," I said with a friendly smile, "and I didn't want to take a chance on hurting you."

He was lost in thought a few moments. Then he shook his head side to side and made an emphatic, drawn-out comment that summed it all up: "Mother*fucker!*"

He was thinking about what he could have done in the woods with his loaded gun.

I was too.

It was foolhardy to arrest Cool with an unloaded gun. And instead of following him deep into the woods, I should have stopped at the road and forced him to come back to me. I knew it at the time, but felt confident I could handle whatever came up—so I forged ahead. I had been working undercover for six years by that time, nearly always alone, often without surveillance, completely on my own. I was not only surviving, but thriving. I was confident and took greater and greater risks. Because I had faced danger frequently, it didn't seem as dangerous to me at the time as it would to most people. Nevertheless, it was foolhardy. Luckily, it worked out.

The day wasn't over yet. Agents raided the mobile home and found two hundred pounds of marijuana in the trunk of the Lincoln and arrested several white guys, a drug ring that obtained quantities of marijuana in Texas for distribution in the Vicksburg area. They seized weapons and thousands of dollars in the mobile home. The ringleader had $9,000 in cash on him.

When the ringleader indicated he might be willing to cooperate, the MBN chief of operations and a local detective left with him while other agents continued the search. The chief stopped at a pay phone next to the road and he and the detective got out to make a call. The ringleader was handcuffed and sitting in the backseat. They had left the car running and a gun on the front seat. While they were at the phone, the ringleader climbed over the seat, jumped behind the steering wheel, and shot at them as he sped off. The detective fired back and one of his bullets went through the door and wounded the ringleader in the leg.

Others were alerted and gave chase. The ringleader sped through back-county roads, leading MBN agents and local officers on a wild chase. Careening and sliding on gravel, police cars crashed or side-swiped each other. It was truly a *Dukes of Hazzard* chase. The ringleader finally bounced through a field, where he abandoned the car and fled on foot. A search for him came up empty. However, he was caught in the early-morning hours as he crept back on his wounded leg to the mobile home. Agents had staked it out.

Starting the night before, it had been an eventful and nonstop eighteen or twenty hours for me. It took a while to decompress and fall asleep late that night.

Occasionally I still think about what could have happened deep in the woods. And since then, I shy away from cough syrup.

The Right Words

Aside from direct undercover encounters, I usually can't think of the right response until later, when it is too late, and then wish I had said this or that at the time. A couple of times, though, providence granted my wish. I was working undercover around McComb, Mississippi. I heard that the Pines Club in Louisiana, just across the state line from Mississippi, was a popular place where a lot was happening, so late one night I drove to the Pines. It sat at the junction of two narrow blacktop roads, surrounded by a large gravel parking area filled with cars and pickup trucks.

What I didn't know, but quickly realized when I went in, was that it was a Cajun and redneck honky-tonk, and that I didn't fit in at all. With a full beard and long bushy hair, I stood out from the crowd of clean-shaven, short-haired, blue-collar good ole boys. I looked like a hippie, the kind of person they didn't tolerate. I was greeted with hard stares and it took only a minute to conclude that I'd best leave. The club was packed tight—all the tables were full, men were standing clustered in small groups, and the bar was crowded with customers sitting and standing two or three deep. I squeezed up to the bar to order a beer to go. Two bartenders were working nonstop and I stood waiting for service. I was pressed against a man on a bar stool.

"Hey, you," said the man on the bar stool, looking up at me with a frown. He had a heavy Cajun accent. "Hey, *you!*" I didn't like the tone. It sounded like trouble looming.

"Me?"

"Yeah, you," the Cajun said angrily. "I'm talking to you." His buddy sitting beside him glowered at me.

"Hey, man, what's that *shit* on your face?" the Cajun sneered.

I raised my hand and felt my beard. "You mean this?"

"Yeah, what's that *fucking shit* on your face?" he said, snarling at me, a taunt, not a question.

"Yeah," his buddy joined in, "what's that *shit* on your face, man?"

Despite the loud din and jukebox music, others around us heard the exchange and jostled closer, staring at me. I realized there wasn't going to be a fight. Instead, it would be a stomping by an angry group, which was now pressing in on all sides. The Cajun and his buddy were ready to be the first to pounce.

Looking at the Cajun, I started gently rubbing my beard.

"Oh this," I gave a wide-eyed look. "Well, see, I was wounded in Vietnam in the face—and I can't shave because of the wounds to my face," I innocently explained. "So that's why I have this beard now. I can't shave because it hurts too much from the wounds."

The Cajun's mouth dropped open and a look of amazement spread across his face.

"Huh? What? What'd he say?" his buddy asked impatiently, half-rising from the bar stool. "What'd he say?"

The Cajun twisted toward his buddy. "He was wounded in the face in Vietnam."

"Oh?" He looked at me.

"That's why he has a beard. He can't shave because of his wound."

"Oh!" The glower had turned into a wide-eyed look of respect.

The Cajun looked up at others pressing around us. They were straining to hear. "He can't shave 'cause he was wounded in Vietnam in the face," he announced loudly, turning on his bar stool to reach everyone pressed in close. "He was wounded in the face and that's why he has to have a beard. He can't shave." This information was greeted by understanding nods and sympathetic looks in my direction.

I rubbed my beard gently while trying my best to look pitiful, reconciled to my awful fate of having to look like a bearded hippie because of my war wounds.

"Oh man, I'm so sorry, yeah," said the Cajun. "Here, man, let me buy you a beer."

"Yeah, man, we're gonna buy you a beer," agreed his partner.

A few others reached for money as they competed to treat me. They started buying me beers and patting me on the back. I left after a couple of beers, relieved to still be in one piece.

My response didn't come from my being clever; instead, it was pure self-preservation. Or, as one person later said, "out of scaredness and afraidness."

The *Gulf Stream*

The worst predators in the swamps are not always alligators. It had become almost routine: drug cartels in South America sent cargo ships carrying tons of marijuana to the coastal waters and swampy inlets on the coasts of Mississippi, Louisiana, and Alabama. Far out in the Gulf of Mexico, mother ships off-loaded bales of marijuana onto shrimp boats or other vessels for the final trip to shore. To avoid detection, drug-laden boats made their way under the cover of darkness along isolated inlets to remote sites where the cargo would be quickly off-loaded onto trucks that would carry the cargo to nearby storage sites. The drugs would later be transported to destinations across the country for distribution.

Trying to interdict the shipments, MBN, DEA, Louisiana State Police, and other agencies shared information and worked closely on investigations and stakeouts.

During one of these joint operations, three of us were staked out in a forward position during the night at a wooded, swampy inlet on the Mississippi Gulf Coast. A narrow, winding road angled through the forest and ended at an isolated industrial warehouse near the inlet, a dark bayou that snaked its way from the Gulf of Mexico deeper into the interior. Overhanging trees and tangled brush crowded the sides of the bayou, a remote and hushed world that evoked scenes from the movies *The African Queen* and *Creature from the Black Lagoon.*

Two hundred yards from the bayou, MBN agent Fred Macdonald; Jefferson Parish, Louisiana, sheriff's narcotics detective Kenneth F. Smith; and I watched in darkness from the windows of a small office on the second floor of the empty warehouse. The windows of the office faced the road that ended at the building, and side windows looked out on dark woods and swamps on the north side of the warehouse. The bayou was to our backs. We didn't have a view toward it and, even if we had, we wouldn't have been able to see anything because of the trees and brush and the black night. Other agents waited in their cars several miles away, just within range of our two-way radio.

Shortly after midnight, Macdonald suddenly jerked his head in the direction of the bayou. "What's that? You hear it?" he asked. Soon, Ken and I heard it too: muffled noises as a blacked-out shrimp boat slowly navigated its way up the bayou. Rumbling engines grew louder as the boat came abreast of the warehouse and then gradually became fainter as it picked its way further inland.

While the boat was being unloaded, we spread out and picked our way on foot through a swamp toward the sounds of its engines. We soon lost both sight of and contact with each other in the black night. Neither Ken nor Fred responded when I called to them in low whispers. Before we could reach the scene, the unloading was completed and the truck left on a sandy track that led through the woods and swamp. The boat was still idling at the landing when Macdonald came across the sandy track and reached the boat first. He charged the boat single-handedly, firing his .44-magnum pistol at the three smugglers on the boat. One of his bullets blasted a hole in the windshield of the pilot house. The smugglers jumped in the bayou and were captured after daylight trying to escape from the area. One later said he felt like he had run over the backs of alligators after jumping off the shrimp boat, swimming across the bayou and rushing through the woods and swamps. Meanwhile, other agents followed the tractor trailer to an isolated warehouse in the middle of a forest near the coast. They raided the warehouse and seized the shipment of marijuana.

In the hours before the *Gulf Stream* seizure, Fred and I were with Ken while waiting for the boat to arrive. We had never met Ken before and we engaged in whispered small talk as we got to know a little about each other. I recall Ken saying that he was married, had two small children, and was attending college at night. Ken had been with the sheriff's office for two years. Not long after the drug seizure, Ken Smith was shot and killed while conducting a narcotics raid with other agents in Jefferson Parish, near New Orleans. Ken was only twenty-five when he was killed.

I returned to southwest Mississippi after the *Gulf Stream* bust, but would soon be back to the Gulf Coast. After winding up undercover in Natchez with a roundup of drug dealers who had sold to me, I went to the coast next to try to infiltrate groups of heroin dealers who flourished in Gulfport and Biloxi. They were supplied by dealers in New Orleans and Mobile, and, if possible, I would also try to make cases on some of the suppliers.

5

MISSISSIPPI GULF COAST HEROIN OPERATION

A Cabdriver in Sewer City

Driving a taxi is interesting work. For one thing, when I started out, I wasn't very familiar with the Gulf Coast area, so it was a challenge at times to find the locations to pick up my fares and then take them to their destinations. The dispatcher for the taxi company would give me directions over the two-way radio and I could always ask my fare to help direct me, so it worked out and gradually I became familiar with the area. Undercover is a people business, and the people I drove were interesting and I enjoyed our conversations. It also made for better tips. I wasn't getting paid by the taxi company, but I could keep my tips, although they didn't amount to much.

John Souder, the MBN supervisor on the coast, had worked out the undercover taxi job for me. I needed the cover. A new informant, Jim (not his real name), provided information about heroin dealers on the coast and agreed to introduce me to make drug buys. The heroin dealers were black, as was Jim, and even though he vouched for me, they nevertheless would be wary of me—a stranger, a white. With Jim's help and the cover of being a taxi driver, I hoped to break into the heroin trade.

As "Michael Warren," equipped with my taxi driver's ID, taxi driver's badge, and a big marked taxi, I began work. In the first few weeks I picked up most of my fares in a black-populated area of Gulfport known as "Sewer City," which was where many of the heroin dealers lived. I gradually became known and started making heroin buys.

A good problem soon arose when a late-model yellow-and-white Lincoln Continental became available for my undercover use. It had been forfeited to the state from a big drug seizure and I thought it would be perfect for impressing the heroin dealers. But how could I explain to the drug dealers how I suddenly went from driving a taxi to driving a big Lincoln and having plenty of money?

The answer was a car accident and a greedy lawyer. I started telling my fares and the dealers that I just heard from my lawyer and I was excited. The lawyer was handling my lawsuit from a car accident several years ago, and he just told me that the lawsuit was finally going to settle for a large amount of money. I would soon be rolling in money. I could stop driving a cab and buy myself a big car. I had Jim spread the word: "Man, that Mike's gonna be rolling in the money," he told them. "He's got a lawsuit over a car accident that's about to pay off big time! I'm talking 'bout *big* time!"

To make it look credible, I not only pretended to be excited about the prospect of the money, but I also complained about my lawyer. "My lawyer's getting a third of it off the top," I grumbled, "and he ain't done nothing for it but file the damn lawsuit. That ain't right. Lawyers are like that—greedy—trying to make every penny they can off other people." That usually elicited knowing nods of agreement.

After a couple of weeks preparing everyone, I stopped driving my taxi, and Jim and I began riding around Sewer City in my big yellow Lincoln. The cover about lawsuit money also provided me with the perfect explanation for having unlimited money to buy heroin, and I started buying larger quantities. For the next six months I made several heroin buys each week from dealers on the Mississippi coast and from dealers who flocked from Mobile and New Orleans.

Everything went smoothly, except for a few incidents. The first occurred when I went to Jim's house for a buy.

Undercover Buys Are Routine—Except When They're Not

I drove into a cul-de-sac and parked in the driveway of the informant's house, arriving to meet and buy from a heroin dealer waiting for me inside. As Jim, the informant, let me in the front door, his wide, anxious eyes met mine and signaled a warning. His lips trembled and his eyes flicked sideways twice to his left and I looked in that direction. A tall figure stood at the front window peering out between the blinds, checking for surveillance. His right hand gripped a black semiautomatic handgun, probably a 9-millimeter. He glanced at me and returned to watching the outside.

I cringed and prayed the agent doing surveillance would not be foolish enough to drive into the cul-de-sac. If he did, I would be in deep trouble. It would broadcast to the man with the gun that I was an under-cover agent. The gunman kept a vigilant watch even after I came inside. This man is wary, savvy, and dangerous, I thought. I understood why Jim was scared.

An armed drug dealer is not unusual, but it is unusual for one to have a weapon out and holding it at the ready. It signals exceptional wariness and proclaims a commitment to use it.

Not knowing whether the agent would drive through the cul-de-sac and not being able to see if he did, I coiled tight inside and watched the gunman for any reaction as he peered outside. Distress and agony can weigh time down, and it stood still now. After a few moments, the man's shoulders relaxed, he took a deep breath and turned away from the blinds. The dealer planted himself on the sofa and Jim and I took chairs across from him. He laid the gun on the coffee table, the barrel pointing toward me. His right hand rested on his knee next to the gun. He stared at me.

"Man, this here's Mike," Jim said, his voice high-pitched and trembling, "the dude I told you about."

With his gun out and ready, the dealer was in control and he knew it. I expected him to be confrontational. I needed to seize control and set the tone before he did.

"Hey, man, why you got your gun out?" I asked. "There ain't no need for that." I spread my arms wide and palms up; body language showing openness and nothing to hide.

"Jim told me you all right, man," I continued, "that you're a business-man, that I can trust you. If Jim tells me you all right, that's good enough for me. But I can tell you're not sure about doing business with me, about selling to me. Well, don't do it!" A quizzical look spread across his face.

"Yeah, that's right—don't sell anything to me. *Don't do it*," I said force-fully. I had his complete attention. "The money ain't worth it, man. The money ain't worth *the worry*." This reminded him about the money he would be making by selling to me. Hopefully, the last thing he would expect of an undercover agent would be for the agent to try to talk him out of a drug sale. "See, I did that a couple of times," I continued, "sold when I was worried about it, but did it anyway and then worried for days after that. It turned out okay every time, but it just ain't worth the worry. The money ain't worth it, man! So don't do it."

We talked, he asked a few questions and then he sold heroin to me. He had been suspicious and ready to be confrontational and violent, but my approach disarmed him. It made me appear to be an experienced drug dealer, maybe even a wise mentor.

I walked out of the house relieved, but mentally and emotionally drained, knowing that the outcome could have been much different.

Selling Stolen Goods Has Side Benefits

For a month or so I was buying heroin steadily in the Sewer City area, but then the buys abruptly slowed down. I picked up Jim, my informant, and we rode around discussing the problem.

"I'll tell you what it is," Jim offered. "It's Frank. He's telling peoples to be careful of you."

"Who's Frank?"

"Frank, he's the man that has Frank's place. You know, that bar in Sewer City. Frank's in Sewer City. Everybody goes there."

"What's he saying about me? What's he telling them?"

"He's telling peoples to be careful about you."

"I don't even know him. Why's he putting down on me?"

"Frank says no one knows you and they need to be careful, that's all. But see, they listening to him, so some of them done got nervous about you."

"Well, can you get up with Frank and tell him you know me?" I suggested. "Let him know I'm all right."

"See, I already done that, but it didn't do no good. He's still telling peoples to be careful dealing with you."

"Does Frank deal himself? Does he sell?"

"Naw, he ain't into that. But he's telling people selling the shit to look out for you, and they listen to him. They pay attention to what he says, and he's scaring people away from you."

"Is there any way we can bring him around? Get him to stop putting down on me?"

"Hah, ain't none I know of," Jim said, shaking his head. "And you ain't gonna be buying shit with him warning these people. I don't know if we gonna be able to do much more."

"*Damn*. Well, we need to figure out *something*, Jim. Let me think about it. And let me know if you come up with anything."

It was frustrating to be stopped just when things had been going so smoothly. I hadn't done anything to make Frank suspicious, but unlike the dealers I was buying from, Frank was not blinded by greed. And he was smart enough to figure out that they should be wary of the white guy who was frequently showing up and buying heroin. I had deliberately paced the buys so as not to generate suspicion, but still, I wasn't a life-long resident of the area—I was an outsider, a stranger, notwithstanding Jim vouching for me. I needed to figure some way to overcome Frank's suspicions.

A few days later, an idea formed and I decided to give it a try. I bought six large cases of beer, loaded them in the trunk of my Lincoln, and drove to Frank's bar. It was early afternoon and I wanted to catch him before his business started for the day. I went inside and found Frank standing at the end of the bar, making notations in a notebook, probably his accounting records. Two men were sitting at a table talking and drinking beer. They stopped and watched me. Frank straightened up, a questioning look on his face. He was maybe in his late forties, stocky, with a weathered face.

"You Frank?"

"Yeah," he said hesitantly.

"Hey, man, I'm Mike." I held up my hand and we shook. "I heard about you and I've been wanting to meet you."

"Yeah, I been hearing about you too," he said wryly.

"Good. It's about time we got up with each other. People tell me you all right, so I thought we might be able to do some business together."

"What kinda business?" Frank said warily.

"Some of my people ripped off a truckload of beer, a whole truckload of beer. We already moved all of it, sold it outta the area because it was hot. But I got a few cases left over from the truckload and thought you might be interested in it at a good price." I saw a look of instant relief on his face.

"How much you got?"

"I got six cases left, twenty-four cans to a case."

"How much you gonna want for 'em?"

"Tell you what, I just want to get rid of them now, so I'll let you have 'em for a real good price. Two dollars a case. How about that, you want 'em?" At such a low price they had to be stolen.

"Hell yeah, I'll take them." Frank beamed with a broad smile. "When can I get 'em?"

"Got 'em right outside in the trunk of my car. Come on."

We went outside, got the cases out of my trunk, and carried them inside, making a couple of trips. Frank paid me twelve dollars for the "stolen" beer and shook my hand with a grateful smile.

I told Jim about my selling "hot" goods to Frank and asked him to drop by Frank's soon and see what he was saying. A few days later Jim reported back with a broad grin.

"Man, Mike, that man's talking *for* you now."

"*Great.* What's he saying?"

"When peoples asking about you, Frank's saying, well, all I know is I did some business with him on some hot stuff and he's all right far as I know."

Soon my heroin buys began picking back up and gradually resumed the previous pace.

Out of Buy Money: Taking "Me" with Me

During the heroin undercover operation on the Gulf Coast I tried to be clever and it backfired. At the time it seemed like a good idea. But it may have led to a meeting of heroin dealers to decide whether to kill me.

Bad timing. My plans for a rare relaxing day off on the breezy Gulf Coast beaches wouldn't happen. As luck would have it, minutes before on that Saturday morning, Tom, a heroin dealer from Mobile, Alabama, had stopped at a supermarket in Gulfport, Mississippi, and called me at home from a pay phone, asking for Mike, my undercover name. He had driven from Mobile to sell heroin on the coast and he knew I might buy some. We had never met but others had recommended me as a fellow dealer who would buy quantity for resale.

I was temporarily out of buy money but didn't want to miss out on making a new case. Unfortunately, caught on a weekend without cash to buy drugs, I wouldn't be able to get any more money until the banks opened Monday. In the days before ATMs there was no ready way to quickly get several hundred in cash for a drug purchase and I didn't have time to try to round it up from other agents. The more sensible response would have been to pass up the opportunity, but I knew from years of undercover work that some opportunities occur one time and one time only. If I missed this deal I might never have another chance to make a case on the Mobile heroin supplier.

Over the phone I quickly agreed to meet him, thinking that I would first try to get him to "front" me the heroin until I could pay him on his next trip to Gulfport. My hastily formed backup plan would be to try to get him to take a check. I would try to pay him with my own personal check, but it had my real name printed on it instead of my undercover name. This presented two problems. First, to convince a drug dealer who dealt in cash to accept a check for drugs, especially a check from someone he had never met. Second, to overcome suspicion caused by trying to give him a check that wasn't in my known undercover name. All these calculations and issues flashed through my mind in seconds during the phone call.

I would need someone to help carry out the check scheme. Bruce Childers, a close friend who had been an Intelligence and Narcotics officer with me years before at Baton Rouge PD happened to be visiting me for the weekend and I enlisted Bruce to help out. But we had to hurry because the dealer was waiting and I could tell by his voice over the phone that he was already nervous.

As Bruce and I reached the supermarket parking lot I spotted the car the dealer had described, a late-model, dark-gray, two-door Buick with Alabama tags, and we parked a couple of rows away. I walked to the Buick while Bruce waited in my car. As I neared the car, the dealer's eyes met mine and then swept the parking lot. He was careful.

Inside the car, quick introductions and a handshake followed with the dealer glancing nervously about the parking lot. He introduced himself as Tom. Tall and rangy with a stubble of a beard, Tom looked to be in his thirties.

"Man, I heard about you too and I heard you do good business," I assured him, "and that I can trust you. People told me when you say something is good or it weighs so much it always will be right. That's the way I am too, and I appreciate someone like you, a real businessman who does business that way." He had to agree. It not only stroked his ego but also helped calm him a little.

"Like, you know," I continued, "instead of trying to get over on someone and make fast money, when people know they can trust you on business, you make more in the long run that way."

"Yeah, that's the way I am," Tom nodded. "They told me you all right too."

"Let me see what you got," I said.

Tom scanned the lot quickly and then pulled a baggie of brown heroin out of his pocket and handed it to me.

"This some good shit, Mike."

"This been stepped on? How many times?" I asked, wanting to know if the volume had been increased by adding a cut to it.

"Only one time. Most times, shit been stepped on several times before it hits the street. This only been cut one time," he promised. "Man, this here's some good shit."

"Good. Good. 'Cause to make mine, I gotta step on it at least one time, maybe two. So I need some good shit."

"Well, this here's it, Mike."

We haggled over price and finally agreed on $650.

Now came the hard part. Tom was ready for me to pay him, but I explained I was out of cash and asked for a "front," which of course made him think I would rip him off and never pay him.

"Naw, man," Tom said, shaking his head vigorously, "I can't do that. I ain't wit' that. I don't front shit." I knew he wouldn't do it, but it was good for my cover to try. Asking for a front can help reduce suspicion because drug dealers expect that undercover agents always have money to buy drugs. An agent wouldn't show up without money and ask for a front.

Now came the hard part. "Well, look man, I don't want to miss out on this," I said. "I've already got it sold. Here's what I'll do. Since I'm out of cash right now I'll just give you a check for it."

He arched an eyebrow. "A *check!*"

"Oh, *don't worry, don't worry*," I assured him, "the check will be good. Everybody knows me, man, I've got a reputation for being straight up, and I can't afford to rip you or anybody off. You're a businessman, you know what I mean." His brows were furrowed but he nodded in agreement.

Now the hardest part.

"One thing, man, I don't want my name on the check," I explained. He gave me a quizzical look. "See, if my name is not on the check then nobody can link me and you together, see what I mean?" That made a little sense to him.

"So, you see my friend in my car over there?" I said, pointing toward my car. He looked at Bruce sitting in the passenger seat. "Well, that's my friend Charlie Spillers. We do business together and he sometimes backs me when I'm short. I'll get Charlie to write a check to you. That way my name won't be on the check and you and I can't be connected together. You won't even have to meet him. I'll get the check for you. I guarantee the check will be good. How does that sound?"

"Well, yeah, I guess so," he said tentatively.

"And not only that, I'll have Charlie make out the check for $650 and sign it, but leave the line blank for who it's to and you can fill that in yourself with whatever name you want. That way he doesn't even know your name and it's safer that way for both of us."

That made sense as long as he didn't think about it. I was fast-talking like a carnival barker doing a sleight of hand, but trying to make the pitch sound reasonable.

"And don't worry, the check will be good, *I guarantee it.*"

Don't stop now. Keep the momentum going.

"Here, you hold onto this," I said, handing the heroin back to him, "while I go get Charlie to write out the check. Be right back."

I rejoined Bruce. "Bruce, quick," I put my checkbook on the seat between us, "look down at the seat between us and act like you're writing out a check."

As he did so, I wrote out the check, then looked up and nodded at Bruce like I was getting it from him.

I returned to Tom and handed him the check. The account holder printed on the check was "Charles W. Spillers" with a post office box address in Gulfport. "See," I pointed to my name on the check and then to the amount, "it's from my friend Charlie Spillers for $650. Later you can write in the name of the person it is to." He handed me the heroin. We shook and I left, elated at making a buy that ordinarily couldn't have been made.

It seemed like a good idea at the time.

You can only go so long making undercover buys in an area until dealers might happen to compare notes about you and realize that you were supposedly a heroin dealer too but you never sold heroin to anyone they knew of.

The MBN office on the coast was in a multistory office building in Gulfport. There was a bank on the ground floor and the office was discreetly located on one of the upper stories behind a secured, unmarked door. I could easily slip into the office unnoticed a few times a week to write reports of buys and to process evidence for the lab. If anyone saw me go into the building, they would assume I went to the bank. I spent little time at the office, just long enough to take care of reports and evidence, and then would slip out again.

Brenda Breaux was the secretary. Remarkably efficient, Brenda was a smart, attractive woman who was a cheerful presence in the office. She made the office an inviting and comforting place, a brief respite from my undercover role.

A couple of months had gone by after making the buy with the check. I had been rolling hard, making several heroin buys each week, accumulating cases on more and more coast dealers. It was dark when I picked up my informant, Jim, on a deserted street several blocks from his house. In his late thirties, Jim stood just over six feet on a lean, almost thin, frame. He hurried to the car, looking around to see if anyone saw us together, which was not a good sign since being seen together normally wouldn't be a problem. As far as the dealers knew, we were good friends and Jim had vouched for me when I first showed up in the drug trade. He used the cover that we had done time together at the federal pen at Atlanta, and I could be trusted. Now he was clearly nervous and agitated. "What's wrong, Jim?" "Mannnn, Mike, you got some heat on *you*." He was shaking and tension made his voice high-pitched and cracking. "I'm talking 'bout some mutherfuckin' heat."

"What's going on?"

"Man, Mike, they asking questions about you, a lot of questions, man! Whoooo, man, goddammit." He shook his head side to side to emphasize the point, also signaling he thought everything was hopeless. He was hunched over, defeated. He looked over at me.

"Mike, you hot as a *mutherfucker*. And these mutherfuckers ain't *playing*. They'll hurt ya." He was talking to himself as much as to me.

"Who? Who's asking questions?"

"Sting, Frank, Smooth, the whole bunch, Mike! They came to see me. Man, these mutherfuckers stirred up and . . ."

"What kind of questions?"

"Man, they wanna know how long I knowed you, how we met, where you living, who you sell to, all kinda shit. They know your real name! They asked me who's Charles Spillers? Who's Charles Spillers?" Jim was trembling. "These mutherfuckers even looking at me funny." Shaking his head, staring at his lap, "I knew I shouldna done this, I knew it! Shit, man. Goddammit!" His whole world was crashing. This was the worst thing that could have happened. He had pushed the possibility to the back of his mind while everything was rolling smoothly, but now . . .

"What you tell them?"

"I told them *I don't know no Charles Spillers*, and they said, well, he was with Mike on a deal. I said, well, I don't know him."

"Jim. Jim, hey man, it'll blow over." I needed to calm him down and keep him on my side. If it was a choice between me and him, he might set me up for them to prove himself.

"But—," he protested. I cut him off, trying to get him under control.

"Jim, these things happen, you know that. Remember when everybody was scared of that guy Spider, but that blew over didn't it? They all thought he was giving information to the police, remember? Everybody gets suspicious of everybody at some point. It don't mean nothing."

"Yeah, but . . ."

"Plus, they don't know anything about me and they can't find out anything because no one knows I'm the heat. The police don't know, no one knows, only you and other MBN agents. So there's no way they can find out that I'm the heat. They just guessing."

"And no one's been busted, have they?" That struck a chord with him. A glimmer of hope. "Have they?"

"Well, naw . . ."

"That's the key thing. Remind them ain't no one been busted. You see, they just guessing."

"Well . . ."

"Here's what you do." I told him to start rumors that two of the other dealers were working for the police. That would help dilute the significance of any suspicions being circulated about me—if there was word going around on several people then it wouldn't mean much on anyone.

"One more thing, Jim. If anyone says something to you about me or about you being the police, then you say, 'Man, I heard the same thing about you!' Understand?"

I dropped off a still-shaken Jim.

The next day, Brenda Breaux answered a call at the office. Just a routine call and she didn't know I had heat on me. The caller had gotten my real name from the personal check I had given for heroin.

"MBN, may I help you?" said Brenda.

"Yeah, I'm calling for Charles Spillers." Brenda's normal and instantaneous response would have been to say, "He's not here right now. Can I take a message?" Because I was undercover, the only people who might call for me were fellow agents or headquarters, but they would ask for Charlie, not Charles, unless it was another agency trying to reach me.

Brenda hesitated, "Who?"

"Charles Spillers. Is Charles Spillers there?" She heard street noise in the background and thought the caller might be using a pay phone.

"Who are you? What do you want?"

"I wanna talk to Charles Spillers." Acting on instinct, she made a crucial decision.

"Charles Spillers? There's nobody here by that name," she replied. "You must have the wrong number."

Click. The caller hung up.

It would have been natural for Brenda to have responded that Charles Spillers wasn't there at the moment, which would have confirmed that I was an agent. She called me at home right away and told me about the call. I knew immediately it had to have been one of the dealers. Her usual response to someone calling for me could have been lethal and a shiver ran down my spine. Without Brenda's quick thinking, they would have been certain I was the police and I would have unknowingly walked into a trap the next time I went out on the streets for a heroin deal.

It was a close call. Too close. Sometimes an undercover agent may have a close call and never know it, never know how close he came to being injured or killed. And I wouldn't have known it if she had not told me about the call and her response. In Vietnam, "grasshoppers" defined one close call, which was measured in inches. Here, the close call was measured in words—six beautiful, meaningful words that comprised of Brenda's quick-thinking, instinctive response to the caller: "There's nobody here by that name."

After Brenda warned me about the caller asking for "Charles Spillers," I called Jim and warned him about it. We agreed it had been a close call—for me and for Jim since he had vouched for me. We were still uncertain about whether this would put suspicions about me to rest, but it should help. I told Jim to get out and visit his friends and go by the joints to see if he could pick up any word on the streets. Jim called me back late that night.

"I found out that some of the peoples who sold shit to you, they had a meeting about you, the night before that phone call to your office. The call where they asked for Charles Spillers."

"About me? A meeting about me?"

"Yeah. They was talking about if you the heat and if you are, about if they gonna kill you."

"So what happened at the meeting? Do you know?"

"I heard it got pretty heated. Some of them argued that you the heat and some others spoke up for you, saying you ain't. They got pretty mutherfucking hot, what I hear, and they couldn't agree on you. Musta been after that that somebody decided to call your office to see."

"How about now, Jim? Any idea how things are since the call to the MBN office?"

"Far as I can tell, things seem okay," he paused, "but I don't know."

"All right, Jim, good work. Look, I've got an idea. Let me make a call and I'll call you back."

I called Jeris, one of the guys I had bought from.

"Yeah," Jeris answered.

"Hey, man, it's Mike," I said.

"Yo' man, wazzup?"

"If you're interested, man, a dude I know, he got some white stuff in. Some good shit. He's only letting it go in L-Bs. If you want one, I can get you an L-B for seventeen five. But if you gonna want some, you need to let me know tonight 'cause it won't last long before it's all gone. We moving it fast."

"Well Mike, seventeen-five, I don't know. I—"

"Man, this is some good shit, Jeris. Some good shit."

"Well, I ain't gonna be able to handle that. At least right now."

"How about checking with dudes you know, man, and see if anybody wants an L-B, okay? But I need to know quick."

"All right, Mike, I'll do that."

"Good. Later, man."

"Later."

I had just offered to sell Jeris a pound of cocaine for $17,500. That should help dispel suspicions about me, I thought. I called Jim back and told him about my talk with Jeris. I told Jim to let people know that I had just moved some pounds of coke. By insisting that the cocaine could only go in quantities of one pound or more and by charging a higher-than-normal price, I knew no one was likely take me up on the offer. I gave a short time frame to limit the possibility that people would have sufficient time to pool their money. As a last resort, if anyone did want to buy a pound of cocaine, I would call them back with news that the source had just sold out. As expected, no one took me up on the offer of cocaine and it helped allay suspicions about me.

With Brenda's quick thinking and the cocaine ploy, things cooled down and I was soon buying heroin again.

Taking "me" with me on the heroin buy was a wild scheme. I was sometimes bold and audacious, but this may have been pushing it too far. Ironically, while working undercover I always pretended to be someone else, but this time I pretended that someone else was actually me. And it didn't work out very well. Fortunately Brenda Breaux kept it from turning disastrous. I'm still in her debt for saving me from myself.

After many long months, the Gulf Coast undercover operation concluded with teams of agents and investigators arresting many dozens of heroin dealers on the Gulf Coast, along with several suppliers from Mobile and New Orleans.

When I first started working on the coast, we intended to permanently transfer and Evelyn and I moved from Jackson to Long Beach. Terry was taken out of school in Jackson and enrolled in school in Gulfport and Evelyn went job hunting again. Months later we purchased a new home in the Orange Grove subdivision north of Gulfport. Because of my undercover work, we didn't tell our neighbors where I worked. To cover my odd hours of coming and going at home, Evelyn told the neighbors that I was doing research to earn a PhD and we were living on her salary, a stipend, and money we had inherited. The neighbors had to wonder though when I started driving the big Lincoln and when they saw young agents sometimes meet me at home. When the undercover operation finally concluded, it was front-page news and covered by the local television news programs. When our neighbors learned I was an agent who had been working undercover, their responses to Evelyn were nearly always the same: "I knew it! I knew it! I knew he either had to be a drug dealer or a narc!" They were relieved it was not the former.

6

MBN INTELLIGENCE

MBN Intelligence

After working undercover in the heroin operation on the Gulf Coast, I transferred to MBN Intelligence in Jackson and worked at headquarters under Claude Stuckey, a former military intelligence officer who had developed MBN Intelligence into a professional, cutting-edge unit. Claude's enthusiasm, sense of humor, and professionalism were infectious, and I think he appreciated my extensive field experience as a valuable addition to the unit. MBN was respected nationwide as one of the premier state drug agencies in the country, and under Claude's leadership, MBN Intelligence was the bureau's jewel.

At that time, being an agent in Intelligence at MBN headquarters primarily consisted of supporting the agents in the field with tactical and strategic intelligence. Each week Intelligence received numerous written and telephoned requests from MBN agents, other agencies, and states, sometimes urgent, for information on suspects or organizations. For example, an agent might request help in identifying a white male known as "Red" who sold drugs in the Delta and drove a blue pickup truck. Another might request any information from Georgia or South Carolina on someone called "Big Ed" who sold heroin and reportedly did time in one of those states. A third might want to know if there was any information on an organization nationwide known as "Peashooter." We prided ourselves in quickly producing the requested information and in supplying more than requested. To the agent who requested help identifying "Red," for example, we might discover and provide Red's full name, biographical data, address, phone numbers, driver's license information, criminal history, vehicles associated with him, his criminal history and associates, and a summary of intelligence reports pertaining to him.

The key to producing a wealth of valuable intelligence quickly lay in our extensive database of intelligence reports generated by agents, and in our personal contacts with intelligence units in other states. MBN

Intelligence had an immense database of intelligence reports concerning not only drug traffickers, but also career criminals in other fields, corruption, and criminal organizations, including the Mafia and the "Dixie Mafia." Street agents were also regarded as intelligence collectors and they regularly generated intelligence reports.

The most valuable information came from thorough debriefings of every informant. As part of the process of officially "coding" new informants, an agent was required to debrief the informant using a debriefing outline filled with more than thirty pages of questions. The debriefings covered every conceivable crime and subject, including drug trafficking, air and marine smuggling, homicides, gangs, aggravated assaults, burglaries, drugstore burglaries, firearms trafficking, armed robberies, labor racketeering, gambling, auto theft, fraud, corrupt law-enforcement officers and public officials, organized crime, illegal possession of machine guns and explosives, and diversion of drugs by pharmacists, physicians, and nurses. The debriefings were recorded and transcribed, and the lengthy transcripts were filed and indexed for quick access to particular information. Intelligence was also indexed by subjects' names, organizations, and criminal activities. In addition, agents regularly generated reports on every bit of information informants reported from the field.

MBN Intelligence permitted access to reports only on a "need-to-know" basis. As further security, reports were stamped with different levels of security classifications: unclassified, confidential, secret, and top secret. Reports with higher-security classifications required more secure storage and restricted access. Secret and top secret reports often contained sensitive information about allegedly corrupt public officials—including sheriffs, district attorneys, judges, legislators, and governors.

MBN intelligence on corrupt officials was so extensive, detailed, and sensitive that when one particular governor-elect was about to go into office, MBN spirited a mass of intelligence files from MBN headquarters and secretly hid the files in a storage unit. We were concerned that as governor he might try to access the files—which included allegations about him and his associates.

We also compiled a separate intelligence file for each county in the state, with duplicate copies of every intelligence and offense report pertaining to that county. Thus, a "county file" would contain detailed information on all intelligence and criminal activity pertaining to the county. When I was going to work undercover in different areas of the state, I would first go by MBN Intelligence and read the county files for the area. I found them helpful in forming a picture of the main drug traffickers and their associates, and in identifying career criminals, crime organizations, and corrupt law-enforcement officers and officials. If a particular intelligence report from a coded informant seemed especially relevant, I could contact the agent who obtained the information and ask for more information or request that follow-up questions be put to the informant.

Our contacts with other agencies were invaluable and we developed sources nationwide with state police agencies and intelligence units. I typically had regular contacts each week with agents and analysts with Texas DPS Intelligence and DPS Narcotics, the Georgia Bureau of Investigation (GBI), the South Carolina Department of Law Enforcement (SLED), the Alabama Bureau of Investigation (ABI), the Tennessee Bureau of Investigation (TBI), Illinois Bureau of Investigation (IBI), the Florida Department of Law Enforcement (FDLE), the North Carolina State Bureau of Investigation (NC SBI), as well as agencies in other states, the FBI, DEA, Customs, and regional law-enforcement groups such as the Regional Organized Crime Information Center (ROCIC).

My transfer to Intelligence meant another move for our family. We sold our home on the coast and moved back to Jackson, where we rented an apartment. Terry was uprooted again, changing schools, and Evelyn again went job hunting. MBN was a close-knit family, and agents and their spouses were a support network of friends that welcomed us back to Jackson.

The Strip Club Bartender

Under Claude Stuckey's leadership, MBN Intelligence conducted some "special projects." One such project was a deep secret even within MBN—Intelligence ran its own deep-cover operation, a dangerous and successful adventure that lasted two years. Under Claude's direction, new MBN agent Richard Allison infiltrated a group of career criminals on the Gulf Coast, working for them as a bartender in a strip joint and helping run their used-car lot, gathering invaluable intelligence in the process.

Before anyone could learn that Richard was with MBN, Claude asked him to volunteer for a deep-cover assignment on the Gulf Coast. Richard did readily, but with some trepidation, knowing what difficult challenges he would face. The coast was notorious for crime and corruption. The mission was to be a purely intelligence-gathering operation targeted against the Dixie Mafia and other career criminals who operated freely on the coast, especially in Biloxi and Gulfport, in an area of joints and strip clubs known as "the strip." Criminals on the coast had an ally in the Harrison county sheriff, Leroy Hobbs, who was later convicted on federal corruption charges. Elements of organized crime operated along the coast, with the Carlos Marcello family, based in New Orleans, and the Traficant family, based in Florida, sharing the area.

It was extremely hostile territory for an undercover agent. The targets were dangerous and Richard's only hope of success—and survival—lay in complete secrecy. He worked alone, without backup. Except for his brother Pete, a Secret Service agent stationed outside Mississippi, even Richard's own family didn't know he was an MBN agent. Claude didn't want to take a chance that a family member or friend might unintentionally confide in the wrong person about Richard's work. For his own safety, his cover had to be complete and unassailable.

Working "cold"—without an informant—and completely alone to take on the fearsome Dixie Mafia was an intimidating undertaking, but Richard turned out to be ideally suited for the assignment. He first got a job as a bartender at White Pillars in Biloxi and through that work met Blackie and Sonny (not their real names), who were among the targets of the operation. Sonny owned a used-car lot, and with Blackie and Sheriff Hobbs had a strip joint called "Blackie's" (not its real name). Because Sonny was an ex-con and couldn't get a liquor license, Blackie fronted as the owner with the sheriff as a silent partner. Sonny and Blackie asked Richard to go to work for them as a bartender at Blackie's—a golden opportunity—and Richard jumped at it.

Soon Richard was not only bartending at Blackie's, he was also working for Sonny at his used-car lot. Sonny owned several small house trailers clustered right behind the used-car lot. Richard began living in one of the trailers, which was ideal for intelligence gathering. The other trailers were used mostly by prostitutes and strippers who worked for Sonny and Blackie. Dixie Mafia and other criminals sometimes stayed in the trailers when coming through the area or hiding out.

With the constant action at the strip joint, the car lot, and the trailers, Richard stayed busy documenting conversations, license-plate numbers, names, events, and the comings and goings of Blackie, Sonny, and their numerous criminal colleagues. On a couple of occasions he saw the sheriff meet with Blackie and pick up a white envelope.

Richard was in the middle of everything, but it was dangerous and he could never relax. As Richard later described it, he literally tried to sleep with one eye open. It was an unnerving assignment, one that would be stressful for even a short period, but Richard did it nonstop for a full year. Following a ten-week break to attend a DEA narcotics course in Washington, Richard volunteered to go back for a second year.

Like any undercover operation, with the opportunities came problems. Richard called Claude about one: "Claude, some of Jane's girls just came by the club. They want me to hook them up with some johns." Jane (not her real name) ran another strip club and some of the women who worked for her also operated as prostitutes.

"Great! That's great!" Claude exclaimed. Claude saw it as an opportunity for Richard to work himself in even closer.

"But Claude," Richard protested, "if I do that, aren't we breaking about a dozen or so federal laws?"

"Heck," Claude laughed, "I don't know about that. Anyway, who's going to report it?"

Richard began hooking the girls up with some of the customers at Blackie's, which helped increase his acceptance along the coast.

One day another problem arose: Richard was arrested. Blackie had forgotten to renew his liquor license and state ABC agents raided the club and arrested all the employees, including Richard. After being booked and fingerprinted, Richard was released along with the others. While the arrest was good for his cover, it presented a serious problem. Because it was a deep-cover operation, neither the ABC nor any other law-enforcement agencies were made aware that Richard was an undercover agent. As usual, in order to prevent an inadvertent disclosure of undercover activities, only those with a real "need to know" were brought into secret operations. The ABC would find out, however, when the FBI processed Richard's arrest fingerprints. A routine fingerprint report from the FBI to ABC would reveal that Richard's prints had been previously processed as an applicant and an employee of MBN. If that happened, Richard would have to be pulled out of the assignment immediately because of the risk of compromise.

Claude scrambled to contain the damage. It wasn't easy, but he was finally able to get the FBI to send another fingerprint report on Richard to the ABC, one that did not contain information about Richard's employment with MBN.

During his two years undercover, Richard had collected a tremendous amount of valuable intelligence about crime and corruption on the coast, and he had done it alone and at great risk. He had performed heroically in an intense and dangerous assignment. Like others in law enforcement, he didn't do it for money or acclaim or recognition, but because it needed to be done. Except for a small number of people within MBN, his remarkable deep-cover work has never been known or recognized—until now.

7
NORTH MISSISSIPPI

Undercover Operations

Pizza, Beer, and Cocaine

MBN operations ran its own deep-cover operations, some of which were in north Mississippi. MBN went into the bar business. We opened and ran our own beer joints, The Hut in Columbus and later the Pizza Haze at Southaven. Undercover MBN agents and informants managed the bars, served as bartenders, made pizzas, and waited on tables. Agents sold beer and bought cocaine.

Jim Wallace, the MBN regional commander for north Mississippi (who later became MBN director), was innovative and the idea of opening and running our own bar as an undercover front appealed to him. We didn't buy or lease an existing bar, but instead started from scratch. Going into the bar business required finding a location, renovating a building, obtaining bar equipment, signs, glasses, mops, brooms, shelves, tables, chairs, beer coolers, beer taps and stocks of beer, and obtaining permits and licenses—and doing it all in undercover names or informants' names while preserving the secret that the bars were MBN undercover fronts. Just one small leak and the operation would be compromised along with all the work, time, and money that went into it.

At our first bar, The Hut in Columbus, a crisis developed just before it was to open. Jim Wallace was not only the regional commander; he was also our tech man. The evening before the bar was to open Jim parked at the rear door of the bar and he and agent Mike Tyson removed video and audio equipment from the trunk of his car and carried the gear into a small office in the back of the bar. Working quickly, Jim rigged the office with a two-way mirror and a concealed video camera for recording drug buys. Upon entering the office with a drug dealer, an undercover agent could activate the video camera with a hidden switch. Jim and Mike were about to test the equipment when two drug dealers Mike had met in

Columbus wandered into the bar by the open back door, squeezing right past Wallace's big police car. Although the car was unmarked, it was an obvious police car, a big dark blue Ford Crown Vic, the sedan commonly used by most police departments and state police agencies at the time. Wallace's car not only looked like a police car, it sported a forest of radio antennas on the trunk. Wallace had so many police radios that his car resembled a Russian trawler, a spy vessel used to monitor US communications off our coast.

As the two men walked into the bar, Wallace quickly hid and Mike ushered them into the office. Anxious and tense, Mike got ready to parry onslaughts of suspicious questions about the car as best he could. As it turned out, the two men were oblivious to Wallace's police car, and the planned test of the equipment turned out to be an actual drug sale instead. It was just the first of many, many drug sales recorded on video. After selling drugs to Mike, the men left by the back door and again squeezed past Wallace's car. Undercover operations need luck to succeed and this operation was clearly favored from the start. The only explanation for the narrow escape was that it was inconceivable that a bar would be an undercover front and the men apparently assumed the police must have parked at the bar and gone into another nearby business.

As hoped, agents working at The Hut made numerous undercover drug purchases, all duly recorded on video. After many months, the operation was concluded with a big roundup. Teams of agents fanned out in the Columbus area and rounded up dozens of drug dealers who had sold drugs at the bar. Following the success of the Columbus operation, we opened a beer and pizza bar in Southaven, the Pizza Haze, and it too proved productive. MBN agents were again selling beer and buying cocaine and other drugs.

One key to these successful fronts was our main informant, Harry (not his real name). A large, silver-haired man in his late forties, Harry was handsome, intelligent, and charismatic. Harry was a professional informant. He had assisted the DEA in major cases in Texas and now he was circulating to state drug agencies across the nation. MBN was highly respected by the DEA and state law-enforcement agencies in other states, and they often referred professional informants to us. Harry and his sidekick, D. J. (not his real name either), were among the very best. Harry and D. J. knew more about making drug cases and doing it professionally than most agents. They knew the importance of marking evidence, maintaining the chain of evidence, climbing the ladder to get to higher-level suppliers, eliciting incriminating comments from drug dealers, and avoiding any hint of entrapment. When Harry and D. J. helped make a case, the case was solid and was a certain guilty plea. They were professionals and as good as informants get. Working with them was like working with fellow agents.

As the Pizza Haze undercover operation at Southaven neared its end, the DEA warned MBN that a drug-trafficking organization in Texas had put out a contract to kill Harry. Harry had helped the DEA on a big case in Texas, and through a wiretap and informants, the DEA learned that the drug organization had ordered a hit on him. The danger was taken seriously and MBN district supervisor Jerry Dettman gave agent Mike Tyson a special assignment at the Pizza Haze, where Harry was working. "There's a contract on Harry and a hit man is gunning for him," Jerry told Mike. "I want you to sit at a table in a corner inside the bar with your gun ready. Watch the door and sit there like you're eating pizza. If anyone comes in and tries to kill Harry," Jerry said, "*you kill him.*"

Mike realized the import of his assignment. Although MBN agents were attracted to the excitement of undercover work and the dangers and the opportunity to do something meaningful, this was an eye-opener for Mike. But Dettman had chosen well. Although young, Mike Tyson was mature beyond his years, fearless and astute, perfect for the assignment of protecting Harry. Fortunately, no one tracked Harry down to the Pizza Haze and the only damage was to Mike's waistline from eating so much pizza. Mike eventually left MBN for US Customs and went on to an illustrious career, including an undercover role on smuggling boats picking up large shipments of cocaine and marijuana off the coast of Colombia from the drug cartels.

After the Pizza Haze closed down with dozens of arrests, MBN finally went out of the bar business. The front operations were successful, but word eventually began spreading about the new MBN tactic. The large investments of time and money and the increased risk of compromise outweighed the advantages. The informants, Harry and D. J., moved on to assist other MBN undercover operations around the state. Harry was still going strong and helping MBN when he was killed. He had eluded hit men—only to be killed in a plane crash.

The Radio Disc Jockey

In addition to operating its own bars in Columbus and Southaven, MBN also ran a deep-cover operation in the Tupelo area. MBN agent Dennis "Mac" McAnally worked undercover as a radio disc jockey for a popular station in the Tupelo area. Mac had worked as a radio disc jockey while going to college, and when he joined MBN, the bureau arranged for the FCC to issue a license in Mac's undercover name. It was a perfect cover: no one would suspect that a disc jockey would be an agent and drug networks readily accepted him into their midst.

A graduate of Delta State University, Mac was blessed with good looks, a charming smile, quick wit, and a cool head. A little under medium height, Mac had reddish-blond hair and sparkling blue eyes that hinted at humor and mischief. He was likeable and his role as a disc jockey made him even more popular.

Operating deep cover, Mac first went to work as a disc jockey at a radio station in Water Valley. Then he was hired as a disc jockey by a popular Tupelo FM radio station, which wasn't aware that he was an agent using the job as a cover. With his deep, resonating radio voice and quick wit, Mac quickly gained a wide audience. Using the radio name "Mac McAnally," he became one of the station's most popular disc jockeys.

MBN and the Tennessee Bureau of Investigation (TBI) arranged for TBI undercover agent Donna Pence to occasionally join Mac undercover in Tupelo, where she would circulate with Mac as his girlfriend. After his daily radio show, they would patronize the bars and make drug buys together.

Donna was unique in a couple of ways. She had been trained in knife fighting by her husband, a SWAT officer in a large police department in eastern Tennessee, and she carried a dagger concealed in a holster held by a harness in the middle of her upper back. Donna's martial skill was welcome because of the dangers she and Mac faced. Mac brought his own martial skills to the job—he was a black belt in karate.

Donna was also a master of disguises and roles. Like an actress, she had a portfolio of photographs of herself. Each portrayed her in a different role. In one she was a demure, conservatively dressed secretary in horn-rimmed glasses and a brunette wig. In another, she was a young woman appearing to be eight or nine months pregnant. She was a corporate executive in one photo, a bleached blonde bar girl in another, and a nightclub stripper in yet another. Using a combination of wigs, makeup, props, and clothing, she had more than a dozen disguises, all different and all convincing.

For Mac, the undercover operation was grueling, nonstop work. Between the full-time cover job as a radio disc jockey and his undercover work, Mac averaged over one hundred total work hours per week and seldom had a day off. The operation went smoothly and after many months it concluded with a roundup of dozens of drug dealers, which came as a shock to the dealers and a surprise to his radio audience. Mac finally got some long-overdue rest and then resumed undercover work elsewhere, although not as a disc jockey. MBN had retired its one and only radio disc jockey, along with its bars.

■ ■ ■

In an undercover operation to infiltrate the Banditos motorcycle gang, agent Steve Campbell reported to a state probation officer for a year while posing as a convicted felon on probation. Steve's state probation officer was unaware of Steve's true role. Only MBN, the commissioner of state probation and parole, and his deputy were aware of the undercover operation. For a year Steve met with his probation officer once a month, was drug-tested each time, and had to sit through probation interviews. Through the probation visits, Steve developed a friendship with another probationer, one of the "ole ladies" in the Banditos motorcycle gang, and she introduced him to Bandito gang members.

Agents Sara Niell and Shelby Boles worked full time for four months as bar girls at a lounge in Meridian, which led to making drug purchases. They initially stayed in a motel, lounging around the pool during the day and going out all night to work at the bar and make undercover drug purchases. But the manager thought the two young women were prostitutes and kicked them out. They got an apartment and continued their bar and drug work.

Other agents also briefly worked cover jobs. Agent Steve Mallory worked cover jobs with a wholesale grocery distributor in Jackson, a construction company, and a meat-packing company for short periods. Agent Jim Walker worked at a service station in Senatobia. The tractor-trailer truck seized in the *Gulf Stream* drug-smuggling case was forfeited to the MBN and agent Mike Tyson and an informant drove it around the state to infiltrate drug-trafficking rings operating out of truck stops.

Infiltrating drug trafficking in small towns in the state was especially difficult because local drug dealers were suspicious of newcomers. Consequently, an undercover agent would need a plausible excuse for showing up in the area. One undercover agent who wanted to circulate among several small towns came up with an ingenious idea to explain his presence at local honky-tonks frequented by drug dealers. He purchased cases of yo-yos, stacked them in his car, and drove from town to town as a yo-yo distributor to small stores. He actually sold to some stores and was eventually accepted by drug dealers, who thought he was just the regional yo-yo salesman. "Oh yeah, that's the yo-yo guy," said some, just before they sold drugs to him. Undercover agents had to be creative and resourceful in order to succeed.

But to survive was another matter, as some agents found out.

Sara: The Ambush and the "Arizona Territory"

After Sara and I worked together undercover in Jackson, we split up and headed to different parts of the state. She eventually began working northeast Mississippi while I went to work around Natchez, Vicksburg, and McComb, and then to the Mississippi Gulf Coast, and finally to Intelligence in Jackson. Her work proved much more dangerous than mine.

On the Sunday after Thanksgiving, Sara and fellow undercover agent Jerry Dettman drove through sleet on a deserted country road outside Columbus to meet a drug dealer named Jimmy Ray for a heroin buy. Somewhere along the icy road, Ray would be waiting in his pickup truck, parked on the roadside. As they drove farther and farther past barren fields, ice crystals pelted the windshield and frosted the edges, the incessant tapping accompanied by grinding and scraping windshield wipers. Wooly mists and dark-gray gloom turned afternoon into dusk, shrouding empty fields and dim tree lines in a thick veil and increasing the agents' sense of isolation. The desolate surroundings were chilling reminders that regardless of how close other agents might be to provide surveillance, undercover agents are all alone at critical times—if a deal erupts in violence, it would be over in seconds, much too quickly for help to arrive. A gun comes out in a blur of motion and a bullet suddenly bursts a heart, shatters a lung, or explodes a head. In those first decisive seconds, undercover agents are on their own. Agents conducted surveillance including DEA agent Tom Dial and several MBN agents. But they couldn't follow Jerry and Sara closely because the road stretched out flat with long, straight stretches, making it too easy for anyone to spot their cars from a long distance.

Sara and Jerry didn't know exactly where the deal would take place. Ray had told Jerry to drive along the road until he saw Ray's pickup truck parked on the roadside and they would do the deal there. They had $10,000 with them to show Ray. The plan was to buy four ounces of heroin from Ray and arrest him during the deal, a buy-bust.

The two agents knew that buy-busts are more dangerous than regular drug deals. When large quantities of drugs and substantial sums of money are involved, drug dealers will likely be armed to protect their drugs from a rip-off or to rob the buyer. The dealer will be especially wary, watching the undercover more closely than usual and scrutinizing the surroundings for anything suspicious. The dealer may also have men conducting surveillance of the buy location to watch for the police. For that reason, agents try to choose and control the location where the buy-bust will take place, or at least know the location in advance so that agents can get there before the deal to spot countersurveillance and to watch the drug dealer when he arrives. Now, however, because Jerry and Sara didn't know where the deal would occur, the agents had neither option.

Their disadvantage was counterbalanced somewhat by the fact that the drug deal would take place on a public road and in broad daylight, factors that can lessen, but not eliminate, the likelihood that the violators will try to rob or kill the undercover agents.

Through the pelting sleet, Jerry and Sara finally spotted Ray's pickup parked on the side of the road and Jerry pulled to a stop on the opposite shoulder. The road was built up high off the surrounding fields, with steep embankments plunging down both sides of the road. The surrounding fields were flat and bare except for a small patch of bushes and trees about fifty yards from the road on Ray's side. The road was deserted and no houses were in sight.

While Sara waited in the car, Jerry got out and met Ray in the middle of the road for the deal. Ray gave him the heroin, Jerry handed the buy money to Ray, and when he took it, Jerry whipped out his gun.

"*Police!* You're under arrest!" Jerry shouted. "Get your hands up!" Ray suddenly screamed, "*Don't shoot!* Don't *anybody* shoot! Don't *anybody* shoot!" Jerry realized it was a trap and he dropped into a crouch. Ray's brother, Johnny, was hidden in ambush in the bushes on Ray's side of the road. He aimed a .30-caliber rifle at Jerry and pulled the trigger.

A rifle shot cracked and the bullet hit the road in front of Jerry and ricocheted up, cutting a deep groove in the crease where his left leg and buttock joined. Despite being wounded, Jerry started firing toward the bushes and trees. Gripping her pistol, Sara jumped out of the car and as she did, a second rifle shot cracked, hitting Jerry in the ribs and spinning him around from the impact. Although Jerry wore a bullet-resistant vest, it wouldn't stop a rifle bullet, but it diverted the bullet's path and prevented it from blowing a hole through his chest and lungs. The rifle bullet penetrated the vest, tore across Jerry's chest just underneath the skin, and exited near his left nipple, leaving a trail of bullet fragments in his chest. A third bullet hit his forearm, ripped away a large chunk of muscle and flesh, and lodged in the vest.

Stunned from the shock of the bullets, Jerry staggered in the road trying to stay upright. Sara jumped out of the car and rushed to help him. As she ran around the front of the car, she saw Jimmy Ray reaching into a pocket, apparently going for a gun. She snapped a quick shot at Ray with her .38 pistol, hitting his money hand. Ray howled as the bullet shattered his hand, and bloody buy money fluttered in the icy wind.

Jimmy Ray was wounded but Johnny Ray kept firing. In rushing to help Jerry, Sara ran into the killing zone, fully exposed to the shooter.

Grabbing Jerry, Sara helped him stay upright and tugged him away from the shooter's side of the road and toward the opposite side, trying desperately to get to cover, out of the line of fire. She and Jerry stumbled down the steep, slippery embankment. They were out of sight but the ground was bare and they were still in the open if the men came after them. She saw thin bushes nearby and pulled Jerry until they reached them. When they fell down behind the bushes, she gripped her pistol and scanned the top of the embankment watching for the men. It was clear for the moment and she turned to Jerry to check his injuries. His chest and arm were bleeding badly and he looked bad. She decided she couldn't wait—she needed to get him to a hospital. Sara helped Jerry up and then tugged and pulled and carried him up the steep embankment. Ordinarily that would have been impossible for her, but she was aided by a surge of superhuman strength, the kind that sometimes enables people to accomplish extraordinary physical feats in critical life-threatening moments.

Sara finally reached the top of the embankment and the road with Jerry. The Rays were not in sight, and just then DEA agent Tom Dial and the MBN agents arrived. While the other agents searched for the shooter and Jimmy Ray, Sara helped Jerry into the backseat of her car and rushed toward Columbus to get him to a hospital

Jerry lay bloody and seriously injured in the backseat, but his first words were ones of relief. "Hey, Sara," he called weakly. "You know that first shot? I thought that first shot hit my privates but they're okay. It was pebbles from the road hitting me, making it feel like I was hit there. I'm okay." It was the only good thing that had happened so far—Jerry was bleeding badly but was breathing and able to talk, and concerned about his privates. It was an indication that he wasn't about to lapse into shock, a deadly condition that could quickly kill a person with lesser injuries.

Sara wasn't familiar with Columbus and the location of the hospital so she radioed the police department and the sheriff's office for directions. Hearing the radio traffic, Jerry rose up from the backseat and told Sara how to get to the hospital.

At the hospital, Sara helped Jerry inside only to find that no doctor or nurse was available. A nurse's aide showed them to a hospital room and left to find a doctor and a nurse while Sara tried to comfort Jerry.

About fifteen minutes later, Ray came through the hospital door hollering for help for his injured hand. Sara arrested him at gunpoint and made him lie down on his stomach. When she ordered him to put his hands behind his back to be handcuffed, he yelled, "Don't put them on tight, don't hurt my hand! Don't hurt my hand!" With Jerry seriously injured and bleeding badly in a room just a few feet away, Ray's whining only made Sara clamp the cuffs on extra tight, driving Ray into a fresh round of wails.

Still no doctor or nurse had come. No agents or police had arrived either and Sara was still alone. With Ray secured, she needed to check on Jerry. The only person around was an older man sitting near the entrance who sat wide-eyed and stunned by the scene. Sara turned to him. "I've gotta go in that room right there, just twenty feet away to check on my partner." Pointing to Ray, who was on his stomach, handcuffed, she said, "You watch him and if he moves just a tiny bit you holler and I'll be here in a second, okay?" The man nodded and Sara rushed back to Jerry.

Finally, a nurse came in the room, but when she saw Jerry bleeding badly from the arm and chest, she looked frightened, and Sara thought the nurse was about to faint. The nurse hurried off to find a doctor.

A doctor finally came into the room as other MBN agents began arriving. Sara stayed to look after Jerry, watch Ray, and to provide details about the shooting and Ray's arrest. The long ordeal had begun at 1:00 p.m. and it wasn't until midnight that Sara left the hospital to find a motel room and get some rest, if she could. Jerry was in good hands and other agents were staying with him.

Exhausted and numb, she trudged outside the hospital into the wintry night and found her car windshield crusted hard with a thick layer of ice. She got an extra undercover license plate out of the trunk and used it to scrape off the ice. When Sara got in the car and started the engine, she noticed that the backseat was soaked with Jerry's blood. She drove off in search of a motel. It was well after midnight and the streets were deserted.

She knew the shooter was still at large and that someone had dropped Jimmy Ray off at the hospital. Perhaps the shooter was lurking near the hospital, she thought, and she checked the rearview mirror to see if she was being followed. In light of the day's events, it was wise to be cautious. She checked into a Holiday Inn near downtown Columbus and then radioed agents at the hospital to let them know where she was. Her room was in the rear building, all the lights were out in the back parking area, and it was pitch black. As Sara went to the door of the room and fumbled at the lock with the key, a chilling fear seized her that the shooter could be stalking her. Once inside, she double-locked the door, pulled the drapes closed, and took the pistol out of her purse to keep it handy. She knew she had reloaded at the hospital but couldn't remember doing it.

When she turned on the room lights, she saw her clothes were covered with dark-red splotches of Jerry's blood.

She was exhausted, drained, and chilled to the bone. Taking the gun with her to the bathroom, she took a hot shower; the steaming water slowly thawed her and relaxed tense muscles. Relaxing her mind was not as easy. The dramas of the day swirled in an endless loop, replaying the harrowing shootout, the rush to save Jerry, and the confrontation at the hospital. She turned off the lights and tried to sleep, but tossed and turned for several hours until sleep finally came. It seemed she had slept for only a few minutes when the loud ringing of the phone woke her. It was six in the morning—she had only been asleep for two hours when Jim Wallace called from the hospital for her to relieve him. He had been up all night with Jerry.

Sara went to the hospital wearing the same bloodstained blouse and pants she had worn the day before. She spent the day at the hospital, numb and sometimes staggering from lack of sleep. Jerry had been in surgery and had more surgeries to undergo but would recover.

That night Sara drove from Columbus to Brookhaven, where she was staying at the time. Brookhaven was more than two hundred miles away and the three-hour drive seemed an eternity as she fought to stay awake at the wheel.

Johnny Ray was soon captured. The Ray brothers were convicted and sent to the state penitentiary but the Ray saga wasn't quite over. The brothers escaped from the pen. MBN went on alert because the Rays were believed to be threats to Jerry and Sara. The brothers were recaptured, but years later one escaped again and was finally apprehended in the state of Washington.

Jerry was calm and courageous in the shootout. It would take more surgeries and four months for him to recover enough to return to work. Sara's actions in the face of danger, uncertainty, and chaos were extraordinary, and were nationally recognized. She was brave, coolheaded, and selfless. But the ambush wasn't the end of her terrifying undercover experiences. The next time Sara would be completely alone. She would be going deeper into a hostile area of the state known as the "Arizona Territory" for its lawlessness.

"Tombstone"—The "Arizona Territory"

After the ambush in Columbus, Sara began working undercover in northeast Mississippi. During that time, the rural areas of northeast Mississippi where we worked seemed so lawless and violent that Sara and I referred to northeast Mississippi as "Tombstone" or the "Arizona Territory." Working undercover in the remote areas of northeast Mississippi felt like working in a hostile and alien land: the criminals were dangerous; several notorious, violent families dominated crime in certain counties; the Dixie Mafia was active; and in many areas, local law enforcement was almost nonexistent or had a reputation for being corrupt or ineffective. Good, courageous deputies and police officers worked hard to fight the criminals but we didn't know whom to trust. Even trusted local officers might not understand the need for complete secrecy about undercover operations. The danger for undercover agents didn't come as much from corrupt officers as it did from a good officer confiding in a trusted friend that an agent was undercover in the area, and then that friend telling another until the word was out on the streets and reached criminals. So, with rare exceptions, for our own safety we kept operations on a "need-to-know" basis and usually didn't let anyone outside of MBN know we were undercover in the area until the operation was over.

Moreover, surveillance was a problem. MBN agents were spread thinly around the state and even if agents were available, it was usually impossible to conduct surveillance for undercover agents operating in isolated backwoods areas and small towns. An undercover agent was pretty much on his or her own in much of the "Arizona Territory."

Sara was undercover right in the middle of it, hitting the backwoods clubs and honky-tonks. One night soon after beginning work in the area, she got an eye-opener when she saw several men go outside a honky-tonk to the gravel parking lot to fight. With Sara and the crowd watching, two of the men got chains from the trunk of a car and began beating their victims senseless. A frenzy of violence swirled in the parking lot, the night air ripped by sickening sounds of chains smacking into bodies, cracking bone and pulverizing flesh, and by frantic, animal screams and bloodthirsty yells. The men flailed away with the heavy chains even after the victims lay helpless and writhing in mangled, bloody heaps, barely conscious and moaning. The vicious beatings drove home the cruelty, violence, and lawlessness of the area. There was no law, no help. Worse than that, Sara was there to try to make cases on the most dangerous of the lot, members of a notorious and violent family in Chickasaw County.

The memory of that violent night was still fresh in Sara's mind when she was undercover at a nightclub in Tupelo in Lee County, and was introduced to two men who were part of the Chickasaw crime family, one in his twenties and the other in his forties. From the way the men acted in the bar, she saw they were bullies, used to having their way, daring anyone in the bar to oppose them. She was frightened but it was an opportunity to make a case on them.

They lured her away from the nightclub on the pretext of taking her to pick up some drugs in Tupelo. Instead, they kidnapped her and took her to a house in Chickasaw County, near the little crossroads of Houlka. Once inside the house, they took her into a bedroom and shoved her onto a bed. There was only one reason to kidnap her—rape, and possibly murder to cover up the crime. Lying helpless on the bed, Sara cringed. After throwing her onto the bed, one man looked at the other and nodded his head sideways toward the door to the next room. The men walked into the next room to plot what they were going to do next, and when they did, Sara jumped up and fled through a side door and ran for her life. Watching over her shoulder for pursuers, she made her way into the crossroads that lay silent, dark, and deserted. Alone and desperate, she didn't know where to turn—if she knocked on the door at one of the few houses it might turn out to be members of the crime family. She found a phone booth and called MBN agent Jay Moore at Oxford. He made record time driving to rescue Sara while she hid in dark shadows to keep from being found by the men.

Sara had escaped and had done so without blowing her cover, which coincidentally helped protect the role of an informant who was working with her in Tupelo. Later, Sara and other MBN agents met with a prosecutor to press charges, which could have included kidnapping, assault, and perhaps attempted rape, but the prosecutor refused. Local officials who went against the Chickasaw crime group might well fear for their own safety. The prosecutor's decision was likely based on the lack of physical evidence and having only Sara's word against that of the two men—even though agents who worked with Sara would readily stake life-and-death issues on just her word alone.

An insight into how women were treated on sex crimes was revealed when the prosecutor asked the other agents to leave the room so he could talk to Sara alone. After they left, the prosecutor turned to Sara. "Now," he said, "I need to know. Are you a virgin?" For the times, it was the customary way that prosecutors handled sex crimes, but she was speechless, offended, and outraged. After risking her life working undercover, being kidnapped and nearly raped, she felt victimized again. And the two men were never charged. It confirmed what Sara already knew—female undercover agents face more dangers and difficulties than male agents.

Working undercover in northeast Mississippi had been an ordeal and an eye-opener for Sara. She had no idea what the "Arizona Territory" would be like until she started working the area. Neither did I, but I would soon find out. I would be going to the "Arizona Territory" next.

Infiltrating Auto-Theft Rings

Gripping my pistol I sat in the dark peering out the trailer window, watching the empty drive that wound in the night past it and three other trailers, all vacant and blacked out. My car parked outside marked mine as the only one occupied. Ten minutes ago a car had driven in and slowly circled back out to the road. Now I grimly waited to see if it would come back. Although I wasn't certain, I thought a car had followed me from a meeting with auto thieves. I was still working to be accepted and perhaps they were checking me out. I gripped the gun tighter. It was hot and stuffy inside and beads of sweat dripped off my brow. I had turned the noisy window air conditioner off so that I would be able to hear a car motor, car doors opening and closing, or sounds of anyone trying to approach. After an hour I finally left the window, turned on the air conditioner, and lay down to an uneasy sleep. If my cover was holding, tomorrow would be busy—I would buy a stolen car.

If my cover was holding was a constant benchmark of danger. In churches on Sundays, pastors preached about living the "golden rule" and treating others as one would want to be treated. By stark contrast, among the groups I circulated in, men bragged, whether truthfully or not, about killing other men and about their readiness to commit murder. Among such men I had to be alert. I had been accepted by some, but others continued to be wary. "I was shaky about you for a while," one said. Another suspected I might be a federal agent until he was reassured. Referring to me, still another declared how easily "I can have him killed." Thus, my armed lookout that night in Lee County was driven by prudent caution.

I thought about how I had come to be in this position. Twists of fate drive the directions our lives take. In my case it came in the form of two angry sisters in Prentiss County, special funds left over from another investigation, and an itch to return to undercover work.

Two sisters from Prentiss County, Sadie and Patty (not their real names), had contacted MBN and reported that a thug who ran a bar near Baldwyn was selling marijuana. The sisters were rough, tough good ole gals who normally would not have anything to do with the law, but they discovered the man had sexually abused a friend's young daughter the year before. Now they wanted to help make a drug case on him. When they met with an MBN agent to provide information, it turned out that the women knew career criminals involved in auto-theft rings and "chop shops" that dismantled stolen cars for their parts.

Meanwhile, MBN agents in a specially funded undercover operation in another part of the state had tried to infiltrate theft rings but had limited success and the operation ended with $10,000 left over. At the time, I worked in Intelligence at MBN headquarters in Jackson but longed to return to undercover work. If the sisters could make some introductions, we might be able to infiltrate crime groups and use the special funds to purchase stolen vehicles. I quickly volunteered and prepared to head north to meet the sisters.

Among auto-theft investigators across the United States, northeast Mississippi was notorious for auto-theft rings and chop shops run by career criminals, including members of the "Dixie Mafia." Working my way into these tightly knit auto-theft rings would be difficult. Living in small towns and communities scattered among rolling hills, members of theft rings were longtime colleagues; some were related and many were lifelong friends, tied together through years of crime. Operating in a sparsely populated corner of the state, they knew everyone else involved in the auto-theft business or knew of them, and could easily check out anyone claiming to be from the area or in the business. They would be suspicious of outsiders. That was me.

My cover would be that I was a member of a multistate auto-theft organization based in Florida and Mobile, Alabama. Acting as a broker for the organization, I bought stolen vehicles and sent them to be chopped or resold in other states.

Though I had worked undercover for years, I wasn't familiar with the auto-theft business and therefore could easily be uncovered as a fraud. I needed to learn fast. Mississippi Highway Patrol auto-theft investigators Virgil Luke and Bob Wallace came to the rescue and briefed me about how professional thieves stole cars and switched VIN numbers, how chop shops operated, and how the professional car-theft industry worked. I might be able to bluff my way through rough spots.

There was still the problem of infiltrating established criminal groups wary of anyone new. The new informants, Sadie and Patty, would vouch for me, but they were not involved in the stolen-car business and their influence among criminals would be limited. I needed to find a way to break through.

I decided to try two ploys. One was to have Sadie and Patty talk me up around their criminal friends long before I showed up. I told the women to spread the word that their friend Mike who was in the stolen-car business in Alabama and Florida would be coming up to Mississippi in a couple of weeks. We agreed on colorful tales they could relate about Mike. I wanted the suspects to visualize me through the stories, to form a mental picture and begin thinking of me as being in the stolen-car business. I hoped my cover would be partially ingrained and they would be inclined to accept me before I showed up. This would take advantage of an important facet of human nature: once a belief is held, it is difficult to dislodge it or change to a contrary belief. Sadie and Patty threw themselves into it with relish, talking about their man Mike, spreading stories about me to cement my acceptance. In their enthusiasm, they went a little overboard when they boasted, "Mike is *bad*. Mike is *sooo bad*, he'll cut off your head and *shit down your neck*."

Spreading tales might help dampen some suspicions, but I needed to do more to be able to infiltrate cautious criminal groups. I decided to use the same ruse I had used on the Gulf Coast when a bar owner warned heroin dealers to be careful of me. After I sold "stolen" beer to the bar owner, he stopped warning dealers away and began vouching for me. It was time to go back into the stolen-goods business. Instead of starting out by trying to buy stolen vehicles, I would begin by selling stolen goods. According to Sadie and Patty, Fred (not his real name), a bail bondsman and pawn-shop owner in a small town near Tupelo, was close to some of the car-theft suspects. If I did business with him in stolen goods, he might spread the news and vouch for me.

Soon after arriving in the area, I went by Fred's pawn shop with Sadie. Fred was in his late fifties with thin brown hair, dark-rimmed glasses, and a stomach that bulged over his belt. Sadie introduced us. "Fred, I want you to meet my man Mike," Sadie said. "He's the one I told you about. I think y'all might be able to do some business together." Fred gave me a sharp, guarded look. I asked Sadie to wait in the car so Fred and I could talk privately. I watched her go out the door and then turned to him.

"Fred, I trust Sadie, but I like to keep my business private," I explained. "I don't like anyone knowing about my business that don't have to know. It's safer that way." I had signaled we were about to venture onto perilous ground. He would be taking a risk by simply talking with me.

"Yeah, hell, I'm that way too," Fred said warily. His guard was up but he probably appreciated my precautions because he wouldn't want a witness either.

"Sadie told me I can trust you and that's good enough for me. So I wanna see if you might be interested in buying brand-new televisions. My people ripped off an entire truckload of TVs. *Don't worry*," I held up a hand, "don't worry, *it wasn't around here*," I assured him, knowing the thought probably flashed through his mind that the theft of a truckload of goods would bring some heat. "It was in another state. I've got two TVs left over and just want to get rid of them. I can let you have them at a good price if you're interested."

"Well, I dunno, that depends," he said, falling into bargaining mode. "What kinda TVs? And how much you gonna want for them?"

I described the televisions. "They're still in the box," I added. "I'm not really interested in making money on it; it's the last two and I just want to move them, so I'll let you have both for, say, $120." The new TVs cost great a deal more, so for a price of $120, they were obviously stolen.

"Well," he said, rubbing his chin, "I might take them if I can get 'em both for eighty bucks."

"I tell you what, just give me a hundred and you got a deal."

"All right," he grinned, satisfied with a good bargain.

"I can bring them to you tomorrow but I don't wanna do it with anybody around. You want me to bring it here?"

"Yeah, you can bring 'em here. I close at 5:30. Can you come about six? That way nobody'll be around." We shook on it, both happy about the deal.

The next day I purchased two televisions at Walmart in Tupelo, stripped identifying store labels from the boxes, and delivered the TVs to Fred and collected the money. He was interested in doing more business with me and I told him taking off truckloads of goods was just a sideline. That led to a discussion of my main business, acquiring hot vehicles to funnel to my out-of-state organization.

I let things rest for a few days to let the word get around. Then I sought out the head of a notorious crime family located in Prentiss County. I drove to one of his businesses, introduced myself, asked to talk privately, and made him an offer. "I've got an entire truckload of new washing machines and dryers," I said. "My people took it off in another state and I wanna move the whole load at one time. You can have it at a good price if you take it all." He was interested in buying some, but I insisted on moving the entire shipment at one time and, as I expected, he declined. If he *had* been willing to buy a whole truckload, I would have quoted an unattractive price or would have gotten back with him later and explained that he was too late, it had already been sold. If I had had the resources to enhance the ruse, I would have had a tractor-trailer truck nearby packed with washers and dryers and would have taken him to see it. But I was operating pretty much on my own and had to conjure up some things out of pure imagination. The offer helped ingrain my cover and spread the word about me.

A cover also involved getting a place to live and having a contact phone number. Initially I stayed at motels in Tupelo. Later on, using my undercover name Mike Warren, I rented a house trailer in Verona, just south of Tupelo, got a telephone for the trailer, obtained a post-office box, and opened a bank account. This was before cellular phones, and the telephone was crucial: other than using pay phones, it was my only means of contacting suspects, the informants, MBN agents, and my wife and son in Jackson. Like other MBN agents working deep cover around the state, I was alone and out of contact much of the time. After getting a phone and a mailing address, I obtained business cards in the name Southern Auto, Inc.

As far as the theft rings were concerned, Southern Auto was a shell company that served as a front for my criminal business.

■   ■   ■

The ruses to infiltrate criminal groups paid off. Fred, the pawn-shop owner, introduced me to two men involved in auto theft and burglaries. Within two weeks after selling the "stolen" televisions, I made my first purchase of stolen vehicles. Late on a crisp November night, three men,

Ed, Clayton, and Robert, met me at the Ramada Inn in Tupelo with two stolen vehicles, a Ford pickup and an Oldsmobile. I purchased both for a total of $1,700. MBN agent James Newman played the role of my accomplice-driver and other agents provided surveillance. After the purchase, we drove the pickup and the Oldsmobile down the Natchez Trace to Jackson and parked them behind Mississippi Highway Patrol headquarters around 3:30 a.m. Later that day I met with Highway Patrol investigator Virgil Luke and we took the vehicles to a warehouse on Interstate 55 for storage.

I began purchasing other stolen vehicles. Each buy usually followed the same pattern: late-night deals occurring in the parking lots of motels, bars, or restaurants in Lee or Prentiss County with one or more agents acting as my accomplice-drivers, then driving the vehicles to Jackson in the early-morning hours and returning to northeast Mississippi the next day. During the first two months, I bought two Cadillacs, two Chryslers, one Chevrolet, two Ford pickups, two Ford automobiles, and one Corvette. The accomplice role players included MBN agents James Newman, Lane Caldwell, Randy Day, Rick Ward, and J. H. Newman.

Vehicle Thefts, Insurance Fraud, Arson, and Murder

Days of solitary undercover work normally preceded each purchase of a stolen vehicle. Usually working alone, I frequently dropped by suspects' homes in Prentiss and Lee Counties to find out what was going on in the criminal world. Sometimes we met at a joint or rode together to meet with others. During these daily visits and meetings, I picked up more and more intelligence as the suspects began confiding in me. They also started confiding more in the informants, Sadie and Patty. Soon, information about other criminals and crimes became a steady flow.

One night when Clayton and I rode around together, he claimed he had helped kill three men, but he wouldn't share any details. I suspected he was exaggerating his importance, but might actually know something about unsolved murders, especially when he said, "I'll shoot a man in the back. I won't shoot him in the front." That seemed more of a statement of fact than a boast. Several days later, he and his sidekick Bruce talked about the murders again when they were with Sadie and Patty. They told the women they had killed three men, and named one of the victims, a used-car dealer. They said the victim was involved with them in stolen cars and the killing arose out of a dispute about the cars. Clayton and Bruce named another man who was serving a prison sentence in Illinois as also being involved in the murder of the car dealer. They said they shot the victim in the back while he sat at a table in his house. To me, their claims of personal involvement seemed bogus, although the unsolved murders were real.

One day when I was with Robert and Clayton, one said, "You don't have to worry about the law around here."

"What do you mean?" I asked.

"'Cause we got three deputies, a police chief, and some city policemen under control." They didn't elaborate and I suspected they were exaggerating, although corruption was in fact a problem in the area.

The more I circulated with suspects, the more information it produced. For example, during one typical three-day period, it was difficult to keep up with the information coming in.

"I've got six cars lined up," one man told me. "Three will be insurance jobs," he added. In an "insurance job," the owner secretly provides the car to the thief and then falsely reports it stolen to collect insurance.

The next day, two other men told me they had a stolen heavy-duty farm tractor loaded up to take out of state. Another man told the informants the same day that he had a stolen vehicle to sell to me.

Meanwhile, Robert planned to burn down his house trailer for the insurance. He asked Sadie and Patty to rent a self-storage unit for him in Corinth so he could move his good furniture and possessions into the unit before he burned the trailer. After the arson, Robert told me how he first replaced the good stuff with a junk washing machine and dryer and old furniture before burning the trailer.

That same week, another man told the informants he had just burned down his house in Ellisville to collect the insurance. Before the arson, he removed his guns, TV, and camera equipment. He had heard that I purchased stolen items and he had eight stolen guns, all high-powered hunting rifles, that he wanted to sell to me. He had bought the rifles several months ago from another career criminal. When Sadie and Patty passed along this information, they also told me that the man made porno movies of girls who had been doped and he used the movies for blackmail. One night earlier in the week, the informants saw him in one of the joints with a fourteen-year-old girl.

Clayton, Robert, and Bruce offered to supply me with stolen heavy equipment, including large farm tractors, Caterpillars, backhoes, and diesel tractor-trailer trucks.

Sadie and Patty said they were in Lee Ann Restaurant and Lounge when a stranger came in with some money and Ed busted his face open by hitting him five or six times with a pool stick. Ed then took his money and the law was called to pick up the victim for being drunk. Later, the victim swore out a complaint against the wrong man, who was arrested and had to pay a small fine.

Leroy Pettigo, who was recently released from prison, told the informants and others at Lee Ann Restaurant and Lounge that he would kill the MBN agent who busted him if he ever saw him. I called the agents involved, Jay Moore and Eddie Berry, and warned them.

I learned one man sold a stolen gun and other hot items to Fred at the pawn shop. To find out if Fred had them, I stopped by the pawn shop and warned him there was heat on the items. Fred said he already sold the gun and it had been taken to the Gulf Coast, but he still had the other stolen goods.

Crooked Crooks

Sometimes things took a bizarre turn. I had been buying stolen cars in Prentiss County from Carl and asked him about getting a Cadillac or Lincoln. "Well, see," Carl said, "Buddy and Albert, they used to work together. They would probably be the ones coulda fixed you up with Cadillacs, but they don't get along any more. They outta the business." Carl sounded like he had a story he wanted to confide.

"But they used to get cars?"

"Yep, back when they was good friends before."

"Before what?"

"'Fore Albert got in that there car accident."

"He was in an accident? How'd an accident get them crossways?"

"Well, see, here's what happened. Buddy and Albert, they was gonna ram two cars together and make it look like an accident and collect the insurance money. So they got two old cars that weren't worth nothin' and went and got insurance on 'em. Then they gonna drive 'em out where two roads cross way out in the county, where ain't nobody around. Then see, Albert, he's gonna sit in the car in the intersection of them roads, and Buddy's gonna drive into the side of Albert's car. Then they make like both cars are totaled out, plus Albert's gonna pretend like he's hurt real bad with his neck and back, and it's all Buddy's fault and all. Then they get the insurance companies to settle up."

"Pretty smart."

"Yep, pretty good deal," Carl said, nodding. "They'd make some good money."

"How come they got crossways? Because of the split on the money?"

"Naw, that wasn't it at all," Carl shook his head. "See, Albert didn't know it, but Buddy'd been fooling around for more a year with Albert's wife, Mary Ann."

"Albert found out?"

"Naw, that ain't it," Carl said, shaking his head. "See here, what happened was, see, Buddy and Mary Ann decided that instead of Buddy driving into Albert's car easy like, he would ram it real hard, so it'd kill him. Buddy was supposed to hit Albert's car on the side, the driver's side, and hit it where the engine is in Albert's car. But see, instead, Buddy drove real fast and hit right where the driver's door is. Bam! He hit that sumbitch right where Albert was. Bam! I mean he hit that sumbitch hard! See, that way, it would probably kill Albert dead, and Mary Ann'd get the insurance money and she'd collect on life insurance on Albert too. And they pay double when it's from an accident." Carl raised an eyebrow. "Pretty damn smart, wudn't it?"

"Damn right," I agreed. "So, what happened?"

"It would have worked good except for one thang."

"What's that?"

"He didn't die. Albert got hurt real bad, but hell, it didn't kill him. And see, when Buddy rammed him like that, then Albert knew Buddy done double-crossed him. 'Course he can't say nothing to nobody, see," Carl said frowning. "But it worked out anyway, 'cause with Albert hurt so bad they got *lots* of money from the insurance. But it took Albert a long time to get over it, he was stove up pretty bad, had to go to the hospital and all. He was in there a real long time. After he finally got right, Albert said he's gonna kill Buddy if he ever catch him out somewhere, and Buddy says if Albert ever come around, he's gonna fill him fulla holes. So see, they don't get along no more."

"What about Mary Ann? How'd she come out on it?"

"Well see, Albert got to suspecting her, and then Albert's brothers, see, they told him he needed to get away from Mary Ann or he'd probably wake up dead one day. So they split up. But after she left Albert, she didn't take up with Buddy and that's a good thang 'cause there'd be a shooting for sure if she hadda."

Albert was lucky he wasn't killed in the staged accident. All three still collected from the insurance-fraud scheme, but his survival foiled his wife's double cross and Mary Ann and Buddy missed out on a big life insurance payoff. And Albert learned a hard lesson: sometimes you just can't trust crooks.

■ ■ ■

In addition to buying stolen vehicles, I had opportunities to purchase other items. Jim offered me a sawed-off shotgun and dynamite after I mentioned we wanted to get rid of someone in Mobile. We met one night at a motel room in Tupelo. While I waited at the open door of the room, Jim paused at the trunk of his car and checked out the parking lot. Then he opened the trunk and took out a duffle bag and carried it into the room and set it on the bed. I locked the door and pulled the curtains shut.

"All right, Jim," I said.

Jim lifted out a sawed-off shotgun out of the bag and handed it to me. Manufacturer's markings had been drilled and gouged out of the shotgun, a mean-looking, black 12-gauge, with a short barrel, sawed off so it was only about twelve inches long. He reached back in the bag.

"Here's the rest," he said. He took out six sticks of dynamite and laid them gently on the bed.

Laying the gun aside, I picked up a stick of dynamite and made like I was examining the markings, although I had no idea what the markings meant.

"All right, good, Jim," I said, putting the dynamite down. "Like I said, my people in Mobile will use this to take care of a guy down there who's been giving us trouble. This'll do the job."

"Good, Mike, glad to help out."

"Let's see, that's a hundred altogether, for the gun and the dynamite, right?"

"Yeah, that's right, Mike, a hundred."

I took out a wad of hundred dollar bills, peeled one off, and handed it to him.

"Here you go."

He pocketed the money. "Just let me know if I can do anything else for you." He picked up the empty bag and left.

Undercover with Good Ole Gals

In circulating around the area I was learning that the backwoods and honky-tonks in north Mississippi had their own culture and that just rambling around with Sadie and Patty could be exciting. We usually ended up at backwoods bar, a decrepit joint in the middle of nowhere.

A few times they drove me around in their old, rusted sedan that had long faded from blue to dingy gray. It was rusted in spots with strips of chrome trim missing in several places along the sides. The windshield was bug spattered and smeared with a hazy film of old caked-on dust. Two long horizontal cracks snaked across the windshield, dividing it into three portions and seriously interrupting the view from inside.

When cranked, the motor began with a slow, strained grinding and then whined, coughed, and belched until it finally sputtered to a start and ran with a nervous clatter. A bluish-black cloud billowed from the tail-pipe and hung over the top of the trunk and the roof, along with the odor of burned oil. As the car started moving to ramble down the road, the tailpipe spewed oily smoke, obscuring the vision of any drivers behind it. When parked, the car tilted down heavily on one side and when moving it squeaked, rattled, and swayed from side to side as if it wasn't quite attached to the frame. Because the shock absorbers were worn out, the front end of the car bounced up and down over every small bump in the road, which made it feel as if we were riding deep rolling waves in the ocean. The car was in constant motion, as much from side to side and up and down as going forward. Any lawman would reasonably assume the driver of the weaving car had to be DUI. The car was begging to go to the junkyard, where it could rust in peace.

Like the car, Sadie and Patty were a little worn too, the way hard living, good times, and bad men can wear a good woman down. Sadie, the oldest, was an imposing presence. With long blonde hair piled high on top of her head, she stood a good six feet tall and her large-boned frame held 240 pounds well. Under a blonde pyramid of hair, her plump rosy cheeks and blue eyes stood out. Patty was shorter and weighed less, maybe 180 pounds, a fireplug with dark-brown hair falling just below her shoulders and a ready grin that could be replaced in a flash by a quick temper and fierce eyes.

Rough and tough, they also loved to banter and tease. But beyond their lively chatter and rowdy laughter, a close look during unguarded moments revealed weary eyes that hinted at despair. The two women affected brash, lighthearted attitudes and pretended it didn't matter how life had turned out. As we worked together and they became comfortable with me, they shared their burdens.

Their life changed when we started working together—at least in the short term. It brought something new and exciting into their existence: a sense of doing something meaningful, intense, and risky. And now someone cared about what they knew and what they thought. I questioned them about criminals they knew and paid close attention to what they said and thought. They were important and I treated them that way.

They could affect my success and safety. If they did well, I did well. If they slipped up, I could be hurt, and if I didn't play my role well or slipped up, they could be hurt. We depended on each other and developed the deep trust that characterizes the best relationships between undercover agents and informants. Beyond that, we enjoyed working together.

■ ■ ■

Swaying down back roads in their old car one afternoon, we had ranged outside their usual stomping grounds when I noticed a remote honky-tonk, one they had never visited. We pulled in to check it out and went inside. At midafternoon, only two pickups were in the parking lot and the joint was almost empty. I stood at the bar with Patty and Sadie on either side of me while we drank beers.

"Hey, fellar," said a deep, gruff voice behind me and I felt a hand on my shoulder. The *hey, fellar* was enough to warn me that something bad was brewing.

I turned around and found myself confronted by three large, beefy men. One who looked to be in his fifties had big, thick logs for arms and wore overalls without a shirt underneath. One side of his face was swollen wide with a big chaw of tobacco and a thin brown stain dribbled from one corner of his mouth to his chin. Another's grin was marked by a missing upper front tooth. The third was as wide as a doorway and flat faced with a scraggly beard. They looked like a delegation from the backwoods in the movie *Deliverance.* Or they were three surly rednecks looking for trouble in a hillbilly honky-tonk on the Lee and Itawamba County line in Mississippi, which is where we were that afternoon.

"Hey, fellar," overalls repeated in a slow, nasal drawl, his lips curled up on one corner and eyes narrowed in a hard stare. "How come you got two women and we ain't got *none?*"

"Yeah," the missing tooth added, edging closer, "that jest don't seem right, *do it?*"

"No, it don't," said the flat face with the scraggly beard. "And they's *purty* women, too! How about it, fellar? How's come you got two women?"

"*Yeah*, that's what I wanna know," snarled overalls, as he moved in closer, his huge tree-trunk body so close I had to lean back against the bar to look up at his oversized ruddy face. There's a difference between good ole boys out for fun and mean-spirited bullies spoiling to hurt someone.

"Well, I guess I'm just lucky," I said with a tight smile, "and—"

"What about it, fellar?" overalls glowered, "you gonna share them women?"

"Hey y'all," Sadie spoke up, her chin jutting out. "Y'all don't be messing with our man Mike, you hear."

"Yeah," Patty said, her eyes flaring, "y'all mind your own business. We jest here with our man. We don't even *know* you fellars. Y'all go on now."

"Leave us alone," Sadie demanded. "Y'all go on. *Git.*" She turned to me. "We were jest leaving, ain't we, Mike?"

I had never run from barroom fights before, but I was smart enough to run from a bad stomping, which was in store for me if we didn't get out fast.

"Whale, *you girls* just need to git to know us," overalls said with a big grin. He turned to the other two men and nodded, "Ain't that right, boys?"

Before he could turn back to us, Sadie grabbed my arm and we all flew out the door.

"Hey!" someone hollered behind us. "Hey, whar *the hale* y'all going? *Whar the—*"

We jumped in the car, the motor whined and sputtered to life, black oily smoke billowed from the tailpipe, and we sped off, spinning tires throwing up gravel and clouds of dust as we fishtailed out of the parking lot.

"Whew boy, Mike, them's sum bad ones!" Sadie exclaimed as we hit the blacktop road, tires squealing, the old car swaying, bouncing, and listing to one side. She shuddered, "They sure scared me. Whew." By that time I knew that if Sadie was scared of anyone, I should be too. After a moment she turned to me beaming with a smile and patted my shoulder.

"But I knew you were gonna protect us from them," Sadie teased. "Weren't you, Mike? You're our man, ain't ya."

"*That's right,*" Patty added from the backseat, "Mike'll take care of us, ain't that right, Mike?"

Actually, when I was out with Patty and Sadie I always figured it was the other way around. They were so rough and tough that I depended on them to protect me. In any event, I didn't see any benefit to going back to that honky-tonk and neither did they.

Guardian Angels

I occasionally brought another agent with me to meet the two women, especially when I was going to buy a stolen car, and Patty and Sadie took special pleasure in shocking the agents with their graphic, sexually flavored language. To this day, when I mention Sadie and Patty, retired FBI agent Orrin Fuelling and former MBN agent James Newman, now Franklin County sheriff, immediately react with similar views: "Holy cow! Those two women were something! They'd make a sailor blush." Orrin and James usually added another observation about Patty and Sadie: "They thought the world of you. They'd do anything for you." And I thought the world of Patty and Sadie. They were my guardian angels.

Sadie and Patty introduced me to some car thieves, but were not directly involved in the car purchases. The less they were involved, the better: they would not have to be trial witnesses, and when the big bust finally came, they could pretend they didn't know I was an agent and had fooled them too. However, for my benefit they became involved in one particular purchase.

I had arranged to buy two stolen Cadillacs. The cars would be supplied by two notorious career criminals. One was suspected of committing torture murders, including the murder of a witness. We considered him one of the most dangerous criminals in north Mississippi.

The delivery of the two Cadillacs was set for late night in the parking lot of the Natchez Trace Inn at Tupelo, a mostly vacant, out-of-the-way motel. I was cautious and earlier during the day I called Sadie and Patty and told them about the deal, in case they had heard anything about it, but they had not. After the call, I went out working on other deals and we were out of contact for the rest of the day and night.

Late that night, MBN agents took up surveillance positions at Natchez Trace Inn and I headed that way for the deal. Meanwhile, Sadie and Patty learned that the two men had the Cadillacs but planned to rob me. The women knew how dangerous the men were, so when they couldn't reach me to warn me, they jumped in their old car and drove like mad for the Natchez Trace Inn, arriving shortly before I did.

Agents conducting surveillance told me about it later. As the thugs waited in the parking lot with the Cadillacs, an old car roared up and slid sideways to a stop. Two large women jumped out and rushed up to the men. The women appeared to be arguing and shaking their fingers in the faces of the thugs. Agents watching were puzzled by the confrontation.

A few minutes later, the women left. Then I drove up and the deal went smoothly. I bought the Cadillacs and my accomplice-agents drove them off. After learning about the confrontation, I contacted Sadie and Patty and they told me about the robbery plot and rushing to save me. After sliding into the parking lot, they rushed up to the men and warned

them, "You don't mess with our man Mike, you hear! He's got big connections all over and if you mess with him, they'll track you down. You
mess with him, you mess with us."

I was astonished Sadie and Patty had exposed themselves to the wrath
of two dangerous men to protect me. An attempted robbery would have
resulted in a shootout and my accomplice-agents and I would have been
in the middle of it.

The Ringleader

I continued buying stolen vehicles. Some of the car thieves mentioned
the name Dean, indicating that he was a boss in the stolen-car business.
I asked Sadie if she knew of anyone named Dean.

"*Oh, Mike!*" she said, "that's gonna be Dean Hill. He's *a bad one*, a real
bad one. We don't mess with him." She held my eyes. "Mike, he can hurt
you. You need to be real careful of him, you hear. *Be careful.*"

As I became more deeply involved in the stolen-car business, Hill
and I circled each other from a distance. Some of the people I dealt with
told me that they had told Dean about me. It would probably be only
a matter of time until we met up, either as adversaries or allies. Obviously he wasn't warning people away from doing business with me so he
didn't suspect me—unless I was being set up and would go to a car deal
one night and never come back. That might be the way it would happen if they discovered who I really was, which was possible if anyone
checked my cover in depth or if Sadie or Patty confided to anyone that
I was an agent. But my cover seemed to be holding and the possibility
of being set up was remote, I thought. A meeting with Hill would be a
major step forward.

Finally, Dean Hill paid a visit to Sadie and Patty and told them he was
ready to do business with me. But first he had a warning for them and
me.

"Let me tell you one damn thing," he declared. "If I ever get arrested
because of you two or this Mike, I can have you and him killed. Easy. All
of you. I can do it even while sitting in jail. I can make one call and have
anything done. And I would get out on bond sometime."

Referring to a sheriff, a police chief, and a justice court judge by name,
Hill declared the law would be useless to protect Sadie and Patty because
the officials he named "are not going to mess up anything they are making money on."

Hill said he had stayed away from me out of fear I might be a federal agent. Hill told the women he had supplied some of the cars others had sold to me. "I can get him counterfeit money and anything else he wants," Hill added. He said he had a farm tractor and three stolen cars on his property: a Lincoln, a Corvette, and a Ford. He mentioned a large farm tractor he and Jerry had stolen and said he had Bruce burn down a house trailer for him for the insurance.

Using Sadie and Patty as go-betweens, Hill and I arranged to meet the next day.

That afternoon he drove up to Sadie's house and I walked outside and looked through the open passenger window. A big, thick, ruddy-faced man sat behind the steering wheel.

"Dean?"

"You Mike?"

"Yeah."

He nodded toward the passenger seat. "Get in." His voice was strong, authoritative, assured. Big hands and thick fingers gripped the steering wheel. As soon as I sat down he took off and sped down the road, his eyes flickering to the rearview mirror. No cars were in sight. Just after topping a hill, he swerved right onto a narrow blacktop road that cut through forest; the road was hilly and curvy. Thick woods crowded the edges and we were swallowed up by a wall of trees. If anyone had tried to follow us from Sadie's, they wouldn't have seen us turn and we would have seemingly disappeared into thin air.

After rushing through a sharp curve, Dean braked and slowed to a crawl and fixed his eyes on the rearview mirror. I twisted in the seat and glanced toward the rear, relieved I didn't have surveillance for the meeting. No one could have followed us without being discovered. Anyone trying to follow would have rushed through the curve, come out on top of our rear bumper, and been burned—and me along with them. Finally, Dean inhaled deeply and let it out with a rush; he took his eyes off the mirror and gradually accelerated to a normal speed, cutting his eyes sideways to glance at me. I know how to do this, his eyes said. He was no fool.

I had taken a chance and had a small microcassette recorder hidden on me to record our conversation. It might be our only meeting and I wanted to make sure I had a recording if Dean incriminated himself. A large, beefy man with cold eyes and thinning red hair, Dean Hill struck me as someone used to intimidating others and getting his way. Before he could say anything I decided to jump right to the point to show I was used to being in charge.

"They told me that you could deliver regularly," I said in the same assured tone he had used, "and that's what I'm looking for." Uncertain of how he would react, I tensed. This was a critical moment.

He hesitated a moment and then snorted, "I can get you just about anything. Just tell me what you want and I can have it. Just about anything you want." Excited and relieved, I tried to keep those emotions out of my voice.

"On a regular, weekly basis?" I asked.

"Yeah, sure can. I'll need to know a day or two ahead of time. I go and show my drivers what I want." We had come on several scattered houses and Dean pointed to a car in a driveway as we drove past. "If I want that car sitting right there," he said, "I tell them I want that car right there. And you just have some place to put it and the car will be sitting there."

"Okay," I nodded. "When can we start doing business together?"

"Anytime you want."

"How about this coming weekend?"

"Be all right." Dean said. He paused, crunched up one corner of his lips, and rubbed his chin. "I've got that Vette. I'm going to have to move that mother. It's a nice sumbitch, it's got 13,000 miles, less than a year old."

"How much you want for it?"

"I'll take $2,500 for it. The other day I could have sold the car for $3,500 to a guy I been doing business with." Wheeling and dealing on stolen cars can be similar to buying and selling cars on a dealership lot, puffing the car and negotiating the price, except no MSRP and no warranties; everything sold "as is"—and don't get caught.

"Has it been turned in?" I asked, referring to whether it had been reported stolen yet.

"It has *now*. See, I had 'til Monday morning on the damn thing."

It was a question of time between when a car was stolen and the owner discovering it was gone and reporting it. If the owner had gone on a weekend trip and left a car at home, he might not discover it had been stolen until his return. That could give the thieves a couple of days to move the car or chop it for parts without having to worry about the police. During that time if a police officer or trooper saw the car and made a routine check of the license plate or the VIN, the car would not come back as a stolen vehicle. Sometimes it was an "insurance job," where the owner secretly "sells" the car for a fraction of its value to a car-theft ring and then defrauds the insurance company by reporting it stolen and collecting insurance proceeds. The car-theft ring would want an owner to give them as much time as he could before he reported the car stolen. When I bought stolen cars, I tried to find out if it was an insurance job or a straight-out theft.

"You still got it in this area?"

"Yeah. I can get it put anyplace you'd want it put."

Dean and I started doing business together and I began buying stolen cars from him and his men. But then I ran into a problem, one that threatened to end the undercover operation.

Before long, I spent the last of the special funds available for buying vehicles. The operation was over unless we could find other funds. Inviting the FBI to join the operation might be an option. Virgil Luke and Bob Wallace worked closely with the FBI, particularly with FBI special agent Orrin Fuelling on car-theft rings. We briefed Orrin and he submitted a proposal for the FBI to join and fund the operation.

But it would take a while for the proposal to work its way through various levels of approval. Meanwhile, I continued working undercover to keep the operation viable, but had to do it without money to buy cars. Car thieves approached me almost daily to buy stolen vehicles and I had to turn them away. They also offered stolen agricultural combines and large farm tractors.

"I can't take it right now," I would explain, "the pipeline to Mobile and Florida is full," or "we don't need that kind right now."

That worked at first but FBI approval still lingered and I became anxious about losing credibility with the suspects. Then a partial solution presented itself. If it worked, it could even help bolster my cover.

Through Orrin, Virgil, and Bob, I had learned about two large-scale undercover operations in Florida and Louisiana. "Operation Gatorbait," a joint undercover operation by the FBI, the Florida Highway Patrol, and the National Auto Theft Bureau, was based in a warehouse in Lakeland, Florida, near Tampa. Meanwhile, the ATF and other agencies with the New Orleans Metro Organized Crime Strike Force were conducting a storefront undercover operation in New Orleans. There was a big difference in those two operations and what I was doing. They were well-organized, multiagency investigations using "storefront" businesses, elaborate covers, and buildings rigged with audio and video recorders, while I operated on the fly, pretty much out of my undercover vehicle. While waiting on the FBI, perhaps I could direct some of the stolen vehicles offered to me to those operations.

I contacted undercover agents in both operations and explained our situation. They agreed to pretend we were all part of the same crime organization and to buy vehicles I could send their way. That was perfect, especially since my cover had been that I was part of a large organization in other states.

Our arrangement was soon tested. Dean Hill came to me about buying another stolen Corvette. I explained I was backed up and gave him a phone number for "Larry" in Florida and told him to contact Larry about it. A few days later, Hill headed for Florida.

At a large metal warehouse in Lakeland, Florida, the wide roll-up door cranked open and Dean Hill drove a stolen Corvette inside. The door closed down behind him. As soon as the car stopped, a man stuck a shotgun in Dean's ear and ordered him out of the car. With the gun barrel against his head, Dean edged out carefully and stood with his hands held up. Another man searched Dean to make sure he was not wearing a wire. Professionals in the auto-theft business had to be cautious and careful. Although Dean was the head of a car-theft ring in Mississippi and Mike had vouched for him, you couldn't be too careful.

A professional himself, Dean appreciated the precautions. This was a big-time operation, just like Mike had said. And it was only one part of the widespread organization Mike was involved in. It was impressive.

One of the men, Larry, introduced himself to Dean and explained that they had to be careful. Larry led Dean into an office while others got ready to work on the Corvette in the shop. They would change the VIN plates and tape parts of the car to prepare it for a new paint job. After his long drive from Mississippi to Florida, Dean welcomed the opportunity to relax in the office. He leaned back in a stuffed chair with a cold beer in one hand and puffed on a big cigar while he and Larry talked. The office door leading to the warehouse shop was next to Dean's chair. As Dean puffed on the cigar, the door beside him opened and one of the men leaned in and held out the license plate from the Corvette.

"Hey, Dean, is this Vette hot?" the man asked.

Dean took the cigar out of his mouth. "Is it *hot*?" he said, an eye cocked. "That mutherfucker'll *burn your goddamn fingers!*"

"Thanks, Dean."

A hidden video camera recorded the scene.

After Dean returned to Mississippi, he told me it had been a pleasure to do business with my people in Florida. Dean called later and told me he was sending a Mercedes to Larry.

A week later I arranged for Dean to take a stolen Corvette to sell to the New Orleans storefront operation, but as he was about to head that way, the undercover agent in New Orleans canceled the deal and Dean came to me about it. The Gaterbait operation in Florida and the New Orleans operation could take a few of the stolen vehicles offered to me but couldn't take them all.

I was still out of funds but saw a way to make a case on him for stealing the Corvette anyway. If I could get him to show the Corvette to me, it would confirm he possessed a stolen vehicle. I told him I might be able to take it. We met, I looked over the Corvette and gave it a test drive, and then put him off about buying it.

Several days later, another case-making opportunity arose. I got word that Fred, the pawn-shop owner who had bought the stolen televisions from me, wanted to meet someone. I called him.

"I know some people who got some things you might be interested in buying," Fred said.

"What kind of things?"

He lowered his voice. "Some guns, a whole bunch of them. Hold on just a minute, one of the guys is here now and I'll get him to talk to you." After a pause, Fred came back on the phone. "This is Rickey's partner. He can tell you what you need to know."

"Mike, this is Cobb," David "Cobb" Berryhill said.

"Fred said you had something I might be interested in."

Cobb explained that he and his partner Rickey had stolen thirty guns and would let them all go at a good price. Since I was still out of funds, I asked if they could take the guns to Florida or Louisiana but Cobb said they didn't want to move them. I told him I would call Florida and Louisiana and call him back.

I called agents at the undercover operations in Florida and New Orleans and tried to get them to come to Mississippi and buy the stolen guns, but they couldn't do it. Still, I didn't want to let go of making an undercover case. If I could get a look at the guns and get a good enough description of some we might be able to match the guns to a burglary, thus connecting Cobb and Padgett to the crime. It was worth a try. I called Cobb.

"I talked to my people in New Orleans and they're interested, but before they come up they want me to look over the guns and let them know what you got and what I think. If it turns out to be a good deal they'll probably come up and get them, but I need to see 'em first. They'll go by what I say."

"Goddamn, that'll be good if they can take them all," Cobb said, "'cause we need to get them out of this area real quick."

"When can I see them?" We agreed to meet at Fred's pawn shop the next day.

The next day, MBN agent Rick Ward accompanied me to the meeting and acted as one of my accomplices. I went in the pawn shop while Ward waited in the car. Fred hustled over to me. "They got them things for you," he said eagerly and led me next door to a small grocery store and introduced me to Rickey Padgett, an ex-con, and Cobb.

Cobb sized me up and I already had my first impression of him. Medium height, stocky with brown curly hair and a full mustache, David Lee "Cobb" Berryhill was an experienced Prentiss County car thief and burglar. A dark-brown suede jacket hung to his hips, likely covering a pistol tucked in at his waist—just as my sport coat concealed the pistol hidden at the back of my waist. Two armed businessmen.

"So you have guns I might be interested in."

"Yeah, you gonna like this," Cobb said, grinning, "we got thirty guns, expensive guns."

"High-price guns," Rickey added. "All look new. I mean good stuff."

"What kind of guns you talking about?"

"Rifles and shotguns," Cobb said. "They high end, came from a man who collects 'em. We got rifles and shotguns, Remingtons, Franchis, and Brownings. All calibers: .22, .243, .30-.06, .44-magnum. All from one house. The man collected 'em."

"He had a houseful," Rickey added. "We knew he had some, but goddamn, we didn't know he had so many, and man, them sumbitches are some good-looking guns," he chuckled.

"How much you gonna want for all of them?"

"We can probably let you have them all for $1,400," Cobb said.

"Like I told you, I'm hooked up with some people in New Orleans and Tampa who might take the whole lot," I explained. "They want me to look at the guns and let them know about what I think they're worth."

"Will they come up here and pick them up?" Rickey asked.

"Well, if they'll buy everything, can you take the guns to New Orleans or to Tampa?" I responded. "You'll be able to get rid of all of them at one time."

"Goddamn," Cobb frowned, "there's too much heat. If they want 'em, they'll have to come up here; there's too much goddamn heat for us to be moving 'em that far."

"Them sumbitches hot as a mutherfucker around here," Rickey added. "We need to get 'em outta here, but there might be heat on us too so we can't be moving them around. They gonna have to come git 'em."

"Okay, let me see the guns and I'll let my people know what they're worth."

"They're outside Booneville," Padgett said. "Cobb will show them to you."

"Wait, look here," Cobb said. "Take a look at this." He reached into a pocket and handed me a large diamond ring. "Look at that mother," he said brightly. "I'll throw that in the deal for the guns." I looked it over and handed it back.

Cobb and I joined Ward in the car. I drove and Cobb sat up front with me. I had prearranged the seating arrangements with Ward. As a standard practice, you don't want the violator alone in the backseat where he can get the drop on you. Having an agent in back of the violator reduces the risks.

We traveled deep in the country, isolated in a remote valley, miles from Jumpertown, a small crossroads in the northeast Mississippi hills, hostile territory for an undercover agent, home to career criminals, car-theft rings, and chop shops.

Following Cobb's directions, we drove toward Booneville, then westward on empty, narrow asphalt and gravel roads, twisting and winding through forests, over hills, and past distant, lonesome fields. During the drive we didn't see another vehicle and passed only a few houses scattered miles apart. The farther we went, the more remote and isolated the area seemed, as if cut off from the rest of the world. Finally, we turned on a dirt driveway curving uphill to an old frame farmhouse set on a wooded hilltop far from the road. The car crawled up the hill and around the house to a barn about fifty yards behind the house.

I turned on a microcassette recorder in my pocket as we got out of the car.

"They're in here, Mike," Cobb said, leading us into the barn. Was my cover blown? I wondered. The most dangerous position is to be burned and not know it. There was a slight possibility he was luring us into a trap and Rick Ward and I were armed and alert.

The barn was gray weathered wood, dark and musty inside, with hay piled along the right wall. Cobb brushed the hay back and unveiled several long bundles wrapped in quilts.

"We got 'em right here," Cobb pulled back the folds of the quilts. Rifles and shotguns lay in piles. All looked new and even in the dim light inside the barn they gleamed with shining metal and polished wood stocks.

"They all damn good guns. Look," Cobb picked up a bolt-action high-powered rifle and handed it to me. "This is a real nice one," he said proudly. I examined it while trying to note and remember the make and part of the serial number.

"There's lots of other real good ones like that."

"Here, look at this sumbitch," Cobb was holding a shotgun out to me. "Man, they some real expensive shotguns and rifles. Them sumbitches worth some money."

"Yeah, this is a pretty nice rifle," I agreed, putting the rifle down and taking the shotgun.

"This is a 12-gauge, isn't it? What is it, a Remington?" I said, looking for the make on the shotgun, and the serial number.

"Yeah, that's a Remington 12," Cobb replied, while sorting through the pile of guns for another one. Cobb was soon holding out another one.

We went on like this for several minutes while he proudly displayed their loot from the burglary.

"Wait," Cobb said, "you gotta see this one." He handed me an AR-18 assault rifle. "Try it out. You can shoot it out back. It's already loaded." Behind the barn the land sloped gently toward fields and wooded areas.

Cobb watched as I aimed at the tree downhill and fired rapidly, tat-tat-tat-tat-tat, and kept firing until the magazine was empty.

"How about that?" Cobb asked.

"Yeah, pretty nice." I turned it over in my hands, admiring it and found the make and serial number. We walked back to the barn, while I kept repeating part of the serial number in my mind, along with the makes of the guns we had already looked at. We looked over several more and while Cobb was distracted by Ward, I whispered the serial numbers of several guns, hoping the recorder would pick up some of my soft murmurings. Ward also was trying to memorize parts of serial numbers and makes of guns.

During the ride back, Cobb was talkative. "I been stealing cars for Kenneth Robinson," he said. "I been doing it a long time. I can change the VINs and get you fake titles."

With a little prompting he talked about the burglary and theft of the guns. "We took the guns from a house where they were in gun cabinets on the walls," he said. "I knew the owner would be out of town. It just so happens he wanted to go off on a strike about coal mining and he messed up and told the wrong man he was leaving." Cobb grinned. "We got thirty rifles and shotguns altogether. Me and Rickey already had that AR-18 rifle and if you're interested, it would be just the kind of gun you can use to bump somebody off with."

He warned us to look out for someone who was reportedly an informant. "Look out for ——," Cobb said. "He snitched people out on cars and he's under protective custody by the law."

"What about you, Cobb? Any heat on you, other than from the guns?"

He hooted. "Hah, I got arrested for auto theft in Tupelo but got off on little stuff 'cause we were caught before we could steal the car. The law knows me," he bragged, "and they always trying to catch me stealing cars," he said dismissively.

We dropped Cobb off at the pawn shop. I told him I would call after I talked with my people. I called agents in the two operations again and tried to get them to come partway to get the guns if I could convince Cobb and Padgett to go that far, but they couldn't do it. I called Cobb and told him my people would buy if they took the guns to Florida or Louisiana, but Cobb refused. Meanwhile I couldn't take the chance of having agents raid the barn with a search warrant because Padgett and Berryhill would instantly connect me with the raid.

Padgett and Berryhill told me later they got rid of the guns, but we had obtained enough evidence to charge them. A week after looking over the guns, I met with Cobb and Padgett late one night and we drove around back roads in Prentiss County. They wanted to show me a relative's house out in the county.

"He's got all kinds of money he stole and never paid taxes on," one said. "He keeps it in a safe in the house and hell, he can't report it if it's stolen. He's got maybe $80,000 to $100,000 *cash*. We would rob him but he would know it was us, even with masks on. We were figuring maybe *you* could do it and we could all split the money."

To keep them from getting someone else to do it I strung them along about the robbery. The man may have been a crook but he never knew how close he came to getting robbed by other crooks—and *relatives* at that.

When the undercover operation ended, Berryhill and Padgett were indicted in connection with the theft of the guns. But only one went to trial. Padgett and Berryhill got into a dispute and Berryhill shot and killed him. I testified at the stolen-firearms trial in circuit court in Booneville and the jury convicted Berryhill.

■   ■   ■

The FBI finally approved the Mississippi operation and FBI agents Orrin Fuelling and Jerry Marsh joined me to work undercover. Jerry also doubled as the tech man for our recording equipment. They leased a new car and concealed microphones inside and a recorder in the trunk. We rented an apartment in Tupelo and began using it as our base and I moved out of the house trailer. When I first began working in the area, I had rented a cheap house trailer instead of an apartment so as to keep MBN undercover expenses down. Now we didn't have to worry about stretching funds. When we hit the streets together, the criminals I had been dealing with didn't question my associates and readily accepted Orrin and Jerry.

Now that money was available again, it was time to contact Dean. He had told me he could supply brand-new Chryslers and I called him to take him up on it.

"I got an order I need to fill," I said. "You mentioned Chryslers. Can you hook me up with new Chrysler New Yorkers?"

"Yeah, I think so. What do you want, two?" Dean asked.

"Just one," I said, and Dean said he would get back to me about it.

A couple of days later, Dean called and said he had problems getting Chryslers. He had another proposition.

"Well, I'm having hell on them Chryslers," Dean complained. "They got a damn new man. Ain't no way you can substitute a BMW, are there?"

"What kind of price could I get on the BMW?"

"I'll get you a brand-new BMW for $2,500," Dean said. "See, they hired this damn new fellow at the Chrysler dealership and that sumbitch run an inventory and they running them every day. So it's making it bad damn hard to get the Chryslers right now."

"Well, on the BMW," I said, "I'll have to make a call to see if I can move it fast on the other end."

"If you could do that, I'd bring it on in to you. And once things are straightened out at the dealership, I'll get that New Yorker for you."

I called back and agreed to take the BMW and negotiated a lower price of $2,200. A new BMW stolen from a dealership in Chicago was driven to Mississippi. That night, Orrin, Jerry, and I parked in the gravel lot of a honky-tonk in Lee County and waited for Dean to show up with it. Dean drove up, rolled down his window, and told us to wait, he'd be right back. About twenty minutes later he returned and parked beside us. A new BMW pulled in beside him and the driver got in Dean's car. Dean joined us and handed over the keys for the BMW and I gave him $2,200. The deal took less than two minutes and they were gone.

We got the BMW for a good price. Later, we got an even better deal. We bought a tractor-trailer truck, including the trailer filled with 198 boxes of new furniture, for $4,400. The driver transported new furniture from furniture plants located in northeast Mississippi. Clayton and Bruce drove it late one night to a roadside pullover on I-55 a few miles north of Canton. Orrin and I met them and left with the tractor-trailer truck. The driver would share in the $4,400 and fraudulently report the truck stolen. Clayton said the driver was cautious about us.

Referring to the driver, Clayton said, "He asked me, 'How long you known those guys?' and I told him, 'Well, I can tell you one thing—he ain't the man.' See, that's all he's worried about. He's a mean one. But I told him you ain't the man, I guarantee it."

"You sure everything's okay with him?" I asked.

"He's okay now, I got that straightened out. He just asked me, 'You know them real well?' I said, 'Yeah, I know them. He's not the man.' and he said, 'Are you definitely sure?' I said, 'Hell yes, I'm sure,' and he said 'Okay, have him call me.'"

"You sure you can trust him, Clayton?"

"Hell yeah, I helped him unload other deals. He's been stealing off the company for years. And tomorrow he'll report the truck missing."

Crisis Looms

Undercover became hectic at times with buying stolen cars, arranging other deals, circulating among suspects, having meetings, collecting intelligence, and trying to keep up with report writing. But one night the phone rang and suddenly everything changed.

I answered the phone. "Mike, something *bad's* happened," said Sadie urgently, her voice cracking with fear. "*Real bad.* He knows. He knows everything and—"

"*Wait. Wait,* hold on and *slow down.* What are you talking about? Who knows?"

"Mike, it's *Dean Hill,* he just came by here and he knows—"

"He knows what?"

"That we're helping and all and—"

"Slow down, Sadie, and tell me what he said."

"He came busting up in here and he says, 'I *know* what y'all are doing.' And I said, 'What're you talking about?' and Dean says, 'I know y'all helping the law. I know *everything.*'"

"What else, Sadie? Did he ask you any questions? Did he say who you were helping or exactly what you were doing?"

"No, but he knows. He knows. I could tell. And he said, 'By God, I'll tell you one goddamn thing—if something happens, it's gonna be your ass.' Oh Mike, what're we gonna do? I'm afraid."

I got Sadie and Patty out of the area that night and put them up in a motel for several days while trying to figure out what was going on. I suspected they had confided in a relative or trusted friend that they were helping the law. That was a common problem with informants no matter how much I reminded them not to tell *anyone* what they were doing, no matter how much they trusted the person. Once an informant confided in someone, word would soon leak out to the wrong people. The old saying is true: If two people know a secret, eventually it will no longer be secret.

While the women were holed up we decided to visit some of the people we had been dealing with to find out if they had become suspicious of us. It would be a way to find out if word had spread about us. Late one morning, FBI agent Orrin Fuelling and I dropped by Clayton's house out in the country. We had purchased stolen cars from Clayton and hadn't seen him in a while. Clayton was surprised to see us and he invited us in.

"Hey, Mike, Bill. Y'all come on in. How y'all doing?" Orrin used Orrin's undercover name *Bill.*

Clayton led us to the living room and sat down on the couch. We sat across from him. On the coffee table in front of Clayton was a loaded revolver. It wasn't a good sign, I thought, especially since I had never seen him with a weapon. Because of possible heat on us, the gun was a danger signal.

"Hey, Clayton, what kind of gun is that?" I asked.

"Well, it's a .357 Smith and Wesson," he said.

"That'll shoot .38s too, won't it?"

"Yeah," he said, "matter a fact, that's what I got in it now, .38 shells."

"You mind if I take a look?" I picked it up, admiring it. "Man, that's a good-looking gun. How does it shoot?"

"Good," he beamed, "it shoots real good. I can hit damn good with it."

"Hey, you mind if I shoot it?" I held it up. "I'd like to try it out."

"Naw, Mike, that'll be fine."

"Can I shoot it out back? Out the back door?"

"Hell, yeah, whatever you want. Go ahead."

I went through the kitchen and out the back door. After walking several paces, I stopped, raised the gun, and fired at a tree about twenty yards away. I kept shooting until the gun was empty. I went back inside and lay the empty—and now *safe*—gun down. That was a form of gun safety. We were able to relax during the rest of the visit. Despite having a pistol handy, Clayton didn't seem to be suspicious, so perhaps word wasn't spreading.

Later I tried calling Dean but couldn't reach him. Nevertheless, we seemed to be cool with everyone. Several days later I brought Sadie and Patty back and told them to lay low and not try to get involved in anything or with anyone. Things seemed edgy but we were able to continue buying stolen cars, although Dean dropped out of sight and the buys slowed.

■   ■   ■

I had to drop out of the undercover operation because I had been selected by MBN to attend a four-month police management course at the Southern Police Institute in Louisville, Kentucky. I left the operation in good hands with Orrin and Jerry. Eventually the operation concluded and the suspects were arrested on state and federal charges. Dean Hill went to trial in federal court in Tampa and I flew down and testified in the case and he was convicted. He also went to trial in federal court in Oxford. Again I testified and again he was convicted. Hill had been caught red-handed and the Federal Fifth Circuit Court of Appeals in New Orleans knew how it had happened. In affirming Hill's conviction, the court wrote: "The path of Hill's conviction began with his introduction to Mississippi Bureau of Narcotics undercover agent Charles Spillers . . ."

> Agent Spillers, posing as a trafficker in stolen automobiles, had arranged to be introduced to Hill because of information he had obtained indicating that Hill dealt in stolen vehicles. In this initial meeting, which was secretly tape recorded by Agent Spillers, Hill boasted to Spillers of his longtime involvement in procuring and selling stolen vehicles, of the quality of his wares and the reliability of his operation, and of his past success in avoiding prosecution. He agreed, without the slightest hesitation, to furnish stolen cars to Spillers on a regular basis and tried to sell Spillers a stolen . . . Corvette that he then had available.

The operation had originally begun because Sadie and Patty wanted to help make a drug case on the man who had raped a minor. We never got to make the case. He beat a man to death one night in the parking lot of a lounge and was caught trying to drag the body away.

My former undercover partner Sara Niell had found out that rural northeast Mississippi, which we called "Tombstone" and the "Arizona Territory" because of its lawlessness, was a dangerous area for undercover agents. After spending months living among double-crossing, cruel, and dangerous criminals, I had to agree.

Death of an Agent

For months I was buying stolen vehicles undercover in northeast Mississippi. After each buy, I would drive the stolen vehicle to Jackson, Mississippi, and turn it over to the Mississippi Highway Patrol vehicle-theft unit. The trips to Jackson were usually late-night drives from Tupelo down the Natchez Trace Parkway or on deserted two-lane state highways, with another agent following. We would drop off the stolen car at MHP and ride back to Tupelo the next day. One cold winter night, around 1:00 a.m., I was driving a stolen car down the Trace to Jackson, following MBN agent Lane Caldwell, who was in his MBN car.

Lane was a little less than medium height, with black, curly hair. He always had a glimmer in his eye, a cheerful smile, and a funny story to tell. After driving on the Trace that night for more than an hour, we had not met a single car, so to break up the monotonous journey, we left the Trace around Kosciusko, Mississippi, and took back roads, occasionally passing through small towns that were totally dark and shut down for the night.

On an isolated stretch of road, we finally came across a car. It was ahead of us, traveling in the same direction we were, its taillights glowing red in the distance. We were traveling fast and caught up with it quickly. The car slowly weaved back and forth in the road. Lane sped past and I followed. We both began watching the car's headlights in our rearview mirrors. We each had a handheld two-way radio so we could communicate during the trip.

Lane radioed me. "Eight thirty-nine (my radio call sign), he looks a little unsteady, over."

"Yeah, he's weaving a good bit. Let's slow down for a minute and see, over."

"Ten-four."

We were a half mile ahead of the car and we slowed down, keeping a steady pace with it. The headlights began weaving more erratically across the road.

I radioed Lane. "He's getting worse, did you see—Look!"

Suddenly the headlights veered completely off the road toward the passenger side of the road, plunged down a steep embankment, and disappeared from view.

Lane and I jammed on our brakes, backed up, turned our cars around, and sped back to where the car had gone off the road. It had gone down the embankment, rolled over, and crashed upside down in a swift stream. It was almost totally submerged, with only the still-spinning wheels sticking up out of the stream. Smoke and steam were rising around the car and its headlights glowed dully under the surface of the water. The passenger cabin was upside down and under water.

We ran down the embankment and jumped in the frigid water. The driver was the only person in the car. We tugged and pulled open the driver's door and pulled him out, already half-drowned, coughing and spitting up water. We dragged him up the embankment and laid him beside the road. He stank of liquor, his eyes were closed, and he kept spitting water and groaning and mumbling slurred, unintelligible words. We picked him up and carried him to Lane's car and Lane rushed him back to town with me following. We found a small hospital, not much more than a clinic, and carried him in.

Except for aches and pains from being banged around in the accident, the driver didn't appear to be injured, just stone drunk, but the medical staff would fully examine and treat him. When we saw a policeman arriving at the hospital a few minutes later, I discreetly slipped away in the stolen car and parked a short distance away to wait for Lane. Lane identified himself to the officer as an agent and explained where he had seen the man drive off the road. About twenty minutes later, Lane rejoined me and we continued our trip to Jackson, both nearly numb from the waist down from the cold water, drained and sleepy from a long day and night. We ran our car heaters nearly full blast to try to stay warm and dry out a little.

Nearly a year later, after the undercover operation had been wrapped up, I was the MBN district supervisor for northeast Mississippi and Lane, who lived in Corinth, Mississippi, was one of my agents. On September 14, 1979, an elderly man, armed with a handgun, kidnapped a young woman. When they stopped at a service station in Corinth, she got word to the station attendant. Lane was talking to a deputy at the Alcorn County sheriff's office in Corinth when the call came in to the sheriff's office. The deputy rushed out and Lane went with him to help out. They found the man in a parked car at the station. He was holding a pistol in his hand. Lane dove into the car, grabbing for the gun, and during the struggle the man fired into Lane's chest. The bullet tore through Lane's lung, causing his lungs to start filling with blood. Although he was mortally wounded, Lane continued to struggle with the man until his lungs finally filled and he gasped his last dying breath.

The man was subdued, subsequently convicted, and sent to spend his last days in prison.

Most people who become law-enforcement officers do it to serve others, but seldom have an opportunity to directly save someone's life. Harold Lane Caldwell saved two lives, but sadly lost his own. Lane was only twenty-five and he left behind a wife and two young sons. He had planned to leave the bureau and go to law school, but a life and a dream were extinguished in a split second by a bullet. Many years later I was proud to eulogize him at the Law Enforcement Officers Memorial service on the Oxford Square. Lane was the best of us.

In the Arena: Demanding, Dangerous Work

When I joined MBN, it was a small agency, limited by statute to thirty agents, later increased to fifty, for the entire state. However, for a relatively small agency, its agents experienced unusually large numbers of violent clashes.

The violence stemmed from the nature of the work—a heavy reliance on undercover in the early years of the bureau, along with arrests of violent criminals. Several factors contributed to the danger. Drug trafficking was characterized by rip-offs: drug dealers cheated buyers by shorting quantity, selling bogus drugs, and robbing customers. Rip-offs led to armed confrontations when the victims were undercover agents. Arrests of armed and sometimes wired drug dealers also produced close calls. In addition, agents encountered increased hazards in buy-bust deals involving large quantities of drugs and money. Drug dealers would be wary, employ countersurveillance, and arm themselves to protect the drugs, as in the buy-bust ambush of agents Sara Niell and Jerry Dettman.

Another factor that made undercover work hazardous was the constant risk of discovery. Agents faced possible injury or death when drug dealers suspected or discovered they were dealing with an agent, as, for example, when the drug dealer pointed a cocked gun at agent Earl Pierce after catching him in a lie. But even after working undercover, making cases, and arresting drug dealers safely, agents sometimes faced one additional threat: drug traffickers who tried to retaliate. A few examples illustrate the risks agents faced daily.

Rip-Offs

Greenville
MBN agent Doug Walsh was making a drug purchase in his undercover van when the drug dealer pulled a gun and tried to rob him. Walsh grabbed for the gun and as the men struggled, the dealer shot Walsh in the arm. Despite his injury, Walsh managed to subdue the man. Walsh spent several days in St. Dominic's hospital in Jackson recovering from the wound. Sara Niell and I picked up Walsh's blood-spattered van in Greenville, drove it to Jackson, and then visited him in the hospital, a sobering reminder of the nature of our work.

Jackson: "Mister, Are You Going to Shoot Me?"
While working undercover, Agent Steve Mallory discovered that a drug dealer in Jackson had ripped him off by selling him bogus drugs. Accompanied by agents Doug Cutrer and Charlie Lindsey, Mallory went to a second-floor apartment in a complex to confront the suspect. A narrow landing ran along the second floor. The agents crowded close together on the landing and banged loudly on the door, which immediately swung open.

A man suddenly stepped out of a back room with a rifle and started shooting. The agents jumped aside from the open doorway. Cutrer fired his .357 revolver through the wall beside the door and the powerful rounds punched through the wall. Lindsey crouched and grabbed for his revolver in his jean's back pocket but the revolver's hammer caught on his pocket. As Lindsey tried to tug it loose, Mallory reached his arm across Lindsey's shoulder and fired his .357. The loud blasts deafened Lindsey.

The flurry of return fire scattered the occupants. Unknown to the agents, a bullet hit the shooter's rifle, knocking it out of his hands, and he jumped out a back window to the ground two stories below, followed by his girlfriend, who wore only panties. On both sides of the open doorway, the agents gripped their guns and got ready to rush in. Lindsey suddenly saw movement down low and was startled when a three-year-old boy toddled out of the apartment to the doorway.

The little boy looked up at Lindsey with big, fearful eyes and asked in a small, quivering voice, "Mister, are you going to shoot me?"

Lindsey's heart could have melted. He reached down for the boy. "*No, baby*, come here. No one's going to *hurt you.*"

The agents swept the empty apartment and found the rifle. Meanwhile, a crowd had gathered in the parking lot below and in the crowd Mallory recognized the shooter and they grabbed him.

Jackson: Sally the Heroin Addict

MBN agents Jim Kelly and Eddie Berry made a heroin buy from a drug dealer and his girlfriend, Sally. A few days later, the agents met the dealer one night and drove him to Sally's apartment for another heroin purchase. When they stopped at the apartment complex, the dealer suddenly jumped out and ran through Sally's apartment and out the back door. While Eddie ran to the back of the apartments, Jim pushed open the front door. As Jim stepped inside he heard a shotgun rack a shell into the chamber and found Sally pointing a shotgun at his face. Jim pointed his pistol at her and they faced off from five feet.

"Sally, what are we going to do?" Jim asked, breaking out in a sweat. One slight pull on the trigger would blow Jim's head off. "If you shoot me," Jim bluffed, "I'll kill you."

With heroin-dazed eyes aiming at Jim over the barrel of the shotgun, Sally replied, "*I'll kill you.*"

"*Wait, Sally*, we don't need to do this," Jim pleaded. "Let's talk. Come on now."

After more coaxing, Sally finally lowered the shotgun. Jim stepped forward, took the shotgun and racked the shells out until it was empty. Sally plopped down on a couch. Jim took a deep breath and slumped down beside her.

"Sally, you don't have any whiskey, do you?" Jim asked weakly.

"Yeah," she said, and pointed to a cabinet. "It's over there."

"Do you mind if I have a drink?"

She didn't, and Jim sat beside her sipping whiskey to steady his nerves. Following the confrontation, Sally eventually cooperated and helped Jim and Eddie make a few heroin buys. A month or two later, her small child was found wandering around outside the apartment. Sally was found inside, dead from an overdose.

Columbus

Two MBN undercover agents were attempting to make a drug buy one night when drug dealers pulled out guns and robbed them. The next day, the two agents encountered one of the robbers and two of his friends in downtown Columbus, standing near the bus station. When the agents approached him, the man attacked them with a knife, slashing one in the hand. During the struggle, the agents shot and killed the attacker. The wounded agent was treated at the hospital. In less than twenty-four hours, the agents survived an armed robbery and a knife attack.

Corinth

MBN agent Dennis "Mac" McAnally and an informant approached a dealer standing outside an apartment complex to attempt a drug buy. The informant had neglected to tell Mac that he had ripped off the man and owed him money. When Mac and the informant reached the dealer, he started yelling for his money and abruptly slammed the informant in the head with a large metal object. The blow cut a big, bloody gash in the informant's head and staggered him. Without blowing his undercover role, Mac pulled his gun and stopped the attack. The dealer turned and ran to his apartment while Mac got the informant into a car to rush him to the hospital. As Mac was driving away, the dealer ran outside and fired several shots at the car. At the hospital, Mac maintained his cover and managed to keep the police from being called by pretending the informant had accidentally injured himself in a fall.

Grenada

After buying drugs from two men in Grenada, MBN undercover agents Steve Mallory and Gary Robinson negotiated to buy a larger quantity. That night the two drug dealers joined Steve and Gary in Steve's car and directed the agents to a house on the edge of Grenada where they were to do the bigger deal. As the men got out of the car, four armed black men emerged from the woods and surrounded the agents. They demanded money and threatened to kill the agents. One stuck a sawed-off shotgun in Gary's stomach and another held a pistol to the back of Steve's head. Steve heard a snap behind his head, like the sound of a pistol hammer falling, but no shot was fired. In the dark, Steve was able to discreetly reach under his shirt and grip his revolver tucked at his waist, but decided not to use it when he realized that if he made a move, Gary would be cut in half by the sawed-off shotgun.

The agents gave up their wallets and several hundred dollars in buy money. With four guns pointing at them, the agents were allowed to return to their car and leave with the two drug dealers who had led them to the location. The two drug dealers pretended that they were not complicit in the robbery, but it was obvious that the robbery had been planned from the start and that the men had intentionally lured the agents into it. One sat in the backseat with Gary and the other in front with Steve. As they neared town, Gary pulled his gun and arrested the two men. While Gary covered both men from the backseat, Steve drove into town and headed toward the police department.

When Steve stopped at a red light, the man in the backseat jumped Gary and tried to wrestle his gun away. They both gripped the gun in a furious struggle and the barrel swung wildly from one to the other. As Steve swung around with his gun toward the rear, the man beside him grabbed for the gun and the gun fired, shattering the front windshield. Steve jerked the gun away and then swung it backhanded against the man's head, knocking him out.

Steve jumped out of the car and pointed his gun at the man in the backseat and was about to pull the trigger when a sound behind him caused him to stop and look back. Two deputies across the street were pointing their guns at the bearded, long-haired agent. He froze and started yelling, "*We're the police! We're the police! MBN! Don't shoot! Don't shoot!*" The agents and deputies subdued the assailant in the back-seat, and later that night they arrested the four robbers.

The snap Steve had heard behind his head during the robbery was the gun misfiring instead of blowing a hole through his head. He had close calls three times that night—during the robbery, during the struggle in the car, and when the deputies nearly shot him.

Buy-Busts and Arrests

Just Another Day in Greenville
At the request of DEA and MBN agents working the Greenville area, MBN agent Faron Gardner, a former Marine and MBN's only Native American, traveled from Meridian to Greenville to participate in two reverse-undercover operations. The agents planned to arrest the drug dealers during the middle of each transaction.

After arranging a large drug deal with a drug trafficker who owned a liquor store in Greenville, Faron went to the man's store to conclude the transaction. On a signal from Faron, who was wearing a body wire, agents outside the store were to rush in and arrest the man. The owner escorted Faron into the store and then closed and locked the front glass door and the inner door. He and Faron went behind the counter and stood discussing the deal. A few minutes later, the man saw agents approaching the door and he pulled out a revolver and began raising it to fire. Faron grabbed for the gun, clutched the barrel, and the two men fought for control. After a brief struggle, Faron wrested the gun away and subdued the man just as agents forced their way inside.

It had been a harrowing ordeal. But later that same night and just a few miles away, Faron would experience an equally dangerous confrontation during a second drug deal.

Six hours after surviving the struggle at the liquor store, Faron waited in a Greenville motel room in the early-morning hours to conclude another large drug deal. As in the liquor-store deal, agents conducting surveillance outside were to rush in and arrest the drug dealer. But the plan went awry. Believing that Faron had a large quantity of drugs in the room, three armed drug dealers showed up to rob him. When the men knocked at the door, Faron peeked out and thought at least one might be holding a pistol. Holding his gun ready, Faron opened the door just a crack but left the security chain fastened. The men suddenly kicked the door open. Faron reacted instantly and pointed his gun at the first man in the doorway but didn't shoot because he couldn't see a weapon. In the ensuing chaos, the three men fled on foot. Agents rushed in and caught one at the scene and recovered a high-powered rifle. They captured the other two men soon afterward. All three men later pled guilty in federal court on federal drug charges.

Faron survived two close calls within six hours—more than some MBN agents would encounter in their entire careers. Occasionally, however, tense undercover situations had unexpected endings, as Faron and agent Roy Sandefer Jr. found out. A drug dealer in Yazoo County agreed to sell Roy a large quantity of drugs and agents planned to arrest the man during the deal. But the man was wary and he told Roy to meet him on a bridge in an isolated area at midnight, and warned Roy, "If I see any headlights around, I'll know you're the police and I'll kill you."

The area around the bridge was too open for agents to get close without being seen, but Faron came up with a solution. Roy's undercover vehicle was a large pickup truck with a hunting-dog box in the back. Faron volunteered to hide in the dog box and pop out to arrest the dealer. That night Roy drove up to the bridge and met the drug dealer while Faron crouched in the dog box. As Roy and the drug dealer stood talking beside the pickup, Faron edged the lid of the dog box up slightly and grasped the top of the wall with his hand, getting ready to spring up. While talking with Roy, the drug dealer suddenly leaned against the pickup and stretched out his hand to rest it on the dog pen. The drug dealer's hand came down on top of Faron's and as it did, the dealer screamed, Faron popped up and yelled *"State Police,"* and the drug dealer jumped and screamed again.

Fortunately, the man never had an opportunity to carry out his threat to kill Roy. After the agents handcuffed the man, they noticed he had wet his pants, but at least he was the only one.

Senatobia

MBN agents John "Doc" Riddell and Dennis McAnally were doing a buy-bust deal in a motel room for nine ounces of cocaine. When the drug dealer took the cocaine out of a duffel bag, Doc gave the code word for the bust. As agents rushed into the room, the dealer grabbed a 9-millimeter pistol out of the bag and was raising it to shoot when Dennis shoved a gun barrel in his ear: *"Drop it! Drop it!"* The dealer froze and slowly lowered the gun. A shooting was barely averted.

Months later, during a one-kilogram cocaine buy-bust in a motel room in Oxford, one of the suppliers kept displaying his gun to undercover agents Randy Corban and Eddie McCullough. When Randy and Eddie pulled out their guns to make the arrest, the man reached for his gun and stopped only a split second before a shooting occurred. It was typical of many buy-bust arrests, characterized by a drug dealer raising a weapon to fire, agents holding their fire until the last moment, and the drug dealer finally dropping his weapon.

Randy Corban played his undercover roles so well that Bobby "Perk" Gaines from New Albany hired Randy as a hit man to kill Ben Prude, who ran Ben's beer store in Marshall County. Gaines provided Randy with a .44-caliber rifle to be used for the murder and was to pay Randy $3,000 after the job was done. Ironically, a few years later, Prude was murdered at his store. A suspect in the murder later led police in a chase after an unrelated crime spree and killed himself during a standoff.

Randy was also familiar with the rough and lawless areas of rural northeast Mississippi. Just stopping by a honky-tonk for a beer could be an adventure. One night in the gravel parking lot of a honky-tonk, Randy's female informant was shot through the breast by an errant shot, which she dismissed as a minor wound. The same informant believed in being prepared: she always carried a hammer in her purse for fights. She reminded me of my two rough ole gal informants, Sadie and Patty.

Pascagoula

Outside Pascagoula, a drug dealer armed with an assault rifle lay concealed in the woods, waiting in ambush for approaching MBN agents, who moved along a trail toward the man's fortified house. He was dressed in camouflage and had a bag with thirty clips of ammo, each holding thirty rounds. The agents were about to enter the kill zone when MBN agent Jim Kelly, in a helicopter overhead, spotted the man lying in ambush. Using an AR-15 rifle, Jim fired from the helicopter and wounded the man in the leg, a remarkable shot. Jim's expert shooting and cool head were honed by his combat experiences as a Marine in Vietnam.

Jackson

When MBN agent Danny Norton entered a mobile home to arrest a drug suspect, the suspect shot Danny with a .22-caliber magnum rifle. Danny wore a bulletproof vest and luckily the bullet struck the reinforced metal plate at the center of his chest. But the magnum bullet hit with such force that the impact knocked the 220-pound agent down. Struggling unsteadily to his feet, Danny managed to clear his head and concentrate on the armed suspect, who had disappeared down the hallway. Thinking quickly and improvising, Danny ran outside to the suspect's car and broke off the car's mirror. He went back inside the trailer and used the mirror to peer around the corner down the hallway without exposing himself to direct fire. The confrontation finally ended when the suspect was wounded and captured.

Yazoo County

When agents attempted to arrest two men during a drug deal one night in a remote area of Yazoo County, the men fled. One, armed with a rifle, ran into the woods. The second man fled in a pickup. During the ensuing vehicle chase, he fired from the truck and rammed through two roadblocks. Agent Steve Mallory was standing on a bridge with a shotgun when the fugitive's truck came barreling at him. Steve leaped out of the path of the pickup just in time, firing at a tire as the truck flew past. Agents Charlie Lindsey and Doug Cutrer jumped aside and also fired to disable the vehicle. The fugitive jumped out near a dumpster and during an armed confrontation, an agent fatally shot him. The other man was later captured without further violence.

Jackson

While on a drugstore burglary stakeout in Jackson, MBN agents Jim Wallace and Jim Kelly briefly left the detail to visit the hospital for a few minutes. Wallace's wife had just given birth to their son, Randy.

Just as the agents returned to the stakeout, they heard a Jackson police radio dispatch about a shooting at the Elbow Lounge, which was only a block from them. In an alley next to the lounge, they encountered the gunman standing over the man he had shot. The victim was gurgling and blood spurted from his neck. The agents identified themselves and ordered the gunman to drop his gun. Instead, he yelled, "I'll kill you, mutherfucker!" and fired at the agents. Wallace and Kelly fired back, hitting the gunman several times. Luckily, the agents were not hit and the gunman and the victim both survived their wounds.

Tippah County

In a remote area of Tippah County, MBN agent Chuck Smith sat in his car parked on the side of a road watching a distant house for a suspect to appear. Chuck was there to assist federal agents arrest the suspect on child-porn charges. Suddenly a car occupied by two men came barreling toward the front of Chuck's car, apparently intending to ram it. Chuck ducked down and tensed for the impact. Instead of ramming Chuck's car, the car squealed to an abrupt halt next to him and the two men jumped out of the car. The driver was the father of the suspect and the other man was the suspect's brother. The driver pointed a .357-magnum revolver at Chuck and ordered him out of the car. Chuck, who was wearing a marked MBN raid jacket, got out and identified himself as an MBN agent. Glaring at Chuck, the gunman said, "I don't care *who* you are. I'm going to *kill you.*"

Moments later the gunman was distracted by a distant sound and Chuck grabbed his own gun and fired. The bullet struck the gunman in the chest and the man collapsed.

After securing the other man, Chuck, a trained medic and a former EMT, turned his attention to the man he had shot, who was still alive. Chuck cleared the man's airway and radioed for an ambulance. He survived. Chuck had shot a man and then saved his life.

Compromised

Belzoni

After MBN agent Elbert Craig entered a house to make a drug buy, the two drug dealers inside discovered he was an agent. At gunpoint, they forced Elbert to get down on his hands and knees in the bathroom. One held a cocked gun to Elbert's head while they discussed whether to kill him there or in the woods behind the house. MBN lieutenant Shirlene Anderson, who was on surveillance, suspected that something had gone wrong. With agents Kathleen Ragan and Mary Nolden and task force agent Kary Ellington, Shirlene burst into the house, captured the drug dealers, and saved Elbert's life.

Tippah County

An MBN agent attempting to make a drug buy in a crowded house in a remote area of the county was compromised when an ex-informant in the room recognized a disguised body transmitter on the agent and warned the others. The agent ran from the house and fled in his car, chased by carloads of drug dealers. With flashing blue lights, agents on surveillance rushed to the rescue and, following a high-speed chase, they stopped and apprehended the pursuers.

Aberdeen

A group of drug dealers hung out at a car wash in Aberdeen, using it as an open-air marketplace to sell crack. When an agent and an informant pulled up in an SUV to try a drug purchase, the group at the car wash became suspicious. A concealed video camera in the vehicle showed them swarming to the driver's window, crowding close, shouting questions and demanding answers. One man suddenly thrust his arm through the open driver's window, trying to grab the vehicle keys from the ignition. The informant floored the SUV in a desperate attempt to escape the onslaught. As the vehicle sped out of the lot, the drug dealers shot at the two men, hitting the vehicle several times.

The action was captured on video. As the car roared off from the car wash, a series of gunshots erupted as five or six distinct pops. Driving wildly, the informant ducked down below the window, his face filling the camera, and yelled, "These mutherfuckers're shooting!" The SUV was hit in four places, including the driver's door, but the bullet hit at an angle and narrowly missed the informant.

Later that night, in the same area, someone jumped out of a side street and fired on MBN agents who were in a surveillance van. The man fled after getting off the shots. For agents, Aberdeen was reminiscent of the Wild West that night.

Water Valley

MBN agent Leon Williams and an informant rode together in the informant's car attempting to make drug buys, while agent James Catalino and a local officer provided surveillance. The agents didn't know it, but word had just spread among drug dealers that the informant was helping the law.

Leon and the informant were turned away at two houses. At a third house, a young gangster-looking guy came out toward the car but stopped when he saw the informant, and started backing up. "What ya'll doing coming to my house asking for dope?" he yelled. "I ain't got no dope." Leon radioed surveillance that something wasn't right. He suspected that word had gotten out about the informant.

As Leon and the informant drove away, two cars occupied by several men started following them, right on their back bumper. One of the cars pulled up beside them and the passenger yelled, "Get your snitch-ass and police mutherfucking ass out of town." The car sped up and swerved in front of the informant's car and stopped, blocking the front as the other car blocked the informant's car from behind. The passenger door in the front car flew open and the passenger jumped out with a pistol.

"Back up! Back up!" Leon yelled to the informant. The informant backed up and crashed into the second car. "Go forward!" Leon shouted. "Hit the sidewalk! *Go! Go! Go!*" The informant stomped the gas and the car shot forward, bumped up, and flew airborne onto the sidewalk and swerved around the car in front, tearing off the passenger door. The gunman jumped out of the way and fired several shots as Leon and his informant sped away. The attackers chased after them, but agents conducting surveillance rushed in and arrested the men.

Retaliation: Home Is Not a Sanctuary

Oxford

While MBN agent Roy Sandefer was working in the Oxford area, his identity became known to area drug dealers and he started receiving harassing phone calls. Roy lived in a mobile home outside town at the time. One night while Roy was out working, someone shot up and burned his mobile home and killed his dog. Although there were suspects, the crime was never solved. Roy was later stationed on the Gulf Coast, retired after a distinguished career, and served as deputy chief of the Jackson Police Department.

Meridian

MBN agent J. C. Denham worked undercover in the Meridian area, where he lived with his wife. When it finally came time to arrest the defendants in his cases, J. C.'s identity as an MBN agent was revealed when he presented the cases to the grand jury. Shortly after J. C. appeared before the grand jury, three men drove to his home late one night with a 12-gauge shotgun loaded with buckshot.

It was after midnight and J. C. was out working. His twenty-two-year-old wife, Stephanie, was home alone. When the armed men arrived, Stephanie was in the utility room at the front of the house doing laundry. As the men prepared to fire, she left the utility room and walked through the kitchen to a back bedroom. Suddenly, shotgun blasts exploded and double-aught buckshot tore through the windows and walls. Bullet-size lead balls ripped into the utility room where Stephanie had just been standing. Another shotgun blast erupted, then another and another and another. Five times the men aimed and fired, and fistfuls of buckshot ripped into the house with each blast. Buckshot tore through the metal refrigerator and punctured the water line. Dozens of buckshot riddled the utility room, the kitchen, and the Denhams' personal car in the carport.

A total of forty-three buckshot, each the size of a .32-caliber bullet, tore into the car and house. Had Stephanie still been in the utility room or had she stayed in the kitchen instead going to the back bedroom, she would have been killed or seriously injured. She survived only by chance.

When J. C. arrived home, he was stunned by the damage. Stephanie was terrified and crying. J. C. comforted Stephanie and took her to stay with her parents in a nearby town. Then J. C. and MBN went after the attackers.

That same night, MBN director Kenneth Fairly ordered MBN agents from around the state to rush to Meridian, and overnight agents flooded the city. Fairly sped to Meridian and met with the police chief to coordinate enforcement. The governor called J. C. and told him MBN would stay in Meridian until those responsible were arrested. Fairly set up a command post and agents started hitting the streets around the clock. For ten intensive days agents relentlessly pressured drug dealers at bars and hangouts with stops, frisks, and arrests. Tips started coming in and one source provided J. C. with information that helped identify the three attackers. MBN arrested the men; all three confessed, pled guilty, and received maximum sentences.

The brutal attack in Meridian was sobering for agents and their families. An agent's young wife had nearly been killed because of his work. We knew we had opponents who would kill us if they could and with each new incident their numbers grew. Now we realized that our families were at risk too. We soon had another reminder of the danger of our work. And it came from the state penitentiary.

The "K.O.S." List

At the state pen at Parchman, Mississippi, prisoners who had been sentenced on undercover buys made by MBN agents compiled and circulated a "K.O.S." list of agents. K.O.S. stood for "kill on sight." On two pages of paper, prisoners wrote down descriptions of MBN undercover agents, their vehicles, clothing, and undercover names. Through a source at Parchman, we found out about the K.O.S. list and seized it. I was on the list, along with Steve Mallory, Doug Cutrer, and others. A follow-up investigation at the pen did not produce criminal charges but did squelch any further organized efforts to identify and retaliate against agents.

■　■　■

MBN Agents Fall in the Line of Duty

Despite surviving shootings and close calls, terrifying moments, and near-death experiences, there were no time-outs for MBN agents. Agents followed up dangerous incidents by collecting evidence, writing reports, and going home or back to their motel room late at night, exhausted and drained. They got up the next morning and went back to work. But some left for work and never returned.

MBN agent Lane Caldwell was shot and killed when he attempted to arrest a kidnapper. When Lane left home that morning on the last day of his life, he left a wife and two young sons. Lane wasn't the only fatality. Agents Robert Henry McLeod, Spencer Glenn Beckley Sr., Marc Lee Whatley, and Kimbrough "Kim" Sterling died in vehicle accidents while on duty. They gave their lives to clean up the streets.

A Warning for MBN Agents and a Prediction

On an overpass over a rural two-lane road in south Mississippi, someone had painted a warning for MBN agents. An agent spotted the message soon after it was written. The agent stopped, got out of his car, and took a photograph of it. In large black letters, the message read, "NARCS DIE YOUNG."

The death threat was meant for MBN agents—they were the only narcotics agents working the area. Copies of the photograph quickly spread among agents throughout the state. Framed copies of that grainy, black-and-white photograph soon hung on office walls at MBN headquarters on Lakeland Drive in Jackson. MBN agents were a close group and that threat brought us even closer together. By identifying agents as a target, our adversaries recognized MBN as a distinct group and threat. It suggested that MBN was effective; otherwise, there would be no reason to retaliate or warn us off.

Most of all, it was a stark reminder of the dangers agents faced. Beneath the placid surface of everyday life, a constant battle raged between agents and those who would kill us if they could. And over and over again, they did try to kill us—whether it was shooting up an agent's residence, an ambush, or going for a gun during buy-busts and arrests. So the photograph became an icon for MBN—emblematic of the nature of our work. It was an exciting but deadly profession. "NARCS DIE YOUNG." The warning proved to be prophetic. Several did die young—and many came close.

My Last Undercover: Infiltrating Mafia and Mexican Drug-Smuggling Operations

My final undercover role lasted five long months. Wearing a three-piece suit and posing as a wealthy businessman from Memphis, I infiltrated an air-smuggling operation directed by a Mafia-linked group in New Orleans. By the time the undercover operation concluded, it had involved dozens of local, state, and federal agents conducting surveillance in three states, airplane seizures, drug seizures, Mafia links, and a smuggling organization based on the Texas-Mexico border. The investigation covered Mississippi, Louisiana, Texas, Florida, the Grand Cayman Islands, Belize, Mexico, Jamaica, and, at the end, Houston, Texas.

The investigation started in north Mississippi with a Swiss-born pilot, Max Keller, and a meeting between us to size each other up. A new informant, Tommy, reported that Max, a crop-dusting pilot in the Mississippi Delta, had approached him to find a buyer for up to 600 pounds of marijuana, which would be smuggled into Texas. From there Max would fly it to Mississippi in his single-engine Cessna. Max had been in the United States only a year, having lived for seventeen years in Nicaragua, where he owned six planes and a crop-dusting service. He had lost everything in a revolution and now he flew crop dusters out of one of the dozens of crop-dusting airstrips scattered throughout the Mississippi Delta.

I was an MBN district supervisor at the time. This would be quick, I thought. It would soon either lead to a drug seizure or Max would turn out to be just talk, but in any event, it wouldn't be an extended investigation. Was I ever wrong!

My cover story was that I was a wealthy Memphis businessman who backed large shipments of drugs distributed in the northeast United States. I told Tommy to tell Max I was interested in buying his entire planeload. Using the informant as a reference, I called Max at the Delta air service where he worked and he agreed to meet me at the Holiday Inn in Grenada. Playing my role, I wore a three-piece gray suit and had a briefcase full of papers open on the bed in the room. On a table sat a bottle of fine whiskey, a bucket of ice, and two glasses.

When Max and Tommy arrived, I told Tommy to leave so Max and I could talk alone. The informant was now permanently cut out of the investigation.

With thick, short-cropped, salt-and-pepper hair, tanned angular face, and compact frame, Max looked younger than his forty-nine years. His alert blue eyes watched me carefully, trying to discern if I was who I pretended to be.

"I trust Tommy," I said after he had left, "but if it's just you and me, Max, no one else can talk. Why take risks if you don't have to?"

"You never know," Max shook his head slowly, speaking English with a thick Swiss-German accent. "You never know. Look what happened to Tommy." He knew Tommy had been busted on a drug charge.

"Yeah, Max, that's why I prefer just you and me talking business alone."

"My buddy was suspicious too," Max said, referring to his smuggling connection. "My buddy said, 'Do you know the guy?' I said nope, I don't know him. So he said, 'I know you've checked him at least,' and I said, 'Yeah, I've checked him out.' 'Cause my buddy, he's careful. But I trust you because of Tommy, and I know if this comes back to be some crap, his ass is going to be in more trouble than mine," said Max forcefully.

His meaning was clear—if I turned out to be the law or a rip-off, Max and others might go to prison but Tommy would be hurt or killed.

I poured two whiskeys over ice and handed one to Max.

"Look, Max, I'm busy and I only came down from Memphis because Tommy told me you're all right and he said you and I might be able to do some business. He said you might be able to get a planeload of weed. If so, I might be interested in 600 pounds at the right price."

Max wanted $350 per pound and I offered $200 per pound for 600 pounds, a total of $120,000. Max said his buddy in Texas could supply the 600 pounds but I would have to go to Texas to pick it up. I explained that I would be more comfortable on the first deal if they would bring it to me. Max said he would get in touch with his friend and call me.

For the deal to have any chance I needed to meet Max's unidentified buddy, but we had a problem. Max and his buddy were cautious because they were aware Tommy had been busted, and that was more than enough reason not to trust anyone he introduced. And the buddy would be even more suspicious when Max told him I wanted him to come to me.

A few days later Max called.

"I talked to my buddy down there," Max said. "He said, for the first deal you need to come down there, to Texas, because he's careful. We just can't be enough careful."

"What about the price, Max?"

"I talked with him and it's a possibility what you told me you could pay, but the main problem is you have to go down there and meet him first. He told me you go down there by airline and if you want to, you can fly back with him in his plane."

"In other words, he wants me to bring the money down there."

"The first time. Later on, no problem."

"I don't like to go into another man's territory with my money until I've dealt with him. Look, Max, let's me and you get together tomorrow and see if we can work it out." We arranged to meet the next day at the Holiday Inn in Clarksdale.

It looked like the investigation was already stalling out. They were both suspicious. The fact that I had been introduced to Max by someone who had been busted was enough to warn them off. Max was careless but his experienced friend in Texas wasn't so easily fooled. With both wary, my going to Texas with the money was too vague and risky without knowing who I would be dealing with, how a deal would work, and where. I needed to find some way to motivate Max to convince his buddy to come to me, and I had an idea of how to do it.

The next afternoon, agent Ricky Peterson and I arrived at the Holiday Inn parking lot in Clarksdale and found Max waiting in his car. Ricky pretended to be one of the men who worked for me in the drug business.

When we pulled up beside Max, Ricky got in the backseat of our car and Max joined me in the front.

Before Max could say anything, I looked over my shoulder at Ricky.

"Hand me that briefcase." Ricky handed a briefcase over the top of the front seat and I put it down between me and Max. "Max, I want to show you that I have my money together . . ."

"I have no doubts."

"Right. But until you know you can trust my word, I want you to see for yourself." When I opened the briefcase, Max's eyes widened as he stared down at $125,000 in neat stacks of real one-hundred-dollar bills.

I picked up a stack and flipped through it and put it back. "Count it. It's $125,000, all hundreds. This is $5,000 more than we talked about. I'm throwing in the extra $5,000 as a premium to have the stuff delivered—a delivery price." Staring at the money, Max grinned and nodded.

"See, Max," I continued, "I'm willing to pay for stuff to be delivered but I'm not willing to go down on the first deal. If the first deal goes right, then after that I'll be willing to go down there and deal. I want you to know I have the money. I will hold this money for several days, *but* after that I'll be looking for other deals to put it in."

"You know," Max said, "my buddy, he told me, 'you said you checked him out and all Max, but it's hard for me to do this with a whole airplane load. Shit, something could happen.' Because my buddy, you see, he's pretty careful."

"That's the way we've all got to be," I agreed. "Look, I want to get something steady that I can rely on, one load every month. I want you to know I'm completely serious on this. You can explain to your man what my position is."

"I'm going to talk to him tonight by phone," Max exclaimed, his voice rising and accent becoming thicker, "and explain to him *the whole god-damn deal* and then get ahold of you, Mike."

"If he's worried about losing the stuff, Max, then we can just start off small. Instead of doing 600 pounds, we can just do something small the first time."

"Two hundred, or something like that?"

"Right. The first time."

"Maybe I could convince him," Max said, "I'll see. I'll try to catch him tonight and talk things over with him." Max's eyes shone with excitement.

"Maybe later we can get something going *both* ways. If your buddy knows someone down there who can handle negotiable securities, that would be good. I come across them all the time that are hot and they're impossible to trace—they're just like cash." I wanted to put the idea in their minds that I also was involved in other criminal ventures.

"I'll get in touch with him *today* and give you a call."

Because Max's buddy kept asking if Max had checked me out, I knew I had to shore up my cover story. Since I was supposedly a wealthy Memphis businessman, I needed a Memphis phone number, area code 901, where Max could call me. The day after our meeting I rented an answering service in Memphis in my cover name and fake company: "Michael Warren, Warren Property Management." I called Max and gave him the number.

"It's my office number, but I'm out of the office a lot. You can just leave a message with my receptionist and I'll call you back." Perhaps for now Max wouldn't discover that my "office" was only an answering service. I also needed a reason he couldn't call me at my Memphis home. "I live in a gated estate outside Memphis," I added, "but you can't call me there because my wife is trying to get grounds for a divorce. She won't move out because she's trying find out anything she can to use to blackmail me for millions in the divorce. So I can't talk business on my home phone."

Max understood. "Oh. Yah, yah, Mike, for sure." Max said his Texas buddy "Billy" was away and would be back soon. It was the first time Max mentioned his connection's name.

During the next several weeks, Max wouldn't make a commitment on the planeload, but we identified "Billy" as William Wayne Mahaffey, who, in addition to drug smuggling, also operated the Landing Café in Tunica. Mahaffey and his associates stayed busy during those ensuing weeks and so did MBN and other local, state, and federal law-enforcement agencies in Mississippi, Louisiana, Florida, Texas, Jamaica, and Belize.

On August 1, Mahaffey purchased a big twin-engine aircraft, a Beech 18, in Florida and had it flown to Ralph Sharp Airfield in Tunica, Mississippi.

A source told MHP investigator Bob Wallace that the plane would leave Tunica for an airstrip at Crowley, Louisiana, for modifications and then on to South America to smuggle cocaine back into the United States. According to the source, the pilots would be Mahaffey and J. R. Sirmons. MBN agents began a surveillance of the airplane and observed Mahaffey and an unidentified man working on it.

Customs and MBN agents planned to covertly install a law-enforcement transponder on the Beech 18. The transponder would allow the plane to be identified whenever it showed up on radar, although a pilot could evade detection when flying under radar or beyond radar range.

However, the Beech 18 flew from the Tunica airport before they could install the transponder, so we had no idea where Mahaffey had flown or what he was doing. Then, five days later, on August 25, through a stroke of luck, Mahaffey was located some 300 miles away in Slidell, Louisiana. In a remarkable coincidence, Mahaffey was discovered there by one of my closest friends, Louisiana State Police narcotics agent Jack Crittenden, who was unaware of our investigation. It came about through Jack's work on smuggling organizations.

Just before taking off to pick up a planeload of drugs, smugglers usually removed the passenger seats to make room for the drug cargo. Someone would then keep the seats in the back of a camper pickup truck or similar vehicle and wait at a motel for the airplane's return. With this in mind, Jack routinely checked motels near airports looking for camper pickups with aircraft seats in the bed. And that's when he found it.

Jack spotted aircraft seats in the back of a pickup parked at the Ramada in Slidell, Louisiana. When Jack checked the Mississippi license plate he learned Mahaffey owned the truck, which had a shell over the back and aircraft seats and a large vacuum cleaner in the truck bed. It was a major discovery and Jack and other Louisiana agents immediately put the vehicle under surveillance.

Checking motel records, Jack found that Mahaffey and Julian Robert Sirmons were in room 105 of the Ramada Inn. Jack then called MBN Intelligence to run a query on Mahaffey and discovered we were already working on him and that I was undercover on Mahaffey's partner Max Keller.

Two different smuggling crews were active for Mahaffey right then. The night before, Jack found Mahaffey in Slidell. A Beech Queen Air twin-engine aircraft took off from the Slidell airport and flew to Jamaica while Mahaffey waited at the Ramada with the aircraft seats. Early the next morning, the plane crashed on takeoff from Jamaica with approximately 1,720 pounds of marijuana on board. The pilot, Kenneth Martin Robinson, and an unidentified male were killed in the crash. A man from Lake Providence, Louisiana, subsequently identified Robinson's body. Lake Providence would come up again later in the investigation.

Mahaffey and the crew of the plane that crashed worked for a crime organization in New Orleans. The day after the plane crash, Mahaffey met in Slidell with three men from New Orleans. The next day Mahaffey and Julian Sirmons drove from Slidell to New Orleans and went to the French Quarter for several hours and then returned to Slidell. Mahaffey made calls from his room to Max Keller and to Richard Darden

Armistead of McAllen, Texas. Armistead would also show up again in the investigation.

We still didn't know where Mahaffey's plane was located, but he unwittingly led agents to it. On August 28, he and Sirmons left the Ramada Inn in Slidell and drove to a small private airport on the Mississippi Gulf Coast. There it was. Mahaffey boarded his Beech 18, took off flying west, and landed in Galveston, Texas, early that evening. He was followed by Julian Sirmons flying Max Keller's single-engine Cessna. Mahaffey and Sirmons rented a car and drove to a Galveston motel. We alerted Texas narcotics agents, who scrambled to the airport in time to conduct surveillance of the planes' arrivals.

August 29 turned out to be a busy day both for Mahaffey and his conspirators and for agents conducting surveillance. In my undercover role I became involved again that evening. At about 4:00 a.m., customs agents working with us covertly installed a law-enforcement transponder on the big Beech 18 while it was in Galveston. We would finally be able to track its flights by radar.

At 7:00 a.m., Mahaffey and Sirmons took off and flew their planes back to the Mississippi Gulf Coast, where they met with the airport manager and placed the single-engine Cessna in a hangar. Mahaffey was overheard telling the manager, "It will be just like the last package." Mahaffey and Sirmons then drove to the Ramada Inn in Slidell. Meanwhile, the airport manager loaded cases of motor oil and groceries onto the Beech 18.

Late that afternoon, Mahaffey and Sirmons reloaded the aircraft seats from their room at the Ramada in Slidell onto Mahaffey's pickup and drove back to the Gulf Coast airport.

At 8:00 p.m., three men in a black Cadillac with Louisiana tags arrived at the airport and met with Mahaffey and Sirmons in the airport office while the manager waited on them with drinks. Mahaffey and one of the men walked outside to talk and the man appeared to be giving him instructions. Mahaffey then retrieved a handgun from his pickup and rejoined the others in the airport office. All six men then walked to the Beech 18 and fueled the bladder tank in the cabin of the plane, after which the three men left in the Cadillac. The bladder tank held extra fuel for the long flight. Mahaffey and Sirmons took off heading south over the Gulf of Mexico, flying to Jamaica to pick up a cargo of marijuana.

A few minutes later, after being alerted that the plane had taken off over the Gulf, I called Max and expressed an interest in obtaining 400 pounds of marijuana.

Referring to Mahaffey, who had just flown south, Max said, "I'll know something the next day or two, because a guy who is out of town on a trip will be back from 'down there.'"

But Mahaffey didn't make it back as planned. The next day, Saturday, August 30, Mahaffey and Sirmons were arrested in Belize when they landed with 1,500 pounds of marijuana in Belize City. They had run low on fuel and made an unscheduled stop to refuel. Local authorities routinely checked the plane and discovered the marijuana cargo.

The next day, August 31, a Learjet arrived in Belize. On board were five men from New Orleans. They were seen sitting in the back row at Magistrate's Court in Belize during legal proceedings involving Sirmons and Mahaffey.

We were totally unaware of the seizure. I called Max to find out what was going on. Max said he had just received a message that something had gone badly wrong. He was going to check further and would get back with me.

On September 1, three days after the plane seizure in Belize, Mahaffey and Sirmons were sentenced in Magistrate Court in Belize to serve three months in jail. However, two days later they were secretly released and left by road for Mexico and the United States.

Max called me that afternoon. "I have some bad news," he said. "One plane crashed on takeoff from Jamaica killing a friend of mine. He was the pilot. The copilot was killed too. It's really bad. The plane was carrying a load when it crashed."

"That's too bad, Max."

"And the other crew is in a jam too. I talked with the lawyer in New Orleans and they went down there on a Learjet. Now I've got to help organize things."

On September 5, I met with Max in his room at the Holiday Inn in Clarksdale. Max was upset about the two men who had died when the Queen Air that had taken off from Slidell crashed in Jamaica. Then, referring to Mahaffey and Sirmons, Max said, "The other crew were arrested in Belize and lost the plane and the merchandise. Everything. One is my buddy Billy, but it's going to be okay. Both of them got back to the states yesterday. I would really like for you to meet Billy, because in the future he's gonna be my head man."

Max said the seizure and arrests proved beneficial because Billy obtained new smuggling contacts, including growers in Belize and contacts all the way up to the prime minister's office. "Billy's already got an airport lined up and now he just needs to get another plane. We need a market where we know every month we can get rid of so much."

"That's exactly what I'm looking for," I said, "a regular supply, so much every month that I can send to the northeast. We get premium prices up north and the organization I'm connected with up there handles everything: transportation, security, and distribution."

"Good, Mike, 'cause that's what we need, regular business. Billy, he can't go back to Belize right now and I'll be the one to go back down there. I told Billy all about you and I want to set up a meeting for you two to meet each other."

On September 9, Max's Cessna landed in Tunica. The plane had been left in a hangar on the Mississippi Gulf Coast when Mahaffey took off for Jamaica. After returning from Belize, Mahaffey had flown the plane to Tunica.

That day, I finally met "Billy"—William Wayne Mahaffey. Max Keller called and said he and his friend Billy wanted to meet with me. We arranged to meet that night in the restaurant at the Holiday Inn in Clarksdale.

I intentionally arrived fifteen minutes late. As I approached their table, Max beamed and they stood up to greet me. Billy Wayne Mahaffey, forty-two, was medium height and build, with brown hair. Max introduced me to Mahaffey, but before they could say anything, I pretended I needed to take care of other business first.

"Excuse me for a minute," I said hurriedly, glancing at my watch. "I've got to make a call right away to take care of some business that came up just before I left Memphis. Be right back." I hurried to the motel lobby and pretended to make a call on a pay phone. I wanted to reinforce my cover as a businessman and suggest I was doing them a favor by taking time to meet.

After I returned to the table we engaged in small talk and then I brought up the seizure. "Max told me you ran into a little trouble on your last trip."

Mahaffey grimaced. "We picked up a load in Jamaica and flying back toward Louisiana we ran into headwinds and ran low on fuel so we landed at the airport in Belize to refuel. But when we landed they found the load and arrested us. I lost the plane and the entire load," he said with a frown. "Cost me $70,000."

"What did they do to you?"

"They tried us two days later and sentenced us to three months in prison. But some people from New Orleans flew down in a Learjet and paid $20,000 to bribe us out. We spent three days in jail and then they secretly let us go. Took us to the border with Mexico and we made our way back from there. The authorities in Belize are still showing on their books that we're in prison."

"Actually, everything has worked out even better because of it," he continued. "I made contacts with growers in Belize, lined up an airfield, and got a government minister as a contact. I can bring a load from Belize and the trip will be a lot shorter than flying all the way to Jamaica. The minister will be able to let me know if there is any heat on us. I want to fly loads from Belize and wanted to meet you because I need a customer who can take loads on a monthly basis."

"That's good," I said, "because my organization is looking for a regular supply. I would like to do a small load first to see how it works out."

"The loads would have to be at least a thousand pounds," Mahaffey said, "otherwise it won't be worthwhile."

"A thousand is no problem."

"I lost a lot on this deal in Belize so I'll need financing for the first load and I'll need operating expenses."

"How much?"

"A total of about $100,000 will do it. That doesn't include the cost of getting another plane. We'll get a light twin engine and hide the ownership by registering it in the Grand Caymans. The banks there handle huge amounts of drug money and they don't have a reciprocal agreement with the US."

"I'm ready to buy loads of a thousand pounds or more," I said, "but I have concerns about two issues. First is the quality of the marijuana grown in Belize. I've never had any from there. All mine has been Mexican and Columbian. Second, do you have heat on you now because of the seizure in Belize?"

"I'm okay on the seizure. As far as we know, Belize didn't send any details of it to Washington. My attorney and the minister are trying to suppress reports about the seizure and we're pretty sure it can be done. Plus, back here in the States I'm going to be moving in about three weeks and sometimes I'll use another name. So I'm pretty sure there's no heat on me in the US and I'm not being followed."

"On the quality of the marijuana from Belize," he continued, "I really don't know. But I can arrange for you to check a sample in Mexico or Belize. I'm pretty sure it's gonna be as good as Mexican and probably as good as Jamaican. Give me about a week's notice and I'll arrange for you to fly to Belize and check a sample."

"Good, because once my people are satisfied with the quality, then we can work out the details for regular deliveries."

"That sounds good to me," said Mahaffey. "I'll be able to deliver a planeload once a month and can probably supply quantities of Quaaludes made in Jamaica. But I'm really more interested in just doing the marijuana from Belize because the trip is shorter and the price is cheaper there."

"All right. I like what I've heard. I'll wait for you and Max to get back with me about getting a sample to check on the quality."

The next day, September 10, the Learjet landed at Moisant Airport, New Orleans, on a flight from Grand Cayman Island. On board were the pilot and copilot, one woman, and three men. The same three men had earlier flown on the Learjet to Belize when Mahaffey was arrested there.

On board, customs inspectors found three envelopes containing a total of $180,000 in cash. At first everyone was reluctant to discuss the money but finally one signed a customs form indicating that his law firm was responsible for the funds. We suspected that the organization Mahaffey worked for had brought in the money to buy him another airplane.

Two days later, on September 12, two men purchased an Aero Commander 681 twin-engine airplane in Oklahoma for $166,000. They paid $152,000 in cash and wired $14,000 later. They flew it away that same day. The purchasers were from Metairie, Louisiana, and St. Croix, US Virgin Islands. The address given by the Metairie man was same address of one of the men on board the Learjet when it flew to Belize and when the $180,000 cash was discovered on board. It appeared the organization had used cash from Grand Cayman to purchase the Aero Commander for Mahaffey's use. Mahaffey was back in business.

Two weeks later, on September 26, Mahaffey landed the Aero Commander at Hawkins Field in Jackson, Mississippi, and refueled. One engine wouldn't restart so he left the plane for repairs and rented a car to drive to Tunica. Agents saw that the passenger seats had been removed from the plane and all the windows except the windshield and the pilot's window had been blacked out, classic signs of a drug-smuggling plane. Mahaffey was ready for another smuggling run. Max called me and said Mahaffey wanted to meet with me.

The next day, MBN agent Teresa Sheffield and I obtained a suite at the high-rise Rivermont Holiday Inn in Memphis and met with Mahaffey and Max Keller. The spacious suite was near the top of the towering hotel overlooking the Mississippi River. I told the men I had trysts at the hotel with my mistress who frequently flew in to meet me and our room would be a private and safe place to meet.

But my cover was razor thin and it would be a race to complete the investigation before they discovered that I didn't exist. During my first meeting with Mahaffey, in Clarksdale, I had sometimes caught him watching me carefully. If he had any second thoughts about me and checked me out, he would quickly discover that Mike Warren was a fake. My cover wasn't backstopped: I didn't have an office, home address, bank account, or credit history—nothing to show I was a real person and had a real company. Not even a Tennessee driver's license. Even the most superficial background check would burn me down. With such a flimsy cover, I needed to be so convincing that they wouldn't check up on me. The sophisticated organization Mahaffey worked for might make inquiries about me when Mahaffey proposed to his bosses that I be allowed to buy one of the planeloads of drugs. The delicate house of cards I had constructed could come tumbling down at any moment, putting me in serious jeopardy.

So far, my cover was supported only by a three-piece suit, an answering service in my business name, and bogus business cards. Now that Mahaffey was meeting with me for a second time, I needed to somehow bolster my credibility. That's where MBN agents Teresa Sheffield and John Riddell came in.

For the meeting at the Rivermont, Teresa, an attractive, curvy blonde, played the role of my mistress. She dressed for the part, wearing an elegant, pink, low-cut, clinging, and shimmering evening dress. Her partially open suitcase rested on a dresser with flimsy lingerie spilling out, concealing a recorder that captured Mahaffey's revelations about smuggling. As Mahaffey, Max, and I relaxed at the table, Teresa lovingly waited on us, keeping our whiskey glasses filled and iced. At other times she would stand beside my chair, her shapely body pressed against me while her fingers lightly caressed the back of my neck. She was alluring. Mahaffey and Max noticed and were frequently distracted. Sometimes I was too.

I had arranged for MBN agent John "Doc" Riddell to phone the room fifteen minutes after the meeting with Mahaffey and Max started. Teresa answered and handed me the phone.

"Mike, it's Robert. He says he's sorry but he needs to talk to you."

I took the phone. "Yes, Robert? That's all right," I said in a slightly exasperated voice. "No need to apologize. Bring the papers on up and I'll sign them." As intended, Mahaffey and Max heard my end of the conversation. I pretended to be put out at always having to tend to other business.

"Sorry, but I'm going to have to sign some bank papers, stock transactions and property documents that can't wait. It'll just take a few minutes."

Mahaffey's and Max's eyes lit up and they said they completely understood.

Teresa answered the knock at the door and admitted Doc, who came in profusely apologizing. Like Teresa, Doc was perfectly suited to his undercover role. The son of a doctor, Doc was handsome and neatly groomed, with cultured manners and an engaging smile. He was dressed sharply in a dark-blue pinstriped suit and vest. He looked the part of a young, astute businessman accustomed to moving in wealthy and powerful circles.

"Mr. Warren, I'm sorry to bother you, sir."

"That's all right, Robert. Where are the papers?"

Doc opened his briefcase and took out several documents.

"These are the ones, Mr. Warren. They just need your signature on these right here, sir. I'm sorry to interrupt you, sir."

"That's all right. Don't worry about it." I signed the papers. Handing them back, I said, "Take these to the bank and this one to my broker."

"Yes, sir."

"And tell him that I might get another 10,000 shares. I'll let him know."

"Yes, sir. Again, I'm sorry, Mr. Warren."

"That's okay, Robert, perfectly all right. You just run along and I'll see you later to finish up."

"Yes, sir."

After Doc left, Teresa topped off our drinks and Mahaffey began talking about getting caught in Belize with 1,500 pounds of marijuana on his plane and how the organization paid bribes to get him secretly released. For over two hours, Mahaffey freely discussed his smuggling activities and the organization he worked for, revealing an extensive Mafia-linked drug-smuggling operation that used planes and boats to smuggle tons of drugs.

"I work for a large, well-financed organization based in New Orleans," said Mahaffey. "Week after next they're going to fly in six loads of weed. More than a half million in deposits have already been made on them. I'll always work for them but I also want to develop my own independent operation, Mike, and you could help with the initial financing. I can get you 1,500 pounds of weed for $250 to $260 a pound, but you'll need to supply the crew to unload the plane."

"At that price, I'd be interested in getting a planeload," I said, "and send it up north where we get premium prices. Max may have told you that I'm connected with an organization in the northeast US. They take care of my security and distribution."

"I might be able to let you have the fourth load but they'll have to approve it first. I've got an Aero Commander 681 that the organization bought for me. I'll fly the load myself and deliver it to you at one of two airfields on the Gulf Coast. Here, let me show you where." Mahaffey drew a map on the back of a room-service menu, outlining the coast and marking the locations of the airfields. "We bought off the attendant there," said Mahaffey, pointing to an airfield on his hand-drawn map. "He stays at the field. We recently located another field, right here, and bought off that operator too. I've got a third airfield lined up also."

"Since I'll have to supply the off-load crew," I said, "I'll need to know the layout first."

"I'll fly you to the airfield we'll use so we can plan the unloading and transportation of the load. I'm going to make a dummy run at the new place Wednesday. It's a new field we got, and it's isolated, away from any town. We bought off that airfield manager too."

"Great," I said. "The good thing is that you have three airfields on the coast and bought off people at each one. I just need to know if I'm going to be able to get a load."

"I'll contact my organization and let you know if you will be able to get the load, 1,500 pounds. Here's numbers where you can reach me." He wrote two Mississippi numbers on a Jack Daniels card, and the name of a woman next to one number. "You can contact me through them. I use the names B. W. and John Ringo, and I always use pay phones. When we talk on the phone we use *acres of property* for *pounds of weed*. In my organization, *South* means Miami and *Down South* is Jamaica."

Mahaffey was eager to talk and I shut up and listened.

"The organization I work for," Mahaffey continued, "it's large and well organized and based in New Orleans. I've been working for them for two years. Two or three families head the organization and they have connections in Arizona, Chicago, California, and Florida. Our base is exactly five and a half air miles from the DEA in New Orleans. We don't bring in loads at the base; instead, we use it for shop work. Some smuggling does occur at Lakefront Airport in New Orleans; a plane regularly unloads in one of the hangers at the airport."

"After my Twin Beech was seized in Belize, the organization furnished me with an Aero Commander. I just flew it to Hawkins Field at Jackson.

I run this plane for the organization and will continue to work for them, and any deals you and I do will be on the side. I want to get you a load to prove you can trust me enough to provide financing for my independent operation.

Mahaffey explained how he got caught with the planeload of dope in Belize. "I loaded up in Jamaica with 1,600 pounds of weed, but they didn't put enough fuel on board when I was on the ground in Jamaica and it caused me to have to divert from my planned route. I left Jamaica with the load and flew to Cayman and then to Cozumel and then headed north. I originally planned to fly north from Cozumel to a point eighty miles north of New Orleans, but I hit strong headwinds and was running low on fuel. So we turned back and landed in Belize, hoping to refuel but got arrested and they seized the load."

Referring to Julian Sirmons, Mahaffey said, "Me and Julian, the co-pilot, are supposed to be in prison down in Belize right now, but they bribed our way out. They tried to buy all the paperwork on the seizure but couldn't get it all destroyed even though we offered a lot of money for it." Mahaffey stopped and sipped his whiskey and then resumed.

"But it worked out even better for us. Now we have a high-level contact in Belize. He's a magistrate, same as a Supreme Court judge. The magistrate arranged for me and Sirmons to secretly leave the country. Because of him, I can fly into Belize with immunity but I have to wait until my three-month prison sentence expires because they're carrying me on the books down there as serving time. If we go down there before that time, Max here can fly the first trip.

"After I got out of Belize, I met the magistrate in New Orleans during the same week you and I last met. I can arrange for you to meet with the Belize magistrate. We can do it in the US or in Mexico.

"Looking back on it now, when I loaded up in Jamaica and discovered that I was eighty gallons short of fuel, I should have unloaded the weed and then fueled up at Kingston, Jamaica, International Airport. I could have paid off people in Jamaica who are associated with the organization. Our planes in Jamaica are loaded by the military and a high-ranking Jamaican military officer is involved with us.

"Until recently we flew at 10,000 to 15,000 feet, but now with the turboprop Aero Commander we can fly at 20,000 to 25,000 feet and that way we can avoid bad weather, which is our biggest problem. I want to get a bigger Aero Commander 690 so I can fly even higher and faster. We leave and return to the US in daylight hours so as to avoid standing out on New Orleans radar. As for fuel, we have a connection with an oil company dealer and buy sealed drums from him. The organization smuggles a lot by boat too. In fact, they have a boat coming in around October 15.

"I had contacts set up, a strip bought off, got a new plane, but I lost a pilot. Since coming back from Belize, Julian is missing on another flight to Jamaica, and I need to find another pilot." Referring to another pilot by a first name, Mahaffey said, "I'll just get him to take Julian's place. He has an airplane that's been confiscated because it was reported stolen, but it's not stolen." We later followed up on that information and fully identified the pilot and the plane.

Max spoke up about Julian Sirmons. "I've known Julian for eighteen years," Max said, "and I got him to work for Billy here."

"Because Julian's disappeared," said Mahaffey, "our operations have been suspended for the coming week. See, just like when the other plane crashed, a Queen Air, I had to wait a week after the crash before making another run to Jamaica in my Twin Beech.

"On getting you that 1,500 pounds," Mahaffey said, "my organization wanted me to find a buyer and a catch crew because other planes will be coming in about the same time. Three planes will be running at the same time. My organization is not one outfit, but two or three families working together. I do business mainly with three people, but hundreds of others are involved in it."

After we had identified the Aero Commander Mahaffey was now using, agents secretly installed a tracking device on it. During our next meeting, Mahaffey told me when he was going to be leaving in the Aero Commander to pick up another drug load. The plane was tracked on radar as it left the United States heading south over the Gulf of Mexico.

On the return flight, radar picked up the plane and agents tracked it as it neared the coast and headed toward Franklinton, Louisiana. Mahaffey landed the drug-laden Aero Commander at the small Franklinton airfield. The plane was on the ground for only a brief time, just long enough to unload bales of marijuana from the plane into a large van.

As soon as the off-loading was completed, Mahaffey took off and flew to the isolated airstrip on the Mississippi coast, where he cleaned the plane to remove any signs of the illegal cargo. He drove from there to Tunica, Mississippi, where he lived and operated a restaurant when he wasn't in Texas.

Meanwhile, alerted by the hidden tracking device on the plane, state and federal agents rushed to the airfield at Franklinton and arrived just as the van was leaving. They followed it to a warehouse located in an isolated, densely wooded area. Later that night, armed with a search warrant, federal and state agents raided the property and found 750 pounds of marijuana, all in large bales, and arrested seven men on state drug charges. The agents had just missed a much larger load. Mahaffey told me later that two large shipments of marijuana had come in by boat and had cleared the barn just before it was raided.

Among those arrested was Nofio Pecoraro Jr., thirty-one, the son of Nofio Pecoraro, one of the main lieutenants for the Carlos Marcello Mafia family of New Orleans. The drug case on Pecoraro Jr. took an interesting turn. He and his mother, Frances Pecoraro, were later indicted on federal charges for trying to bribe a state judge on the drug case. Each received a two-year sentence on the federal bribery case and he got an additional three years on the state drug charge.

Despite her husband's position as a top Mafia figure (or perhaps because of it), Frances Pecoraro was a high-level state official—she served both as chair of the state insurance rating commission and as the assistant agriculture commissioner. It must have been an embarrassing time for her husband, Pecoraro Sr. In addition to his responsibilities as a Mafia leader, he had to worry about his son facing state drug charges and now his wife and his son facing federal bribery charges.

In 1991, Frances pleaded guilty in another case to money laundering, fraud, and other charges. Pecoraro Jr. fled just before he was indicted in the 1991 case and was a fugitive for thirteen years. He was finally caught in Britain in 2003. Using the alias "John Styker," Pecoraro had been running a pub on the outskirts of London. His capture generated newspaper articles across the United States. One of most creative headlines was by a newspaper in Seattle, Washington: "13-Year Hunt Ends in Arrest of 'Grogfather,'" *Seattle Times*, February 1, 2004.

Mahaffey was also linked to the Mafia through his phone calls to a number in New Orleans. DEA Intelligence reported that the number belonged to a front company for a multi-million-dollar drug-smuggling organization controlled by Carlos Marcello's brother, Vincent Marcello, and one of the men who had flown on the Learjet. After the company closed down, the men became involved with a famous French Quarter establishment.

■ ■ ■

Although Mahaffey had flown the drug load, we refrained from arresting him and seizing the plane so that I could continue undercover. As we had hoped, he didn't realize that his plane had been tracked or that he had any heat on him. He assumed the seizure in Louisiana was related to the boatloads of marijuana probably being traced to the barn. He thought agents had simply hit the barn too late to seize the boat shipments and had lucked into seizing part of his planeload that was still at the barn.

Ten days after the seizure in Louisiana, MBN undercover agent Teresa Sheffield and I again met with Mahaffey at the Rivermont Holiday Inn in Memphis. Mahaffey talked about smuggling and drew a map to show me the location of an airfield they used near Lake Providence, Louisiana. "We've got someone at the airfield. It's a perfect place and we've brought in eight loads there," said Mahaffey. I asked him if he had any heat on him.

"On my last trip the load went to a warehouse in Louisiana and the feds hit the warehouse and got part of the load," said Mahaffey. "But I checked with the lawyer and I'm okay. They called me from the lawyer's office yesterday. They don't really know what happened," Mahaffey said. "But I checked with the lawyers down there and they say there's no heat on me at all," he said, shaking his head.

Mahaffey mentioned the names of the two lawyers. One was on the Learjet when it flew to Belize after Mahaffey was arrested with the planeload of marijuana and was also on the Lear when it arrived in New Orleans with $180,000 cash on board. The other lawyer had represented one of the defendants charged in a Mafia case.

"That's too bad about your load getting hit," I said.

"See, here's what happened." Mahaffey said, leaning closer. "Two boats came in with loads just before I flew in. They were working two boats on the north side of Lake Pontchartrain [the large lake bordering New Orleans to the north]. I think they followed the loads from the boats to the stash place. But when they hit it they missed the loads from the boats because they had already been moved out. Instead of getting the big loads from the boats, the feds caught the load I had brought in. But there's no heat on me and we've already gotten rid of the plane anyway. So," he said smugly, "I'm not worried about any heat on me."

Mahaffey was in a curious predicament because of the plane and drug seizures. A string of reverses had followed him, and the organization he worked for had spent considerable sums. The Twin Beech 18 had been seized in Belize with 1,500 pounds of marijuana. He had not only lost the plane and the drug shipment, but his people from New Orleans had to pay $20,000 in bribes. Then they paid $166,000 for the Aero Commander and afterward lost part of the load Mahaffey had flown in with it, which also resulted in the arrests of some members of the organization, including a Mafia leader's son.

Mahaffey was becoming expensive and the organization had to be getting suspicious that he had too much heat on him or couldn't be trusted. At the very least, it was time to let Mahaffey cool off for a while. Without the prospect of continuing to make money by flying drug shipments, Mahaffey turned to another drug-smuggling organization based on the Texas-Mexico border and offered me 1,500 pounds of marijuana.

Over several phone conversations with Mahaffey, and then with Max Keller and Richard Armistead, we negotiated price and delivery location. Armistead had the connection. I increased the quantity I would take and agreed to purchase 3,000 pounds at $180 per pound, for a total price of $540,000. I would take delivery in Houston, Texas, on November 18.

Negotiating price was fairly straightforward, but negotiating the delivery location was difficult. The suppliers wanted me to do the deal in "the valley," the area around McAllen, Texas, adjacent to the Mexican border. I refused because it would be too dangerous. The suppliers would have control of the area, making surveillance difficult or impossible. I could be isolated and held hostage pending completion of the deal, or kidnapped and murdered for the half-million-plus buy money. I suggested north Mississippi or Memphis and then north Louisiana as a compromise, but they refused. As an alternative, they insisted on Houston, Texas. I agreed.

They would naturally want to control where and how we would do the 3,000-pound deal, which likely would make it difficult for surveillance and would expose me and other agents to greater danger. I had to try to convince them to do it my way.

I told Max and Armistead that I would fly to Houston for the deal, although I actually planned to drive. Max and Armistead would fly commercially from McAllen to Houston. We agreed to meet at the Houston International Airport. They said that after we met at Houston International we would travel to Hobby Airport in Houston and from there fly by helicopter to a ranch located fifty miles outside Houston and do the deal there. I knew that would be a problem but didn't object. I had another idea and would surprise them with it at the airport.

Finally it was time to travel to Houston and plunge into the uncertainty that waited. Other than Max and Armistead, whom I had never met but had talked with on the phone, I didn't know anything about the organization I would be dealing with, who I would meet, where the ranch was located, or how they would want to do the deal.

The next two and a half days would turn out to be nearly nonstop: a long drive and almost constant negotiations and meetings with members of the drug organization.

After a sleepless night, MBN agent Ricky Peterson and I made an eleven-hour drive from north Mississippi to Houston. We were running late and upon arrival we went directly to a hurried meeting at the Houston DEA office. We had called ahead and the DEA agent in charge provided as many agents and resources as we needed, including a flash roll. The first critical event would be the meeting at the airport. From the DEA office we rushed to the airport, arriving just as the flight landed.

Houston International Airport

Max came off the plane with two men following close behind. When Max saw me, his eyes brightened and he broke into a wide grin. He turned and said something to two men behind him while motioning toward me. They hurried over and Max introduced me to Armistead and Ivan Carpenter.

"Mike, we need to hurry, yah, and get to Hobby Airport," Max said eagerly, talking fast. "At Hobby we get a helicopter and fly to the ranch. It's only about fifty miles from here and we'll be there pretty damn quick, yah." The other two were nodding and were ready to rush to Hobby.

"Hold on, Max," I said, holding my hand up. "Let's go over to a table and talk and I'll tell you how I would prefer to do this."

Max's brow creased and he looked deflated. We walked to a nearby table.

"But, Mike," Max protested as we sat down, "we have a helicopter ready to go. We go to Hobby Airport and fly on the helicopter to this place. It's a ranch just fifty miles from Houston, and then . . ."

"Max, wait, I appreciate those arrangements," I countered, "but here's my problem. It's not all my money in this deal. I have investors. Several lawyers help finance my deals and I have to look after their money." Armistead and Carpenter bent closer and I turned to them. "If it was just my money," I explained, "there'd be no problem. We could fly out to the ranch because I know Max," I nodded at Max and looked back at them, "and I trust Max. I want to make this a regular deal, once or twice a month, but I don't know anyone else and on the first deal I have to look after everyone's money. After the first deal we'll do it anyway you want. If it was just my money we'd be on our way to Hobby right now to take the helicopter. Let's get this first deal done and then we'll be doing a regular thing, anyway you want." I looked from one to the other and Carpenter and Armistead nodded, and I kept going before anyone could raise an objection.

"I'm going to get a motel room at the Holiday Inn on Highway 45 close to here," I continued. "Talk to your people and meet me there. I'll get a U-Haul truck and give it to you. You can fill it up and bring it back and I'll pay the money then. Once I get it back I'll have two of my men drive it to Memphis. That's simple and easy. Nothing complicated. So let's get this going, okay?

"To show you I'm ready to do business," I offered, "and to show good faith, I'll take one of you right now to see the money—all five hundred and forty thousand. It's right outside. Pick one of you right now to come with me to see it and the others wait here."

The three looked at each other with questioning eyes and Carpenter spoke up. "I'll go." He glanced at Max and Armistead, and they nodded at him. He turned back to me. "I'm ready." The choice told me that Carpenter was the one closest to the smuggling organization.

Making a surprise show of a flash roll doesn't prevent anyone from attempting a robbery but it does preclude anyone from planning it in advance and coordinating with accomplices. A half million in cash would be tempting to anyone.

As I led Carpenter out of the terminal, a white van pulled up with three men in it, Ricky Peterson and DEA agents Tiffin and Marshall playing undercover roles. The side door slid open and we climbed in and slid onto the middle seat. The van drove off and slowly circled the airport parking lots.

The agent in the rear handed me a zippered sports bag and I placed it on the floorboard and unzipped it. It was stuffed with real hundred-dollar bills bundled into half-foot high stacks. One-half million dollars cash beckoned from the bag. Carpenter stared at the money and his eyes lit up. He shot me a sidelong questioning look.

I waved at the bag. "Go ahead. Take a look." He randomly picked up a few stacks and thumbed them. Finally he nodded, satisfied that the stacks consisted entirely of hundred-dollar bills.

"It's all there—five hundred and forty thousand," I said, "the full amount for 3,000 pounds. By showing you my money is ready, I'm showing my good faith. I'm ready to do the deal. We just need to work out the details." There was a half million dollars in the bag instead of the full $540,000, but I knew he wouldn't take time to count it.

When we dropped Carpenter off at the terminal I reminded him I was on my way to the nearby Holiday Inn to get a room and I would be waiting for them to contact me there.

The Holiday Inn Crisis

After showing the half million at the airport, we had a roadside meeting with the DEA supervisor to fill him in on the airport meeting. It delayed us and I tried to hurry it so that we could get to the motel before they tried to contact me. As it turned out, a surprise and a real crisis awaited.

After the DEA meeting, an agent drove me and Ricky to the motel as other agents converged on it to conduct surveillance. Unfortunately, the DEA car we were in was a large, unmarked police-type sedan, four doors and no hubcaps, readily recognizable to even the most casual observer as a law-enforcement car. The car came to a stop under the overhanging portal of the motel, with another, similar DEA car behind us. The motel doors and adjoining walls fronting on the entrance were floor-to-ceiling plate glass. Ricky and I got out of the car and walked through the doors. Just inside, I almost froze in midstride, stunned to find Max standing in the middle of the lobby watching us. Through the plate-glass windows, he saw us arrive and emerge from the DEA car. Max stared at us with a startled look, his eyes wide and frightened. Then his eyes skipped to the front where the car had dropped us off. I veered from my path to the desk and started walking toward him, smiling. He looked past me at the DEA cars that were driving away. His jaw tightened and he looked like he was about to take off running.

"Hey, Max," I called out casually while strolling toward him, trying to will myself to relax and pretend everything was okay. But he wasn't paying attention. He stared past me toward the front. As the DEA cars drove off, his eyes followed them until they were out of sight, then flickered around the lobby trying to see everything inside at once, sensing danger like a cornered animal. As I neared, Max instinctively backed up a half step, perhaps expecting me to slap handcuffs on him. The huge drug deal might already be lost for good.

From years of undercover I knew that sometimes you have to impose your will on others. Through attitude, energy, and earnestness, you must try to convince others to believe what you want. Now was the time. The old saying zipped through my mind: "Who are you going to believe—me, or your lying eyes?" Max's eyes correctly told him that an unmarked police car had just driven up and we had emerged from it. The

three-thousand-pound deal hung in the balance, on the verge of immediate collapse, moments away from blowing up—if not already gone. My
explanations and attitude in the next several minutes needed to contradict what Max had just seen and furnish a plausible explanation for it.

"You beat us here," I said. "Good. Have you got a room yet?" His eyes
flickered back to me but kept skipping around the lobby and toward the
front. "You got a room?" I repeated.

"Those cars—who are those cars?" Max demanded, nodding toward
the front.

"Cars? What cars?" I said, with a puzzled look. I glanced over my
shoulder toward the front. "I don't see any cars."

"The cars at the door," he said in an accusing tone. "They just drove
off."

"I wasn't paying any attention. I had my men in the van drop us off."

"Those cars, they didn't look right," he said. "Did you come in those
cars?"

"No, I told you, the van dropped us off near the door."

"Mike, I don't see the van outside," Max said warily, eying me suspi-
ciously. He wiped his mouth with the back of his hand and licked his dry
lips.

"It stopped short of the doors because there were some cars in front
of us."

He thought about that for a moment. "Well—"

"You got a room yet, Max?" I asked.

"No, we just got here. I was waiting on you. That's when I saw those
cars. They look like police cars."

"Huh? Police cars? They gone now?"

"Yah, Mike, they drove off after you got here."

"If they were police cars, it's probably just some cops from out of town
staying here," I said easily, "or eating in the restaurant or maybe they
answered a call at the motel. Who knows? Long as they're gone now,
that's good. Plus, they don't know anything about us. Right?"

Max hesitated, then gave a brief nod.

"What about your people, they coming here? We need to get this
thing going."

"Yah, they gonna be here soon. They dropped me off and they're coming back to talk to you."

"Okay, good. Let me get us a room."

Now Max was fitting the pieces together to be consistent with us not
being agents. As I had suggested, if there were unmarked police cars out

front a moment ago, it was probably just a coincidence. Although Max *thought* he saw us getting out of the cars, he must have been mistaken— he saw us walking past the cars after the van had dropped us off. I had given him plausible explanations for the presence of the police and a way of convincing himself that he did not see us get out of police cars. Just as important in overcoming this crisis was my attitude and demeanor with him, relaxed and confident, ready to move forward with business, with absolutely nothing to worry about even if those had been police cars. They had nothing to do with us. He would instinctively know that if I were an undercover agent who had just been found out, I should be tense and anxious. Instead, I was just the opposite. We had made it by this crisis, I thought, but from this point on Max would be watching me closely for anything else suspicious.

Ricky and I got a room, and DEA special agent Tiffin, who had accompanied us into the lobby, quickly warned the agents on surveillance that Max had already spotted two of their vehicles. I returned to the lobby a few minutes later and found Max, Armistead, and Carpenter waiting on me. I was relieved because it proved that we had overcome the major crisis with Max, although he and the others might be wary of me from then on.

"Our people are in the lounge waiting to meet you, Mike," Carpenter said. We went into the lounge and joined two men at a table, both stocky Hispanics. Carpenter introduced me to Pedro and Ramon, and described them as the suppliers. We started negotiations about how to do the deal. They couldn't understand why I didn't want to go the ranch and examine and weigh the dope. My reluctance could seem suspicious, but I explained my reasons and the need to do it my way on the first deal with them. They didn't want to do it my way and instead wanted me to go to the ranch. I persisted in doing it my way and our discussions went back and forth, polite but intense. I felt alone in an unrelenting debate with Pedro and Ramon, who were supported by Max, Armistead, and Carpenter.

Almost two hours passed and I was still in the midst of negotiating when suddenly I felt physically and mentally exhausted. It hit me all at once. After working the entire previous day, traveling all night from Mississippi to Houston, and then pursuing the deal all day, I had been going nonstop for almost two days and nights. Now, fatigue abruptly sapped my energy, dulling my thinking and ability to focus. Having to perform at a high level during the nonstop negotiations had exacted its toll. The hours of constant negotiations were similar to performing an extended one-man show on stage, exhilarating but draining and exhausting.

Too much was at stake and I couldn't let up now. If I gave in on doing the deal their way, it would expose me and other agents to greater risks. If I let down my guard or didn't think quickly enough I might say something that could make them suspicious. I needed to fight off the mental fog and physical exhaustion and push through it. Excusing myself from the table, I went to the restroom and splashed cold water on my face and sucked in deep breaths. Temporarily refreshed, I returned to the table and resumed our discussions.

They eventually seemed to be leaning toward doing the deal my way, but couldn't give me a definite answer. It turned out that someone higher up in the smuggling organization would have to make the decision.

Meanwhile, I had Ricky and the DEA get a U-Haul truck. They parked the truck at the motel and Ricky delivered the key to me in the lounge. I gave the key to Carpenter and while the others waited in the lounge, Pedro, Ramon, and Carpenter led me to room 230. Inside, we met with three men. Two were Hispanics, Roberto Zamora Jr. and a man named Pete. The third man, Jerry, took charge and acted as the leader of the group. Pete did too, but Jerry was more vocal. Tall and lean, with sandy hair and a drooping mustache, Jerry was in his thirties. The other men looked to be in their thirties or early forties.

The standard-size motel room was now crowded with seven men. Most stood during our discussions. I was unarmed. Jerry and Zamora demanded to know why I wouldn't go to the ranch to get the drugs. We started the negotiations all over again. Jerry was irritated, but I continued to insist that they do it my way: take the U-Haul truck, load it with 3,000 pounds, and deliver the loaded truck to me, at which time I would hand over the half million plus. At times, Jerry and some of the men had brief exchanges among themselves in Spanish, which I didn't speak, and once he and Pete stepped to the back of the room and talked in low voices, out of my hearing.

Jerry and Pete said the marijuana was stashed at a ranch house fifty miles from Houston. They finally agreed to load it in the U-Haul, but then raised another problem. They insisted I pay for the marijuana *before* it was actually delivered. I refused and presented a reasonable alternative: I told them to deliver the loaded truck to one of my men near the ranch, while I waited with some of them in their room. When my man verified that the truck was full he and one of their men would call me. Then I would leave the room for a few minutes and return with the money and pay for the load, and my man would drive away in the U-Haul. Jerry said they might do it my way, but threw in a surprise, one that could be a problem.

"I need to see your money," Jerry said. "One of my men will have to see it."

"What? I've already shown the money," I flicked a thumb toward Ivan Carpenter, "to Ivan. This afternoon, at the airport. He's seen it all. I didn't have to do it, but I wanted to show I'm ready to do business and to show my good faith."

"Mike, that was good, but that was *him. We* need to see the money," Jerry declared flatly. "We can't do anything unless we see the money ourselves."

I argued, but it became clear that the deal wasn't going any further unless the money was shown again.

"All right, Jerry," I said finally. "I'll call your room in a little while and let you know something."

For safety reasons you normally don't show a flash roll twice but I was convinced the deal wouldn't occur unless they saw it. But showing a flash presented two problems. First, DEA might have already returned the money to a bank. Second, even if the money was on hand, the DEA supervisor might be reluctant to show it again. A second show would entail more risks to everyone involved. The first time was a surprise flash, but this time the smugglers knew beforehand we would be showing the one-half million.

Ricky and I left the motel with Agent Marshall to meet up with the DEA supervisor. We drove to a field about ten minutes from the motel where a command post had been set up. More than a dozen DEA and Houston PD narcotics cars were parked in the field. A SWAT team was also on the scene. Investigators and agents sat in cars or stood in small groups in the dark field. Many had been rotating with the group of agents conducting surveillance of the motel and others stood by to provide additional surveillance and to make the arrests if the deal ever went down.

I discussed the situation with the DEA supervisor.

"What do you think?" he said after I described the meeting with Jerry. "Do we need to show it again?"

"If we don't show it, the deal probably won't go down."

"All right. Let's do it."

Fortunately, the half million we had shown that afternoon was in a vault at the DEA office and agents rushed to get it.

Using a motel room to show the money would be too dangerous so we came up with another plan. As soon as the agents returned with the money, I used a nearby pay phone and called Jerry at his room.

"Okay, Jerry, I'll show the money again," I said. "Pick out one man to see it. Just one man, and have him standing alone at the motel entrance in ten minutes. Ten minutes—no later than that. If he's not there in ten minutes or if he's not alone, then I'm not showing it again."

"Okay," Jerry said, "I'll have someone there." His tone was business-like, but I sensed a small hint of excitement and satisfaction in his voice. He wants the deal to go nearly as much as I do, I thought, and this needs to be done to clear one hurdle. The money flash wouldn't ensure that the drug deal would occur, but it would add momentum to the negotiations about how to do it and help me maintain some leverage. Without the second flash there would be no chance of doing the deal. We both knew that.

Less than ten minutes later Ramon stood in front of the motel. Using the same white van we had used at the airport, we pulled up, slid open the side door, waved him in and then sped off. It was so quick it looked like robbers making a fast getaway. Ramon settled in on the middle seat beside me while the driver drove erratically, making evasive driving maneuvers that would reveal or shake anyone trying to follow us.

"You're the one picked to see the money, right?" I said. "No one else."

"Yeah, Mike, thees ees right. I am the one to see eet."

"I've already done this once, and later on I don't want someone else saying they need to see it too. This is business and I'm not going to be playing games."

"No, no, no," Ramon held his hands up, "No. Thees ees eet, Mike. Just me. That's eet. We are glad you are doing thees. We just have to do thees to be sure, you understand."

"And I have to take care of my money, especially my backers' money on a deal this size."

"Mike, thees ees no beeg deal for us. Eet's 3,000 pounds, but last week we brought in nine tons, just in that one week. The week before that we brought in six tons. So thees ees no beeg deal."

After we had been riding for nine or ten minutes, we abruptly pulled into a parking lot on Highway 45 and stopped beside a parked van. Ramon and I hustled into the van, onto the rear seat, and the van moved off. An undercover agent handed me the zippered bag and I placed it on the seat between me and Ramon and unzipped it. Ramon reached in and picked up stacks of hundreds, thumbing the bills in the dim light flashing from passing streetlights as we rode. Ramon held one stack of hundreds up to his nose and sniffed the money. He repeated the process at random with several other stacks of hundreds. It dawned on me that he must be checking whether the money was freshly printed counterfeit. He had been around. Finally satisfied, Ramon put the last stack back in the bag and nodded at me.

"Ees goot, Mike, ees goot."

We transferred back to the first van at another parking lot and traveled back to the Holiday Inn. As Ramon got out we shook hands. "Tell Jerry I'll call him at the room in a few minutes," I said.

"Okay, Mike, we can do thees now. I tell Jerry."

We returned to the command post in the field and from a nearby pay phone I called Jerry at the motel.

"All right, Jerry," I said, "we should be good now. What about the load?"

"Yeah, Mike, we are. I appreciate you doing that."

"We need to go ahead and get this deal moving. I've got people in the northeast waiting on the stuff and the quicker they get it, the faster we can turn it over. We need to get things moving. When can I get it?"

"Mike, I can take you to the ranch right now and you can look at the stuff and check the weights."

This was the scenario I didn't want, one I had been resisting from the start of the negotiations. Going to the ranch would put me and any agent I took with me under their control. It would be easy for them to search us for weapons or wires and to hold one or both hostage until the money was paid for the dope. When the bust took place, any undercover agent at the ranch would be completely at their mercy. That's why I wouldn't go to the ranch or allow another undercover acting as one of my men to go.

"Look, Jerry, like I told you. I'll be glad to go to the ranch on any future deals, but on this first one, let's keep it simple. Just load up the U-Haul truck and bring it to me and I'll pay when I get it. I don't want to go out to the ranch with my money, especially since I have to protect my backers' part of the money."

We continued to argue. Jerry said he would call me back in a few minutes and I gave him the pay phone number.

Meanwhile, the U-Haul rental truck and a blue pickup left the motel and traveled to a Union 76 truck stop in Brookshire, Texas. From there,

DEA agents and customs investigators followed it to a ranch about five miles from Brookshire. The U-Haul backed up to a small house located to the rear of the main house. From a distance, agents maintained a continuous surveillance of the ranch.

Jerry called me back a few minutes later and said they were trying to work it out to do it my way, but couldn't understand why I didn't want to go see the dope. The struggle to convince the suppliers to bring the dope to me continued throughout the night in a dozen phone calls between us. Using pay phones, lobby phones, and the room phone, I continued intense negotiations with Jerry, Ramon, Carpenter, Armistead, and Max. I met again with Armistead and Max.

In the early-morning hours, Ricky Peterson and I finally went to our room, rested for a few hours, and got up groggy as dawn was breaking. At 8:00 a.m. I called Ramon in room 230 to check on the status of the deal. He didn't know.

Surveillance of the ranch had continued through the night and into the day. Agents saw pickup trucks arrive and leave the ranch, but saw no movement of the U-Haul truck.

Late that morning, Peterson, Tiffin, and I encountered Carpenter in the lobby.

"Hey, what's the deal? What's going on?" I demanded. Carpenter didn't know.

While Peterson and Tiffin waited in the lobby, Carpenter and I went to room 230 and met with Ramon, Pedro "Pete" Gonzales, and Zamora. The U-Haul was being loaded, they said. I told them I would have my money on standby and left.

As it was nearing noon, Ricky and I returned to room 230 and met Ramon, Gonzales, Carpenter, and Zamora. Ramon wanted one of us to go to the ranch with one of them and get the U-Haul. I told them Ricky would go to get the U-Haul, but I insisted that they deliver it to him away from the ranch at some location like a service station.

"Is there any place close to the ranch like that?" I asked. "A service station or parking lot?"

"There's a truck stop near the ranch," Ramon said.

"All right then," I said, "just drop Ricky off at the truck stop and he can wait there. Bring the loaded U-Haul to him. When he lets me know that he has it and it's loaded with the 3,000 pounds, I'll pay you in the room here."

"Okay, Mike," Ramon said, nodding, "we'll do it that way." He turned to one of the others. "Drive out there and drop him off at the truck stop and then bring the U-Haul to him." Ramon turned back to me. "Okay, Mike?"

"Good. I'll wait here in the room with you for the call from Ricky and then I'll pay you."

"Okay."

Ricky and Gonzales opened the door to leave, and I touched Ricky's arm. "Wait at the truck stop. Don't go to the ranch," I insisted. "I'll be waiting for your call."

They left and I told Ramon I would be back in a few minutes with one of my men. I went to my room and notified DEA to follow Ricky and Gonzales. I got Agent Tiffin and rejoined Ramon and his colleagues in their room. We sat and made small talk. They passed around cocaine in a small glass snorter. Tiffin and I declined. Tiffin and Carpenter left the room and went to the hotel lounge to wait.

When they reached the truck stop, Gonzales insisted that Ricky go on to the ranch with him but Ricky refused and got out at the truck stop and waited.

A short time later, the U-Haul arrived at the truck stop and Gonzales gave Ricky the key. Ricky opened the back of the truck and then called Ramon's room.

"It's for you," Ramon said, holding out the phone. "It's your man."

"This is Mike," I said.

"It's all here," Ricky said. "I've got the key. It's packed full," he said excitedly.

"Okay. Good."

I hung up and turned to Ramon. "Wait here. I'm going downstairs and get my money. I'll be back here with it in five minutes."

"Okay," Ramon grinned.

I left the room and joined Tiffin and Carpenter in the lounge, and we arrested Carpenter, rounded up several agents, and returned to the room. They stood to the side while I knocked on the door. The door opened and we rushed in with guns drawn and arrested everyone. They were taken by surprise and didn't have a chance to react.

By that time it was midafternoon, and a flurry of law-enforcement actions was just beginning. At the truck stop, agents rushed in and arrested Gonzales, who had driven the U-Haul and delivered it to Ricky. Customs agents watching the ranch stopped two men in a pickup who had come with the U-Haul to the truck stop and were waiting nearby. They arrested Juan Ricardo de la Rosa and Mario Esteban Chapa, who had a paper sack containing $23,000.

Other agents with a search warrant raided the ranch and seized 600 pounds of marijuana in the small house where the U-Haul had been loaded. They also seized two pistols and arrested the lone man at the ranch, Thomas Leon Coleman.

I finally saw the U-Haul full of marijuana early that evening after it had been moved to a secure compound in Houston. It was crammed full with 3,000 pounds of marijuana, front to back and floor to ceiling. Houston media were there taking photos and videos.

DEA, Customs, and Houston PD did a professional job of conducting constant surveillance during the two long days and then safely making the arrests. Agents congratulated me and Ricky, who had taken the biggest risk in going to get the U-Haul. There were pats on the back, handshakes, and broad smiles all around. But I was physically and mentally drained, too numb from nonstop undercover to fully enjoy the success.

During the course of the months-long undercover investigation, Mahaffey had revealed extensive details of a large and highly organized smuggling organization involving hundreds of members in several states and countries, using planes and boats to smuggle tons of dope. He told me about airfields they controlled, drew maps, mentioned names and some of the aircraft they were using, and talked about past and future smuggling events. Through surveillance by federal, state, and local law-enforcement agents over the course of the undercover and through follow-up investigations, we identified several airfields and the smugglers' contacts at the fields, and other aircraft and pilots involved. DEA and Customs would follow up nationally and internationally. MBN continued investigations of other suspects on the Mississippi Gulf Coast and in north Mississippi. Meanwhile, Louisiana State Police and Texas DPS Narcotics could pursue investigations of suspects identified in their states.

It was over. More than ten years after I first started working undercover, I had done my last undercover. I was promoted to MBN regional commander and would assume those duties. Now, I would no longer be Mike, Rick, J. R., Glenn, John, or any of the other numerous people and roles I had played. I would no longer pretend to be a drug dealer, a crime-syndicate member involved in stolen vehicles, or a wealthy businessman, and would no longer work undercover jobs such as a laundry man, hospital worker, or taxi driver. Now it was time to go back to being just "me"—whoever that was now. It was over.

EPILOGUE

I am part of all that I have met.
—*Ulysses* by Alfred Lord Tennyson

My undercover career ended with the 3,000-pound buy. After ten years of working undercover, it was over. It had been an exhilarating journey.

But the undercover life came with a price. For years my undercover life had tried to change me, seduce me, and sometimes even kill me. We all change over the years, but prolonged undercover work had tried to permanently replace the "real" me with a very different version of myself. Perhaps some versions might have been better, but others most certainly would not have been. My wife says I had a split personality during those years. There was the "undercover" me and the "real" me. The challenge was in trying to keep the two from merging completely. Some parts did, some didn't. For good or bad, I think the essential core survived fairly intact.

Without a doubt, undercover work did change me in some ways. Justice Oliver Wendell Holmes was right when he wrote, "A mind that is stretched by new experience can never go back to its old dimensions." Most people could never imagine how long-term, intensive undercover work imprints itself on an agent. Even agents who worked undercover only briefly may not know. Because success and survival depended on it, I became hypersensitive to others' emotions and feelings. I could read a micro-expression flashing across a person's face, and detect tension, suspicion, or anxiety in someone's look, in their voice, or through their body language. I could "feel" it in a room. "Sometimes the heart sees what's invisible to the eye," according to Tennyson. I could see a question or a thought in a person's eyes.

Reading people was necessary to self-preservation. But it also became a tool of success. By being able to detect a thought forming or see a question or a suspicion flashing across someone's face, I could interrupt to disrupt the thought or dispel the unspoken doubts. It's not simple to pursue two completely different chains of thought at one time. So to divert someone's thoughts or keep the suspicion from congealing,

I would start talking about something that would force the person to think about what I was talking about. I would lead them down another trail of thought, usually with something that reinforced my credibility as a criminal. Sometimes it would disabuse them of the thought that was forming or cause them to forget about it.

Aside from becoming sensitive to others' emotions, I changed in other ways. As you would expect, spending so much time with people when they're committing crimes can cause an undercover agent to become hardened and cynical. It did me. However, there's also a flip side. By becoming familiar and friendly with people who were committing crimes, I saw them as individuals. Many were bad and dangerous people doing bad things, those who will always prey on others. But some were basically decent people who were doing bad things. Years later, as a federal prosecutor, I divided defendants into those two broad categories and tried to treat the two groups differently when I could.

Of course, undercover life changes one in other, more positive ways. You have to become quick thinking, decisive, flexible, and good at planning, directing, and leading. You need to be confident but not cocky. I came to feel that I could master any situation. Career criminals and drug dealers detected that confidence and it enhanced my credibility with them.

Family was affected by my work and my family life definitely suffered. Undercover work absorbed all my time and energy. I didn't have much time at home, and when I did, nearly all waking hours were filled with work. Even on my rare evenings at home, I was on the phone for hours with informants, agents, and criminals. I wrote reports at home, and often marked and sealed evidence there. At the kitchen table I listened to undercover recordings and made notes for reports. I was often preoccupied, thinking about how to handle my next undercover encounter and the deals I was working on. When the phone rang, my wife would hand me the phone no matter what name the caller asked for, or if I wasn't home my wife would simply say that "Mike" or "John" or "Rick," or whoever, was gone off somewhere right then.

When I wasn't home, my wife spent many hours on the phone with some of my female informants who called to give me information. She would take the messages and then they would tell her how much they enjoyed working with "Mike" or "J. R." and would share their trials and tribulations with her. Undercover also imposed itself on the family in other ways. We had to be careful going out to dinner or to a movie. If a suspect saw us together we would quickly go separate ways. Through the years we lost time together and missed experiences as a family—time and experiences that could never be made up.

Prolonged or intensive undercover work also extracts a physical toll. Stress, terrifying moments, long nights, unpredictable work hours, drinking, lack of sleep and exercise, a diet of unhealthy fast food, and constant uncertainty have both temporary and permanent effects. Years later my physician explained that constant stress had weakened my immune system. I developed ulcers and suffered repeated bouts of pneumonia, bronchitis, and other ailments, catching every bug that came along. I write about this to give the reader a complete picture of the life of an undercover agent, especially those who might be thinking about trying it as a career.

The aftereffects of undercover life continued in other ways. For a couple of years after I stopped working undercover I felt vulnerable and exposed using my real name and it took a long time before I could do it comfortably. Sometimes upon encountering someone new I automatically used an undercover name, even though it wasn't necessary. I did it without thinking and instantly wished I hadn't. For a while I even continued to check into motels using an undercover identification rather than my real name. The real me took time to fully and comfortably surface.

Despite the price paid, I had been given a remarkable opportunity for a unique and exciting career. T. S. Eliot was right: "Only those who will risk going too far can possibly find out how far one can go." We normally don't get to push ourselves and to fully explore our capabilities. Undercover provided opportunities to be tested, to be creative and resourceful, and to gain insights into worlds I would have never imagined. The work was often gritty but occasionally humorous and glamorous. At times I may have taken more chances than necessary and sometimes was reckless or used poor judgment. Through it all I was lucky, although I sometimes think about what could have happened in those hair-raising moments that could have turned out much differently. Most of all, I was fortunate to work with dedicated agents and to get the opportunity to live an undercover life filled with excitement, adventures, and challenges. I had a dream job—and it had me.

AUTHOR'S NOTE

Some of the conversations in this book are etched in my memory word for word and are precisely reported. In other conversations where it is impossible to recall every word, the dialogue in this book accurately reflects the substance of the conversation, the phrases and words used, the attitudes, feelings, emotions, context, and the actions of those involved.

Some undercover conversations and meetings were lengthy and for the sake of not boring the reader, I omitted portions of conversations that were irrelevant and mundane. For example, during a two-hour meeting with a smuggling pilot, we sometimes talked not only about smuggling, but also about other subjects that would not be of any interest. Those topics could be omitted without changing the accuracy of the discussion about smuggling.

Transcripts still exist of some of my recorded undercover meetings. Where a suspect engaged in a disjointed conversation, I sometimes paraphrased or compressed the separate lines into a single paragraph for the sake of clarity and readability.

In instances where I used real names, I used both first and last names. For all others, I used only a fictitious first name.

ACKNOWLEDGMENTS

This book could not have been written without the gracious help of my friend and neighbor, author John Hailman, and my sister Connie Rachal, who is also an author. Both generously reviewed and edited many chapters and in doing so, made the book much better. I am indebted to the people who read and commented on drafts, especially my sisters Carolyn Rudder, Shelia Casselberry, Marsha Bursavich, Deborah Booksh, and my brother Steve Spillers. Many thanks to Craig Gill, editor-in-chief of the University Press of Mississippi, and copy editor Anne Rogers for their guidance and expert work. Thanks also to the rest of the incredibly talented folks at University Press, especially director Leila Salisbury, production editor Shane Gong Stewart, art director John Langston, and designer Todd Lape. Any and all errors and shortcomings of the book are mine alone.

I am grateful to the many people who shared their experiences for the book: Richard Allison, Steve Campbell, Bruce Childers, J. C. Denham, Jerry Dettman, Orrin Fuelling, Faron Gardner, Jerry Gardner, Jim Kelly, Charlie Lindsey, Fred Lovett, Steve Mallory, Fred Macdonald, Jay Moore, James Newman, Sam Pruet, Mickey Robbins, Sara Niell Robbins, Chuck Smith, and Jim Walker. Thank you for allowing me to share some of the extraordinary events in your lives.

During my career in law enforcement I was fortunate to work with outstanding prosecutors, particularly assistant district attorney Frank Gremillion in Baton Rouge, assistant DA Tommy Mayfield in Jackson, and assistant US attorneys John Hailman, Al Moreton III, and Tom Dawson in Oxford. By their example they inspired me to go to law school and become a prosecutor. Thank you for serving as role models for me and others.

My wife Evelyn read and commented on drafts of the book and made valuable suggestions. Unfortunately, she is also part of some of the frightening events described in the book. Beyond that, she was part of every minute of the ten tumultuous years I worked undercover, and she somehow managed to keep our family going despite the fears, uncertainty, and stresses of our daily life. She also lived an undercover life and she did it heroically.

Finally, thank you to the men and women in law enforcement who risk their lives to protect us all.

INDEX